Visual Tools *for* Transforming Information *Into* KNOWLEDGE

SECOND EDITION

D1127604

Visual Tools *for* Transforming Information *Into* KNOWLEDGE

SECOND EDITION

David Hyerle

PROLOGUE BY
Arthur L. Costa

FOREWORD BY
Robert J. Marzano

CORWIN PRESS
A SAGE Company

For information:

Corwin Press
A Sage Publications Company
2455 Teller Road
Thousand Oaks, California 91320
www.corwinpress.com

Sage Publications Ltd.
1 Oliver's Yard
55 City Road
London EC1Y 1SP
United Kingdom

SAGE Publications India Pvt. Ltd.
B 1/I 1 Mohan Cooperative
Industrial Area
Mathura Road, New Delhi 110 044
India

SAGE Publications Asia-Pacific Pte. Ltd.
33 Pekin Street #02-01
Far East Square
Singapore 048763

Printed in the United States of America.

Library of Congress Cataloging-in-Publication Data

Hyerle, David.
Visual tools for transforming information into knowledge/David Hyerle. — 2nd ed.
    p. cm.
Includes bibliographical references and index.
ISBN 978-1-4129-2426-9 (cloth)
ISBN 978-1-4129-2427-6 (pbk.)
    1. Visual learning. 2. Constructivism (Education) 3. Thought and thinking. 4. Critical thinking.
5. Cognition. I. Hyerle, David.
Visual tools for constructing knowledge. II. Title.

LB1067.5.H94 2009
370.15'23—dc22   2008017823

This book is printed on acid-free paper.

10   11   12   10   9   8   7   6   5   4   3   2

Acquisitions Editor:	Hudson Perigo
Editorial Assistant:	Lesley Blake
Production Editor:	Jane Haenel
Copy Editor:	Dorothy Hoffman
Typesetter:	C&M Digitals (P) Ltd.
Proofreader:	Cheryl Rivard
Indexer:	Kirsten Kite
Cover Designers:	Anthony Paular and Michael Dubowe
Graphic Designer:	Brian Bello

Contents

Foreword

In *Visual Tools for Transforming Information Into Knowledge* (2nd edition), David Hyerle takes the concept of visual tools to new heights. He provides a strong theoretical base by starting with the mapping metaphor. Just as cartography increased the speed and efficiency with which new lands and new people could be identified and connected, so too do visual tools escalate the speed and efficiency with which an individual can identify new knowledge and connect it to what is already known. Hyerle reviews not only the theoretical underpinnings of the use of visual tools but also the research supporting it—some of that research my own. Specifically, in the book *Classroom Instruction That Works* (Marzano, Pickering, & Pollock, 2001), I reviewed a number of studies focusing on what I referred to as nonlinguistic representations. This term included instructional strategies such as graphic organizers, mind maps, and the like. The research I reviewed strongly supported the use of such strategies as powerful instructional tools. In my latest review of the research on general instructional strategies contained in the book *The Art and Science of Teaching* (Marzano, 2007), I found even stronger evidence for the efficacy of nonlinguistic representations.

In his work on visual tools, David Hyerle has expanded the frontiers of strategies involving nonlinguistic representations far beyond what I and others have attempted to do. He provides not only a comprehensive theoretical basis for the efficacy of visual tools but expands their application to new and exciting arenas. A short list of the applications of visual tools Hyerle details includes

- Brainstorming
- The use of visual tools for facilitating habits of mind
- The use of software to enhance nonlinguistic thinking
- Collaborative reflection
- Book reviews
- The creation of mindscapes
- Traditional graphic organizers
- Domain-specific graphic organizers
- Chunking content to aid memory
- Process maps
- Mapping lesson plans
- System maps
- Feedback loops

Hyerle also addresses five levels of implementing Thinking Maps and provides criteria for determining whether visual tools are being used effectively by an individual teacher or by an entire school. In short, David's work is the most comprehensive and useful to date on the topic of visual tools and what I have referred to as nonlinguistic representations. This book will no doubt be considered a classic for years to come.

Robert J. Marzano
March 2008

REFERENCES

Marzano, R. J. (2007). *The art and science of teaching: A comprehensive framework for effective instruction.* Alexandria, VA: Association for Supervision and Curriculum Development.

Marzano, R. J., Pickering, D. J., & Pollock, J. E. (2001). *Classroom instruction that works: Research-based strategies for increasing student achievement.* Alexandria, VA: Association for Supervision and Curriculum Development.

Prologue

Deeply rooted in constructivist theory, this book draws on philosophical and psychological models of how the mind works, how human intellectual capacities emerge and grow over time, how humans derive meaning, and how knowledge is structured. The intent is to provide educators with insights into how interventions can be arranged and conditions organized so as to educe, enhance, and refine those human intellectual resources.

In reviewing this book and preparing to write this prologue, I reminisced about other constructivist theorists who influenced the formation of my views of learning and human cognitive development: Bruner, Piaget, Taba, Suchman, Feuerstein. I retrieved several of the constructivist mental models that scaffolded their philosophical and psychological search. I found myself returning to Jerome Bruner's compelling inquiry, "What makes human beings human?" I began to mentally reflect on and list some of those unique intellectual capacities that distinguish humans from other life forms. When I approached the upper limits of my memory span—that magical number 7 (plus or minus 2) items to hold in my head simultaneously—I realized I had to write them down or some might drop out. I therefore represented my thoughts graphically (Prologue Figure 1).

As I mapped, I also came to realize that what I thought in my head was fuzzier than what I wrote on paper. As I refined what was on paper, I mutually refined my inner thoughts. I realized, for example, that many human capacities, while innate, are underdeveloped and will need to be amplified to live productively in the future. Not only did the brainstorming web allow me to see the relationships between these attributes, but it also disclosed overlaps, redundancies, and omissions. I edited here and there to be consistent and then reflected on my map. I felt satisfied that I had a structure that could be decorated with a few insightful contributions about the benefits and potentials of this book. Using the structure, I then turned to composing. As the thoughts flowed from my brain and were translated to individual letters by my fingers and flowed as words onto the computer screen, I again revisited my map altering here and there, combining where necessary, and generating more bubbles as additional thoughts emerged that, in turn, stimulated others.

The gift that David Hyerle has bestowed on us in this book, you see, is a set of tools for exploring, enhancing, and refining those unique cognitive qualities of humanness. I would like to

1. explain what is meant by each of these uniquely human qualities that undergird constructivist theory;

2. describe how David has so masterfully addressed them; and

Prologue Figure 1   What Makes Human Beings Human?

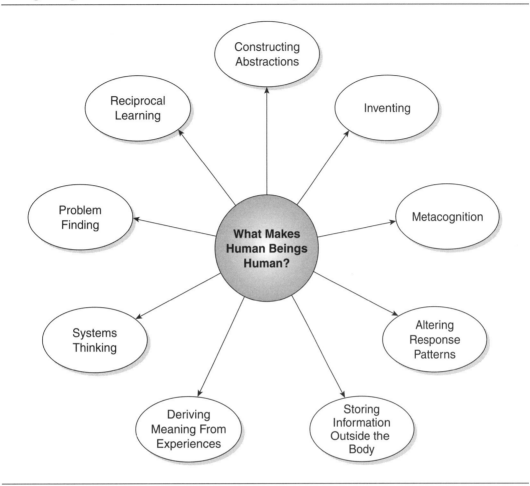

3. make implications for their significance to mindful schools where the staff is intent on emancipating themselves, their students, and their communities from the shackles of nearly a century of reductionism (see Prologue Figure 2).

The following nine human qualities, then, may illuminate my reflections on this book.

1.   Metacognition. To the best of our knowledge, human beings are the only form of life that can reflect on their own thinking processes. Basically, metacognition means that, when confronted with a dilemma or some obstacle, humans draw on their

Prologue Figure 2   Prologue Process

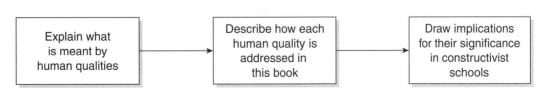

mental resources to plan a course of action, monitor that strategy while executing it, then reflect on the strategy to evaluate its productiveness in terms of the outcomes it was intended to achieve.

The "thinking" visual tools described in this book are forms of metacognition—graphically displayed thinking processes.

We know that what distinguishes expert from novice problem solvers is habituated metacognition; that thinking and discussing thinking beget more thinking; and that thinking and problem-solving capacities are enhanced when students think aloud, discuss, and communicate their thought processes to others, making their implicit problem-solving processes explicit.

2. **Constructing abstractions.** Humans have the unique capacity to synopsize massive amounts of information and to shape raw data into workable patterns. There was a time when human beings lacked access to information in making decisions. Data were scarce, took long periods of time to transmit, and were simplistic in format and immediate in implication. With the advent of the Information Age, however, an overwhelming amount of immediately accessible and often conflicting information became available. Because of the lack of vast amounts of such disparate information in the past, the human intellectual capacity for constructing abstractions may have been underdeveloped. And with the increase in available information, the upper limits of this capacity will be continually tested and exceeded in the future.

This book provides visual tools to assist learners to organize and find patterns in the overwhelming amount of information available today, as well as to make sense of and evaluate it.

We have found that the capacity to construct abstractions has become prerequisite to survival and will need to grow if we are to live productively in the future. Resourceful humans, therefore, will continue to develop their capacity to gather, organize, make sense of, and evaluate the overabundance of technology-generated and -transmitted data.

3. **Storing information outside the body.** I recently had more memory installed in my computer. It was a simple process of installing more modules. I wish I could do the same for my brain!

Human beings are the only form of life that can store, organize, and retrieve data in locations other than our bodies. This "human capacity" probably emerged as a survival mechanism because our ancestors reached the limits of their memory span. They had the need to remember and communicate an increasing amount of information and therefore used tools to record and convey mental visions and concepts. Cave walls, where their dwellers formed their marks and petroglyphs, may be history's first storage locations. Now the World Wide Web, CD-ROMs, blogs, e-mail, and a range of handheld communication devices assist us in accomplishing this human function.

This book fulfills this human intellectual capacity by providing tools to generate, store, and communicate information in such a manner that can be recalled and interpreted at a later time and by others.

Because the archives of the mind are limited and the amount of information is increasing, students will need to learn strategies of harvesting, storing, cataloging, retrieving, interpreting, and communicating vast amounts of information among locations beyond their brains.

4. **Systems thinking.** Humans have the unique capacity to see the parts in relation to the whole and thus to see patterns, congruencies, and inconsistencies. The

human preference for perceiving parts *or* wholes as separate cognitive inclinations, as some cognitive-style theorists would have us believe, is inadequate for productive participation in a quantum world. In dynamic systems, tiny inputs can reverberate throughout the system, producing dramatically large consequences. Systems thinking fulfills a human capacity to understand the boundaries within a part of the total system and, at the same time, to understand the interactions with its interconnecting parts.

Hyerle suggests the use of visual tools to guide thinking when we need to simultaneously pay attention to the whole and analyze whether the parts are, indeed, interdependent and interconnected. Visual tools are one means of describing how a system functions when altered or when innovative thinking in one part of the system affects the total system. Maps serve as tools for examining many processes and interactions, such as how decisions are made, how disciplines work together, how new practices are initiated, and how priorities are established.

Families, weather systems, and national economies are examples of systems. To participate fully in any society, and to protect a fragile environment, citizens must realize that any system involves a synergistic relationship of interlocking parts; as one part changes, it affects the other parts. No one part can operate efficiently unless the other parts of the system work in harmony. This capacity for simultaneously holonomous parts–whole relationships has become essential not only in the workplace but also in solving environmental and social problems.

5. Problem finding. To the best of our knowledge, humans are the only form of life that actually enjoys the search for problems to solve. Being dissatisfied with existing levels of certainty, humans have an insatiable passion for questioning the status quo, sensing ambiguities, and detecting anomalies. Once having intuited such inconsistencies, humans have developed the profound capacity to engage in experimental inquiry, to set up procedures to test and evaluate alternative ideas, and to strive for certitude. The process of modern scientific thought thrives on this human tendency.

Maps are tools for displaying intellectual processes, the clustering of the diverse, complex procedures of experimentation. They represent the sequences, alternative branches, choice points, and pathways that surround the acquisition and production of knowledge. These become the basis for systematic inquiry and scientific investigation.

Process is, in fact, the highest form of learning and the most appropriate base for curriculum change. In the teaching of process, we can best portray learning as a perpetual endeavor and not something that terminates when we leave school. Through process, we can employ knowledge not merely as a composite of information but as a system for continuous learning.

6. Reciprocal learning. Human beings are social beings who have a compulsive craving to engage with others. The most hideous form of punishment is to deprive humans of their quest for reciprocity. Humans learn best in groups. Intelligence gets shaped through interaction with others: justifying reasons, resolving differences, actively listening to another person's point of view, achieving consensus, and receiving feedback.

In this book, Hyerle commends interactivity as tools are developed in cooperative settings. Such tools assist in developing students' and teachers' capacity for flexibility—viewing situations from multiple perspectives, as well as being able to change and adapt based on feedback from others. Using such cooperative tools transcends the sense of self—enlarging the conception of "me" to a sense of "us." And becoming less attached to egocentric orientations permits us to exercise more advanced reasoning processes. Use of such tools provides interconnectedness and kinship that comes from a unity of being, a sense of sharing, and a mutual bonding to common goals and shared values. Students understand that as we transcend the self and become part of the whole, we do not lose our individuality; rather, we relinquish our egocentricity.

Collaboration, cooperation, and interdependence are paramount not only in today's work cultures but also in families, in governmental organizations, and among nations. Schools must enhance students' capacities for holding their own values and actions in abeyance and lending their energies and resources to the achievement of group goals, contributing themselves to a common good, and seeking collegiality and drawing on the resources of others. Students must come to regard conflict as valuable, trusting their abilities to manage group differences in productive ways, to seek feedback from others as a valued source of learning. They must know that "all of us" is more efficient than any "one of us." Interdependence makes possible the most complete and effective intellectual functioning of human beings.

7. **Inventing.** Human beings are creative—they are toolmakers. Although some other life forms may perceive the need for and employ instruments to accomplish tasks and solve problems, only humans are capable of designing and creating new tools.

Further, humans are intrinsically rather than extrinsically motivated, working on the task because of the aesthetic challenge, rather than the material rewards. They constantly strive for greater fluency, elaboration, novelty, parsimony, simplicity, craftsmanship, perfection, beauty, harmony, and balance.

Hyerle disparages giving students ready-made maps to follow and fill in. He emphasizes the need for students to invent their own tools and to hone and refine them as they generate and gather information, process or elaborate that information into conceptual relationships, and then apply and evaluate those generalizations. He believes strongly that each of us has an inherent motivation for this inventive process, which can be capacitated through such visual tool making.

All humans have the capacity to generate novel, original, clever, or ingenious products, solutions, and techniques. We often try to conceive problem solutions differently, examining alternative possibilities from many angles. We tend to project ourselves into different roles using metaphors and analogies, starting with a vision and working backward, imagining we are the objects being considered. Creative people take risks—they "live on the edge of their competence," testing their limits—if that capacity is developed.

8. **Deriving meaning from experiences.** Thomas A. Edison stated that he never made a mistake; he only learned from experience. One of the most significant attributes that makes humans human is their capacity for reflecting on and learning from their experiences. Intelligent people form feelings and impressions about an event; they compare intentions with accomplishments; they analyze why events turned out as they did; they search for causal factors that produced the effects; they summarize their impressions; and, based on those analyses, they project how they could modify their actions in the future.

The human mind, however, is inclined to distort or delete information to suit its own purposes and biases. Hyerle suggests that the use of maps as tools for reflection can assist us by graphically tracking the procedures employed in an event. Reflecting on the visual pathways, strategies, and decisions is a more efficient and systematic way of holding information than attempting to recall it. The experience can be analyzed more honestly and completely if it has been graphically organized.

Autonomous individuals set personal goals and are self-directing, self-monitoring, and self-modifying. Because they are constantly experimenting and experiencing, they fail frequently but they *fail forward,* learning from the situation. A major outcome for any school desirous of preparing autonomous humans is to develop students' capacities for continuous self-analysis, self-improvement, self-referencing, self-evaluation, and self-modification.

9. **Altering response patterns.** Whereas other forms of life are wired to respond in certain ways to stimuli in their environment, humans are self-actualizing and self-modifying—they can consciously and deliberately make choices about whether and how they wish to respond. They can alter their habits and can voluntarily select among alternative responses. We might be inclined to be impulsive, but we can choose to be deliberative; if we are disposed to make premature evaluations, we can choose to withhold our judgments; when we are habituated into perceiving egocentrically, we can choose to perceive allocentrically. This decision-making process requires consciousness and flexibility—being aware of our *own* and others' actions and drawing on a repertoire of response patterns. David Hyerle supports the use of visual tools because they encourage consciousness and flexibility of responses. Deliberately employing mapping tools causes us to restrain our impulsivity, to suspend our judgments, to generate and consider alternatives, and to attend empathically to others' perspectives.

Fully functioning humans engage in continuous learning. If our students believe that their education has been completed on graduation, they've missed the whole point of schooling. Continuous lifespan learning is essential for students today and in the future. With advances in technology and changes in the workplace and human mobility, we may find other underdeveloped capacities continuing to learn how to learn, how to change and grow, and how to relinquish old patterns and acquire new ones.

ENDNOTE

David also proposes that the use of these tools is not just "kid stuff." Cooperatively inventing and employing such tools benefits the human intellectual capacities of the adults in the school as well. When the staff design, generate, and employ these maps, they too become more aware of their data generating, storing, and retrieval systems. All staff members are at once beneficiaries and leaders of the learning organization. They more readily see the parts-whole relationship. They view their particular operation as part of a larger whole and see that innovative/creative thinking in one part of the system affects the total system. Everybody in the entire system is perceived to be a continual learner—a caring, thinking individual capable of complex decision making, creativity. School life consists of not only the continuity and use of visual tools across departments and grade levels but also the use of a shared, common language throughout the organization. Perhaps it is this fractal quality that is the unique characteristic of a mindful school.

Arthur L. Costa
Professor Emeritus
Sacramento State University

Acknowledgments

In the mid-1980s, Dr. Art Costa, then and now a leader in our field, opened my eyes to the complexity and elegance of our human capacity to think. Quietly, Art also opened several doors for me, one that led the ASCD in 1996 to publish and then distribute to all its members my first book, *Visual Tools for Constructing Knowledge*. Art's Prologue to this new book welcomed readers to that first edition. His words stand as a testament to the original nature of his thinking and the universal, enduring qualities of his insights. I am forever grateful to Art for his guidance.

Over all these years, I have been deeply influenced by many people who have developed visual tools. Tony Buzan, Gabriel Rico, and Nancy Margulies have given us rich brainstorming tools; Richard Sinatra, Jim Bellanca, and Bonnie Armbruster have offered an array of graphic organizers and research; and John Clarke, Joseph Novak, and the late Barry Richmond have offered us languages for mapping concepts and systems. These pioneers have built the trails upon which we now walk *and* the maps for navigating the complexity of the present knowledge network.

This revision was a struggle for me, for I wanted to synthesize these pioneering works with some of the new theory, research, and practice that may enlighten a new generation of work. The act of drawing together comprehensive research into the heart of practice is exciting, difficult, and time consuming. This is a task that Robert Marzano has taken on for years, and I appreciate his research and interest in translating research into practice, as well as the focus he offers us in the Foreword to this book.

In this edition, there are several new pathways thanks to Tim Van Gelder, Rob Quaden and Alan Ticotsky, and Christine Ewey, who show us, respectively, how to build mental models for reasoning, for systems thinking, and for integrating multiple forms of information into visual frameworks. The last two chapters of the book are anchored by four authors offering new insights into the practice of Thinking Maps, the work that long ago became central to my life journey. Many thanks to Stefanie Holzman, Sarah Curtis, Larry Alper, and Cynthia Manning for concretely detailing how Thinking Maps are used as a language for learning and leadership across entire schools.

If there is one simple lesson I have learned through my work with visual tools, it is that the form, or design, of knowledge is inseparable from the content and processes of creating that knowledge. Unlike most books in education, this book is rich with the interplay of text and graphics, requiring important design decisions. Thank you, Hudson Perigo, executive editor of Corwin Press, and the team of Lesley Blake, Jane Haenel, and Dorothy Hoffman for the high-quality production of this book, thus giving you, the reader, an opportunity for clearly viewing the form and function of visual tools.

PUBLISHER'S ACKNOWLEDGMENTS

Corwin Press gratefully acknowledges the contributions of the following reviewers:

Mark Bower
Director of Elementary Education and Staff Development
Hilton Central School District
Hilton, NY

Mark Johnson
Principal/Curriculum and Assessment Facilitator
Glenwood Elementary
Kearney, NE

Judith A. Rogers, EdD
Professional Learning Specialist
Tucson Unified School District
Tucson, AZ

About the Author

David Hyerle is an author, researcher, workshop leader, and keynote speaker focused on integrating thinking process approaches into 21st-century learning, teaching and leading implementation designs across whole schools. The creation of the Thinking Maps® model by David in the late 1980s emerged from his inner-city teaching experiences at the middle school level in Oakland, California. His development of Thinking Maps was also informed by his work with the Bay Area/National Writing Project and the Cognitive Coaching™ model. David completed doctoral work at the University of California, Berkeley, and Harvard Schools of Education in 1993, through which he refined the theoretical and practical applications of Thinking Maps as a language for learning and leading. Among the numerous professional books, articles, online/video courses, and resource materials he has authored—including the ASCD book *Visual Tools for Constructing Knowledge*— David has written the training materials for Thinking Maps and guided the professional development process with Thinking Maps, Inc. In recent years, David has coauthored the seminar guide *Thinking Maps: A Language for Leadership* and edited *Student Successes With Thinking Maps*, a book that synthesizes background research and documents the outcomes from the implementation of Thinking Maps. David now lives in New Hampshire with his wife, Sara, and their son, Alex, and works as the Founding Director of Thinking Foundation (www.thinkingfoundation.org), a nonprofit organization supporting research in cognitive and critical thinking development for all children and for the purpose of creating "thinking schools" nationally and internationally. He can be reached by phone at (603) 795–2757 and by e-mail at davidhyerle@thinkingfoundation.org.

Summary Definition of Visual Tools

Visual tools are nonlinguistic symbol systems used by learners, teachers, and leaders for graphically linking mental and emotional associations to create and communicate rich patterns of thinking. These visual-spatial-verbal displays of understanding support all learners in *transforming static information into active knowledge*, thus offering a complementary representational system to more traditional literacies grounded in speaking, writing, and numerating. These linear and/or nonlinear visual forms are also metacognitive tools for self-assessment in each content area and for interdisciplinary learning that may unite linguistic, numerical, and scientific languages together on the same page.

As shown in Summary Figure 1, and investigated in this book, there are three basic categories of visual tools, each with specific purposes and visual configurations:

brainstorming webs for fostering creativity and open mindedness;

graphic organizers for fostering analytical content and process specific learning;

conceptual mapping for fostering cognitive development and critical thinking.

A fourth category is a unique synthesis *language* of visual tools that has been used extensively across schools called Thinking Maps® (Hyerle, 1990, 1996). This common visual language of visual tools integrates the creative dynamism of webs, the analytical structures of content-specific learning, and the continuous cognitive development and reflections fostered through conceptual mapping. Over time, new visual languages may develop that integrate different visual tools and thus enable a greater range of thinking, communication, and reflection.

Visual tools are used for personal, collaborative, and social communication, negotiation of meaning, and networking of ideas. These graphics are constructed by individual or collaborative learners across media networks and mediums such as paper, whiteboards, and computer screens. Because of the visual accessibility and natural processes of "drawing out" ideas, many of these graphics are used from early childhood through adulthood, and across every dimension of learning, teaching, assessing, and leadership processes. Visual tools are also used across cultures and languages and may become keys to new levels of more democratic participation and communication in human systems. Across traditional cultures and new "virtual" cultures, visual languages ultimately may be used for uniting diverse and distant learning communities as people in schools, communities, and businesses and in different countries *seek to understand* each other through *seeing* each others' thinking and perceptions through multiple frames of reference.

Summary Figure 1   Tree Map: Types of Visual Tools

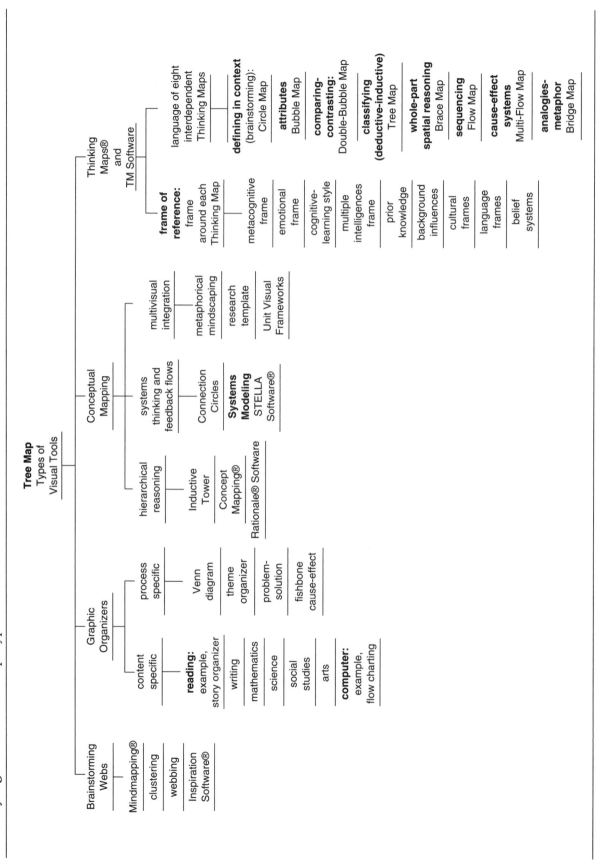

Introduction

Transforming Static Information Into Active Knowledge

BLIND INSIGHTS

The moment I knew that the visual tools described in this book were deeper than the facade of the boxes, ovals, and arrows that we have seen for years was during a return visit to a school in Mission, Texas, in the early 1990s. I had been leading the implementation in this school over time, using a language of visual tools that I developed as a foundation for facilitating thinking skills and for directly improving teachers' instruction and students' performance. During a previous workshop at the school, a participant had asked a question that stopped me in my tracks. At first the question seemed to indicate a resistance to change that we have all felt at one time or another, but then the question turned to a deeper level: "These visual tools may work for most students, but not for my students." I asked, "Why not?" She hesitated and then spoke softly, "They are *blind*. How would you use visual tools with blind students?" As quiet settled across the crowd (and "wait time" proved to be no great strategy at that moment), all I could do was respond with a promise to return with the question in mind.

When I did return a month later, the teacher who had asked the question handed me the answer: a videotape and several pale yellow, bumpy pages. And then I knew: her students were using a Braille machine to generate visual tools on this special paper. We popped the video into the machine, and the whole faculty watched with a focused fascination rarely found in a workshop setting. One of her students, particularly taken by "visual" tools, had created several Braille maps for generating context information about a writing topic using a Circle Map and then prioritizing the ideas into a Flow Map for sequencing. On the video, this boy led his seeing peers in a discussion about the use of the maps and a reading of his description about a visit to a beach as his hands moved over the pages, sensing the spatial display of the bumps. The product was a beautifully descriptive piece of writing. The teacher was delighted with the outcome, and the student was improving his writing *and* thinking abilities. Of course, his "seeing" peers had been using the same array of visual tools: they could see the patterns . . . but he could *feel* them.

What I learned from this teacher, and the key concept that propels this book, is that most *high-quality* brainstorming webs, graphic organizers, and conceptual mapping approaches are not simply isolated visual techniques to be handed out in preformed worksheets. These tools, now often referred to as *nonlinguistic representations*

(Marzano, Pickering, & Pollock, 2001), are not just a few more tools for the proverbial teacher tool belt, but a new foundation for rigorous learning, higher-order systems thinking, metacognition, and formative assessments in classrooms.

Visual tools, in the best cases, are generated from a blank page *by students* for transforming text-based content information into active knowledge using a rich integration of modalities—visual, spatial, verbal, and numerical—to create conceptually rich models of *their* meaning. These acts of transformation take students from the basic information found in texts to the highest orders of thinking seamlessly, from building concrete content facts and vocabulary directly to the abstract conceptual understandings that are the basis for learning knowledge in every discipline. Visual tools offer a third way through the great dichotomies and supposed polar opposites on which we as educators endlessly query: What should we focus on in the context of "too much information" in "too little time" requiring "too many intended outcomes?" Here are some of the dualistic dilemmas we question:

Content or Process?

Factual Information or Conceptual Knowledge?

Linear or Holistic Thinking?

Analytical or Creative?

Recall or Understanding?

The Basics or Higher-Order Thinking?

As shown in this book, educators are seeing in practice and in the research that these tools for transforming information into knowledge are facilitating diverse learners who require differentiated instruction, multiple intelligences, habits of mind, and higher-order thinking. *But most important, students are transforming information into knowledge using "mapping" in dynamic congruence with what is already going on in the brain.* As Pat Wolfe, a leader in the translation of brain research for practitioners, says: "Neuroscientists tell us that the brain organizes information in networks and maps" (Wolfe, 2004). The brain, we have come to understand, is an organism that has a specialized, continuously evolving, multidimensional, and dynamic *spatial* architecture that networks and maps information. Information is stored in distributed circuits—maps—across the brain (Introduction Figure 1).

Most important, the brain is also *dominantly* visual as most brain researchers believe that we receive around 70% of information from our environment through our eyes. We make and store images and pictures of incoming information in our brain, and now our new technologies—mostly visual—are merely reinforcing the visual dominance of the brain.

The breakthroughs shown in this book establish the importance of visual mapping that in many ways replicates what the brain does so well. High-quality visual tools are basically used for surfacing dynamic schemas, graphic representations that externalize in blueprint form the conceptual knowledge structures bound within the architecture of the brain. This is why visual tools are a breakthrough in education and not just another tool on the sagging tool belt of endless and uncoordinated "best practices" for teachers. It is now clear that the traditional linear strings of words students see in textbooks and hear from teachers in dominantly linear-auditory

Introduction Figure 1   Overview

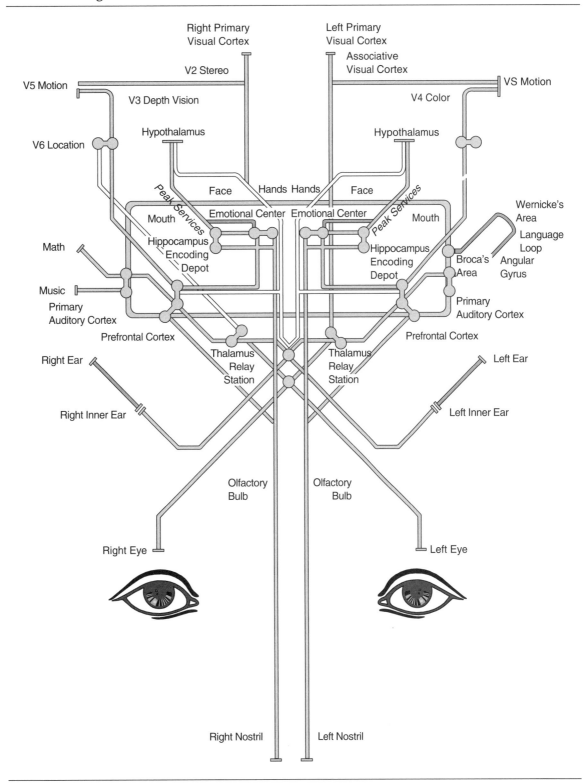

Source: Adapted from Carter, R. (1998). *Mapping the mind*. Berkeley, CA: University of California Press.

classrooms do not even come close to approximating the complex visual-verbal-spatial patterning of what is going on in their heads. Thus, there is cognitive dissonance between

> what is going on in students' minds as their brains are *naturally* mapping information and

> what is happening in classrooms as teachers talk and student see linear strings of information in texts.

Visual tools are a natural bridge between the brain and mind and high intellectual performance on tasks requiring more than linear processing. As one third grader stated about the use of a language of visual tools: "Thinking Maps . . . are the paper of my mind" (DePinto Piercy & Hyerle, 2004). The paper of the mind is not linear text, it is a map.

I now believe even more strongly than ever that visual tools provide one of the most direct routes for most learners—and maybe all but a few learners in our ever more inclusive classrooms—to show and communicate *their* rich patterns of thinking about content vocabulary and conceptual knowledge. These tools leverage learning well beyond the common *linear* presentations of information that are presented in classrooms and that are but a shallow facade of the holism of human thinking based on conceptual understandings.

RIGHT NOW: JUMPING THE ACHIEVEMENT GAP FOR ALL CHILDREN

It is surely an understatement that this book of collected, high-quality uses of visual tools is important for the age we live in right now: the age of information. But schools are not interested in just how to help students remember information, but in how to teach students to transform information into active knowledge. Today's students are the ones who will be responsible for knowledge creation and knowledge transfer in the future—as so-called knowledge workers—so we need to give them tools *right now* for learning how to construct meaningful knowledge from information, not merely regurgitate information.

Of course, this philosophical and political stance has been the foundation for both progressive and conservative educators' seemingly endless critique of public school education for generations: We don't teach children to think. The "ends" of differing political-educational doctrines seem the same in the sense of wanting to create an internal capacity in our children within our democratic system for higher-order thinking, but the "means" always seem in dispute. My concern is that there have been few if any breakthroughs to concrete solutions for *how* to give all students the wherewithal to meet this challenge. Visual tools as documented in this book and in the research have now proven to be such a breakthrough in education: the means to the outcome of facilitating content-specific acquisition of information *through* higher-order thinking through visual representations.

As we come to believe more and more that knowledge is not only interconnected but also interdependent, then we will see how much we need to provide students with these dynamic new mental tools. These tools will help them unlearn and relearn what we have taught them so that they may build knowledge and also have the experience and capacity to create new tools for making their world. It is all too clear, though, that for many children of color and children in poverty, the overriding focus, right now, is often on making it to the next rung of minimum standards through repetitive, basic skills instruction and not on the mediation of deeper learning and thinking abilities. In his newest book, Jonathan Kozol documents the resegregation of schools, especially in urban centers (Kozol, 2005). Kozol documents how it is not just the separate and unequal funding of schools that affect African American, Latino, and other children who may not be empowered in the mainstream language, culture, and economy. It is that which is less visible: the tracking of these children into rote-learning classrooms that ultimately dooms them to an educational and economic underclass.

Unfortunately, some schools are attempting to jump test scores in the short run so that they can make the next rung of *adequate yearly progress*, but in the meantime, many students are receiving instruction that is not matching their natural mental capacities to do higher-order work. My focus on the use of visual tools for promoting higher-order thinking in low-achieving schools, most recently with my own work with Thinking Maps, Inc., and also in collaboration on projects with the nonprofit group National Urban Alliance, has proven to me that educators can deliver a standards-based curriculum that integrates "the basics" with higher-order processes while engaging students' diverse cultures and languages.

Out of necessity, high-quality "knowledge tools" are desperately in demand with students' access to new technologies and communication tools. Teachers, parents, and employers face pressing questions: How are all students *right now* processing and filtering the vast amounts of information they confront through endless media outlets? How are students *right now* working fluidly with the newest technologies to rapidly generate, change, and communicate meaningful knowledge? The concern is real: *right now* few classroom practices or tools exist to explicitly support learners in filtering, organizing, and systematically assessing raw slices of information. Reading comprehension, in the traditional sense of reading a text, is not enough: students must *right now* grapple with data in many forms delivered in high-speed chunks through numerous technologies. At the same time, they must perform at high levels of thinking in high-stakes gatekeeping exams. Few tools provide a concrete means to transform unprocessed information into useful patterns of knowledge that are at once usable and easily communicated to others. And few tools, once mastered, can help learners manage the unknown overflow of information for a lifespan.

While visual tools have been shown to be effective in schools, educators need to become aware that visual tools and software programs are now commonplace throughout the world of work, *around* the world. Graphical software tools for organizing information are now added to word-processing and database spreadsheets to help workers and clients communicate smoothly as novel ideas, information, inventories, and solutions to problems are moved through systems.

The question that drives this investigation of visual tools is this: How may we introduce students to and support their use of visual tools so that they can capably handle continuous change and become lifespan learners, as they progress from kindergarten throughout their senior years and across their work lives? The promise of this book, and the proof within, shows that all students may be engaged with visual tools at the highest levels. It has become ever clearer that visual tools as high-quality nonlinguistic representations are designed as practical, effective, dynamic, collaborative, and learner centered. Importantly, these proven tools are theory embedded, transferable across disciplines, and are becoming part of the assessment and self-assessment processes of learning. As we will investigate, graphic *languages*—which go well beyond simplistic brainstorming activities and generic "blackline master" graphic organizers—offer teachers and students a rich and coherent synthesis of isolated visual tools. Languages such as Mind Mapping®, STELLA® Systems Thinking, Concept Mapping™, Rationale® Software, and Thinking Maps®, when used with depth over time, bring about significant transformations in student performance and offer a pathway for long-term development of their thinking abilities.*

OVERVIEW OF THE BOOK

This book is a synthesis of two prior books, new research in the field, and also new applications with a language of visual tools I developed called Thinking Maps. In *Visual Tools for Constructing Knowledge,* published by the Association for Supervision and Curriculum Development (Hyerle, 1996), I offered a more theoretical overview of visual tools, broken into three basic and sometimes overlapping categories: brainstorming webs, "task-specific" graphic organizers, and conceptual mapping (that I called *thinking-process maps*). This first book was supported and guided by Dr. Art Costa, who wrote the prologue, and who has graciously let me republish it in this edition as a rich framework for seeing visual tools as extensions of what makes us human.

I had explored these three types of tools, highlighting that in practice they sometimes had common visual *forms*, but often significant differences in purpose and *function*. This theoretical work, some of which is still useful, was based on my doctoral research at the University of California at Berkeley and at Harvard University, and is synthesized in my dissertation, *Thinking Maps as Tools for Multiple Modes of Understanding* (Hyerle, 1993). The book you have in your hand is also grounded in the sequel *A Field Guide to Using Visual Tools* (Hyerle, 2000a), a compilation of more practical examples from the field that included excerpted writings and stories from many educators, parents, and businesspeople who had created novel applications of visual tools. The work also showed, in explicit terms, how each of these different tools was used and gave examples from classrooms and publishers.

In this book, I have included excerpts from many of these sources and expanded the "overview" synthesis pages for many of the tools so that teachers can try out the tools with students as a starting point to move from isolated uses to more comprehensive, schoolwide uses of visual tools. These overview pages include a model document that is an exemplar of how to take the tool into practice, but I have not

---

*Many isolated, generic forms of visual tools presented in this book have been used by educators and businesspeople for generations. When a developer or researcher of a set of visual tools, or visual tools software, and/or a language of visual tools that requires specialized techniques, resources, and training has a registered copyright, I have used the appropriate symbol that legally and professionally recognizes their work, and I hope that readers will investigate and honor these distinctions.

provided blackline masters for duplication. Why not? I have learned from over 20 years of experience with visual tools of every kind—and I have tried most of them with students—that if you have to duplicate a blackline master for students, you are asking them to duplicate your pattern of thinking, and not draw out and construct their own. I also have learned from my own experience and from observing other educators that we often *severely* underestimate students' capacities. This occurs especially in those schools and classrooms where teachers are working with students who land in the lower quartiles of testing and those with special needs. For many different and complex reasons, many educators end up coddling and thus inhibiting these students' cognitive development, rather than explicitly mediating their thinking toward high levels and into their own zone of proximal development (Vygotsky, 1936/1986).

This book is most easily understood as having three stages. The first three chapters, as shown in Introduction Figure 2, introduce you to, respectively, the metaphor of mapping, the research on the effectiveness of visual tools, and three types of visual tools, including general guidelines for using them. Chapters 4, 5, and 6 focus in on three basic types of visual tools, with pathways for applying them: brainstorming webs, graphic organizers, and conceptual mapping. The final two chapters document the now extensive use of a synthesis language of visual tools I developed, called Thinking Maps. Chapter 7 introduces Thinking Maps and then reveals how these tools, as a language, have been used successfully for English-language learners, for Mapping the Standards, and for leadership practices across

Introduction Figure 2   Flow Map of Book

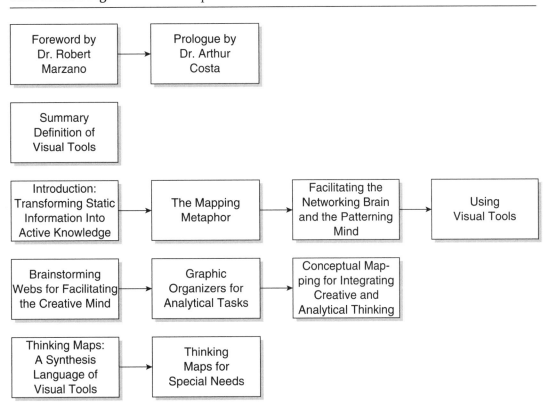

whole schools. After my introduction to the tools, three authors—Stefanie Holzman, Sarah Curtis, and Larry Alper, respectively—give us insight into these three applications. The final chapter documents how a school in West Newton, Massachusetts, Learning Prep School, with elementary through high school students and all with language-based special needs, has fully implemented Thinking Maps over multiple years. The well-documented results show changes in students' cognitive development, performance on classroom tasks and the Massachusetts Comprehensive Assessment System (MCAS) test, as well as profound shifts in how these students *see themselves* as learners through the differentiated uses of Thinking Maps.

This last chapter, written by Cynthia Manning, Coordinator of Thinking Maps at Learning Prep School, is a testament to what can happen when a whole school faculty explicitly and systematically, with coherence and sustained effort, delivers to their students a visual language for learning based on fundamental cognitive processes. One student is quoted as saying that these tools "get me to think." The demonstrated successes described in detail in the final chapter reverberate back across the book as the effort and outcomes portrayed heighten the central premise of this book: empowering students at every level to transform *static* information into *active* knowledge. These visual tools offer direct pathways from lower-order applications to higher-order thinking, from remembering content information to transforming information into conceptual understandings, from being able to map out and write transitional sentences in an essay to envisioning and planning students' dramatic transition from school into the often daunting new world requiring self-knowledge.

The students who are quoted in the last chapter represent the vision of this book: showing how visual tools are enabling students to take control of their own thinking and actions so they can transform information into knowledge that, in turn, leads to these same students' being able to transform the daily journey of their lives into a continuous process of self-knowing and renewal.

1

The Mapping Metaphor

Teachers around the world are often mystified by the mismatch between their perceptions of students' thinking and classroom performance. These perceptions may be positive, as offered in the following statements you may have heard yourself say:

- "I know that he has great ideas, but he can't seem to get them out in his writing! His writing is always a jumble."
- "She has amazingly creative ideas but has a very hard time articulating them."
- "I give my students the information, but when they come back with it—if they can remember it—it's a disorganized mess! They are smart, but they simply don't know how to organize their ideas."
- "I tell them the steps, and I know they can do it, but they often have to be told over and over again to get it right."

The perceptions may also be dangerously negative and detrimental, as some educators work from a deficit model, especially with students of color, students who are learning English as their second language or discourse (Mahiri, 2003), and students who come from families living in poverty. Here are some examples that I have heard over 25 years of working in urban schools with a high percentage of children of color, many of whom also live in poverty:

- "These children just can't think."
- "I ask them to tell me what they are thinking and they just don't say anything. I ask them to write and the words are a jumble."
- "Well, you know, look where these children come from. They just don't have the prior knowledge to make it."
- "How can they think if they don't have any vocabulary?"

These very same concerns may be heard in the workplace as well, as supervisors recognize the talents in people yet are perplexed by the quality of work produced or don't recognize the talents of people because of cultural mismatches or institutional structures.

Our educational system seems baffled by these disconnects, and one of the keys to resolving this disconnect is to move beyond an antiquated view of isolated information and knowledge and realize, in the research and in classrooms, that we are working with a very different mindset and set of student expectations than what existed 50 years ago. We are teaching to a generation of *digital natives:* Web-based, dynamic, visual-spatial-verbal media-savvy futurists who *see* and can visually represent the world in a much more connected way than we show it in classrooms. But in classrooms, many teachers still talk while students passively listen (as John Goodlad's research showed 20 years ago), students read text blocks and write answers at the end of the chapter, students fill in static worksheets and even static blackline masters called *graphic organizers,* or are led through software programs, all structured like books, just electronically. Our children don't feel lost on the Web because they are comfortable with networks of ambiguous information and unstable knowledge, but I believe that many feel lost in classrooms around the country because knowledge is perceived as primarily static and linear.

From the point of view of how knowledge is represented, there is a fundamental disconnect between how students and educators *see* and understand knowledge, and this is one of the subjects that this book addresses. *The primary reason for this is that most educators, as most educational researchers, are primarily text driven and auditory:* we live not only by the idea of text *books* and *the spoken word* but also that information is valid only when substantiated in linear text *blocks* and *strings of sentence.* To find out something, we read text in books. To find out what students know, we have them write text blocks to us or speak to us in strings of words. This has guided our definition of literacy for longer than we can remember. This is our mindset. One of the main reasons that learners, young and old, often have writer's "block" or their thinking is "blocked" is what I offer as a guiding metaphor for information: the WALL OF TEXT. The linear wall of text does not explicitly show the rich networks and patterns of thinking that the author is presenting implicitly within the linear representations. When visual tools are presented alongside text or used by learners to find the patterns embedded in the wall of text, then the rich foundational structures of knowledge is unveiled.

Now, at the beginning of the 21st century, we know that the linear representation of information, concepts, and knowledge does not reflect how our brains work. Linear representations are, to a certain degree, oppositional to how our minds and emotions work. This is a radical statement, but not so radical when you think about it. Linear lessons are not how we remember information. Linearity is not how we think as we connect information and transform that information into knowledge. Actually, the world around us doesn't work that way either; it works as a dynamic, interdependent, highly complex web of connections—much more like how a map looks.

Recently, I was working with teacher and administrator leaders from a school system in New York State, and after presenting an overview of visual tools within the context of some of the conclusive research and practice presented in this book, the literacy coordinator for the district broke through the paradigm for defining "literacy" in classrooms and dramatically offered this epiphany: "For all these years, I thought it was all about my students speaking and writing, but now I understand that what I really wanted to know was how my students were thinking." Please read this quote again. This insight is the way into this book: speaking, writing, and numeracy in the forms most often found in classrooms are predominantly *linear* representations of students' meaning making, while most thinking processes, content information and knowledge, and emotions are held in *nonlinear* associations. There are additional ways, as shown in this book, to represent knowledge that is as "rigorous" as linear text and in a complementary form.

The work presented in this book is not revolutionary as much as evolutionary, as educators who were trained and retrained in the auditory-verbal teaching techniques of the late 20th century enter the integrated visual-spatial-verbal-auditory literacy of the 21st century. *But this is not to suggest that we should discard the wall of text.* We still must live and learn by linear presentations as well as nonlinear and linear visual forms. What we want to do is add visual tools in an interplay with text and thus also bring forth an additional metaphor for how knowledge is represented. As you will see in this book, this breakthrough in how we represent information, ideas, and concepts, which has been occurring over the past 20 to 30 years from the first uses of brainstorming webs for prewriting processes, goes hand in hand with all the linear text that we still hold as important.

COGNITIVE DISSONANCE IN REPRESENTATION SYSTEMS

This book offers an overview of the need for the explicit shift toward a deeper and more expansive use of visual tools across classrooms, whole schools, and whole school systems for teaching, learning, and leadership purposes. Following is a brief summary of the domains and research that show conclusive evidence of the need for this shift:

New sciences: We know that the world is a dynamic, interdependent system or "web of life" that is not linear, that even "time" is not clearly understood as linear, and that in every discipline, including brain research, scientists must map the content knowledge to deeply understand a system.

Brain research: We know from research that the brain is dominantly visual and that the real untapped power of the brain-mind capacity is the natural mapping of incoming stimuli, and memory and meaning are greatly enhanced by visual representations. As Pat Wolfe has said: "Mapping is what the brain does."

Intelligences: We know that multiple intelligences are based on different representations of information and that emotional intelligences as well depend on the capacity of the brain to create visual-spatial-verbal schemas, or mental models. And we know that we must facilitate a full range of habits of mind and mediate these habits to improve thinking and problem solving.

Instruction: We know that nonlinguistic representations blended with verbal forms (dual coding) have a large impact on student learning and that the facilitation of thinking requires the development of habits of mind and metacognitive behaviors. The use of nonlinguistic representations also directly influences content-rich vocabulary development.

Learning: We know that the research on the effectiveness of graphic representations is extensive and conclusive, especially for identifying text structures for reading comprehension in every discipline, and that *student ownership* of visual tools based on thinking skills is a key to high conceptual performance.

These domains and the research within each help educators by guiding us to the use of new tools and strategies. Yet I believe that an additional metaphor—the mapping metaphor based in our dominantly visual-spatial relationship to the world—offers the language for integrating and also moving beyond the wall of text metaphor. Let's look at this additional metaphor for *seeing* how we construct knowledge.

THE ELEPHANT IN THE ROOM

A cartoon by Handelsmen recently published in *The New Yorker* magazine shows an older couple sitting in their living room, reading in their easy chairs. An elephant has picked up the phone by its trunk and is answering: "No, this is the elephant." This plays on "the elephant in the room" idea that we become so comfortable with things as they are, even if they don't work in a changing world, that we come to not even notice the problem. Of course, this cartoon takes it a step further: the elephant is not just a passive bystander in the corner, but has completely taken over the daily life of the couple to the extent that he is taking control of and making decisions about their everyday lives. So let me offer you "the elephant in the living room answering your phone" for educators that is this book's big-picture message:

There is *cognitive* dissonance between the highly constrained linear presentation of information in classrooms as text blocks and the multidimensional mapping of mental models that the brain-mind naturally *performs* when processing and crafting information into knowledge.

This dissonance or disconnect is *the* fundamental barrier to improving students' thinking and teachers' capacities to convey and facilitate basic and complex content and conceptual learning for all students.

This dissonance is like the elephant in the room—so obvious, tangible, and now so comfortable that most of us cannot see it. Teachers are making the transition toward knowledge creation by students' using visual tools and other new processes of teaching, but the cognitive dissonance in the classroom still exists.

The double meaning in the term *cognitive dissonance* is clear: *cognitively* we process beyond the linear mindset, but we ask students to show their thinking primarily in linear terms. This book offers not a replacement of traditional forms of literacy, but an additional way of "showing what you know" that is shifting our perception of knowledge on the most basic level. Why? Because visual tools of every kind, from brainstorming webs and graphic organizers to thinking-process mapping, are all based on the metaphor of the visual-spatial-verbal *mapping of knowledge*. Like any breakthrough technology, this transformational technology of the mind—the mapping of mental models—includes that which came before. The visual mapping of information into knowledge is what the brain does already and what has gone before in the sense of mapping physical space.

THE MAPPING METAPHOR: *TERRA INCOGNITA*

This book is about the richness of the visual-spatial-verbal mapping metaphor for the 21st century, its central role in helping us understand how visual tools and technologies support learners in their human capacity to transform information into knowledge. Ultimately, this is about power sharing of the construction of knowledge. The gulf between our students' technical expertise and their mental fluency is one of the barriers we must transcend to enact positive change in schools and the workplace. To be sure, we cannot go back to a time when information was so neatly packaged in books resting on library shelves. The mapping metaphor opens up our central dilemma as we step into the new millennium: our students may have the technical link to information, yet few have the mental fluency to craft information into meaningful and relevant knowledge.

The unique representations derived from map making are best expressed through the history of cartography, which reveals that this invention was a turning point for human understanding:

> The act of mapping was as profound as the invention of a number system. The combination or the reduction of reality and the construction of an analogical space is an attainment in abstract thinking of a very high order indeed, for it enables one to discover structures that would remain unknown if not mapped. (Robinson, 1982, p. 1)

This quotation is drawn from James H. Wandersee's insightful analysis of the connection between cartography and cognition (1990). He suggests that cartography links perception, interpretation, cognitive transformations, and creativity. Wandersee states that map making serves four basic purposes:

1. to challenge one's assumptions;

2. to recognize new patterns;

3. to make new connections; and

4. to visualize the unknown.

Map making, or cartography, has always been a central form of storing vital information about our surroundings and distant shores, from the ancient mappings of the earth and sky to solar systems. Humankind has always sought ways to discover and map new frontiers and find our way home by land and sea and, most recently, air. Cartography has been both a science and the gateway to new learning, but until the last few decades the term *mapping* has stayed within the intellectual domains of astronomers and geographers. Actually, from Africa to the Mayan astronomers, maps have been the documents of discoveries and ownership, and then, often, of domination. If a "discoverer" could map a region, then ownership was established. Planting a flag was a symbolic gesture, but mapping the region was the act of establishing physical boundaries and territories.

Of course, the attempt to discover longitude in the 18th century was foremost in the minds of seafarers, traders, and governments, as latitude and longitude lines crossed and established the relationships in space that could guide adventurers and conquerors alike to unknown lands. The Lewis and Clark expedition across the western region of North America, like any other journeys into new landscapes, was an attempt to map territories unknown to a new republic so that commerce and land holdings could expand. The "map" that Lewis brought back to President Thomas Jefferson was, of course, technical in the geographic sense, commercial in the description of resources, and ethnographic in depicting cultures new to the adventurers.

> Lewis studied maps in Jefferson's collection. He also conferred with Albert Gallatin, a serious map collector; the problem was that west of the Mandans nearly to the coast was *terra incognita*. And the best scientists in the world could not begin to fill in that map until someone had walked across the land. (Ambrose, 1996, p. 80)

Now we send captainless ships to distant planets to map and in some cases "own" new territories off the curvature of the earth. Now the "four corners" of our globe are known, and our technical expertise has seemingly, and some say recklessly, hopscotched over our practical needs. We have access to electronically mapped terrain through GPS, or global positioning systems. We may be in our car with a map on a screen, guiding us around the corner or into another state. Likewise, and using similar technology for networking information, our children, gazing at a television or computer screen or handheld device, access linked data from points around the world, and from different points of view. Those views may range from electronic explorers of knowledge on the Net to mass marketers of goods to exploiters of graphic violence and other morally repugnant materials.

There are no new territories in the lower 48 states: the new territories are of human imagination, interaction, communication. The terms *network, World Wide Web, integrated,* and *Internet* are concrete expressions for what has become the central metaphor of this age: mapping. Mapping is a metaphor for both connecting and overlapping knowledge structures. As we see in this book, mapping is also the name for practical tools for mental fluency. Mapping is a rich synthesis of thinking processes, mental strategies, techniques, and knowledge that enables humans to investigate unknowns, show patterns of information, and then use the map to express, build, and assess new knowledge. If "the world is flat," as Thomas Friedman proposes (Friedman, 2005), then we will need new maps to navigate on this dynamic technological plane for thinking and communicating.

The brain is based on pattern seeking; our minds consciously create patterns, our emotions are driven by layers of interconnected patterns of experience, our media thrive on the communication of patterns, and nature—that which we are a part of and which surrounds us—is a complex weave of patterns. Some of these patterns are linear and procedural, but the foundation of knowledge, from the basic factual knowledge record to decision making borne of evaluative processes, consists of nonlinear patterns. Are thoughts linear? emotions? an ecosystem? our values? Put in the starkest terms, our educational *system* and educational leaders can no longer lag behind the children who sit before a computer and can access and download and then create complex interweavings of knowledge as we stand before them and speak and write and numerate in linear strings of words and numbers.

MAPPING THE BRAIN

In early studies of the brain, scientists saw two *hemispheres* linked by a bridge; next, *regions* of the brain, specific *locales;* and then the detailed system of neural networks. Figure 1.1 shows how even back in the early days of brain scans, the understanding of brain functioning depended on visual mapping of the contours of activity. In this example, a special camera called a "magic eye" was used for scanning brainwave activity in different regions of the brain.

Figure 1.1   Mapping Brain Activity

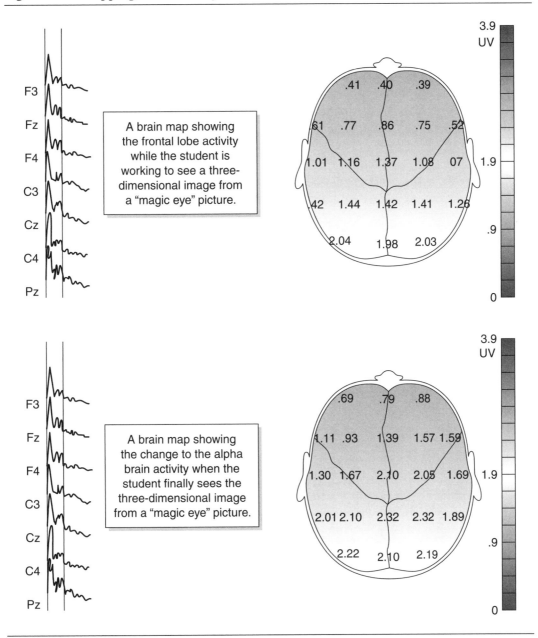

Source: Alcock, M. W. (1997, Spring). Are your students' brains comfortable in your classroom? *Ohio ASCD Journal,* 5(2): 13.

One of the most important technological races of the past decade has been the "race" to map the human genome system. In an article about J. Craig Venter, one of the early leaders in this race, the "finish line" is described as

a map of the entire human genome, the 80,000 genes that are thought to exist within our DNA. Altogether, this means finding more than three billion microscopic pieces of information—nucleotides, or bases, that are the molecular equivalent of letters—then putting them all in the right order and learning how to read them. (Belkin, 1998)

Venter is controversial from a scientific perspective not because he has been attempting to identify every gene (as is the government-sponsored Human Genome Project). Rather, he is trying to extrapolate from a partial sequence of genes in a DNA string that the other genes exist in between—much like making a map of a city with all the streets, but not filling in the details of each storefront. He is also in the center of a conflict from an ethical-commercial perspective: Who will "own" this map, a so-called Book of Life, the complete genetic code for humans? Of course, a power visual representation of our modern age is shown in Figure 1.2: a map of a DNA strand.

VISUAL TOOLS FOR MAPMAKING

Maps are primary guides in our lives: road maps, world maps, transit and subway diagrams, maps for exploring a museum or amusement park, weather maps, and even imaginary treasure maps. Of course, as we consider geographic knowledge on a map, we see key representations of the essential connections among mountains, valleys, and rivers. Similarly, visual tools are used primarily to make and represent connections among ideas and concepts.

Visual tools offer a bird's-eye view of patterns, interrelationships, and interdependencies. They provide guides for making our way in books full of text or among downloaded materials from the Information Superhighway. Unlike geographic maps, which show explicit *physical* models of the world, visual tools generate and unveil *mental* models of interrelationships developed by learners, along with the unique patterning capacity of each learner's mind. The significant difference between geographic and mental maps is that geographic maps represent relatively static, physical entities, whereas the maps we are investigating represent internal, mental, flexible, often quickly changing, and highly generative patterns.

Visual tools as evolving maps reflect our capacities to pattern and reorganize relationships. The similarity of purpose between geographic and mental maps, moreover, is clear: Each is based on the visual representation of a region, a mental space (Fauconnier, 1985) that heretofore may have been unknown. Each simultaneously displays a view of both the holistic "forest" and the detailed "trees" and is leading us into a vision of knowledge as holographic and not on the flatlands of the paper page. Additionally, maps are much like paintings: they are drawn from a certain perspective and thus have limitations. This means that each map is made in the eye of the beholder, with the instruments at hand, and within the intellectual and philosophical paradigm of its maker. This is best illustrated by the continuum in our belief system about our own planet, from the "flat earth" map made by our ancestors to the astronauts' perspective from a valley on the moon.

Figure 1.2   The Complexity of a DNA Strand

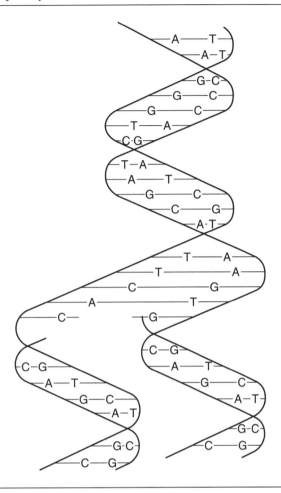

Source: Lowery, L. F. (1991). The biological basis for thinking. In A. L. Costa (Ed.), *Developing minds: A resource book for teaching thinking* (Vol. 1, rev. ed., p. 113). Alexandria, VA: Association for Supervision and Curriculum Development. Reprinted with permission.

The metaphorical relationship between cartography and mental maps of human cognition is useful, though certainly incomplete. *Seeing should not be construed as believing or knowing.* Seeing is one modality for perceiving, though for most of us it is our primary modality. Visual perceptions balance with auditory and kinesthetic access to knowing. Visual tools for mental mapping need to be integrated with other representational and language systems for reflecting different kinds of intelligences.

THE FOUNDATION OF THE MAPPING METAPHOR: SEEING

Mapping may help us to understand how the metaphor of "seeing" is the foundation for and central to the success of visual tools. This metaphor "grounds" visual tools in everyday classroom language. Figure 1.3 is a map of some of the everyday uses of the "seeing" metaphor. This "mapping" as an alternative form of epistemology is easily understood through the metaphor of "seeing." George Lakoff, professor of Linguistics and Cognitive Science, University of California–Berkeley, along with his colleagues has conducted cross-cultural research in the area of conceptual metaphor. Lakoff's most recent book, *Don't Look at That Elephant in the Room*, has caused quite a stir in political circles. His landmark study, aptly titled *Metaphors We Live By* (Lakoff & Johnson, 1980), reveals the centrality of metaphor to cognition, language, and everyday living. Lakoff's work integrates a wide range of cognitive science research and philosophical inquiry into a new framework for understanding human cognition, experience, and action.

As shown, this metaphor does not stand alone, overlapping with other modalities and spatial/physical relationships in the world. As you link these terms and add your own from everyday life, notice the overlapping of visual and spatial metaphors. For example, "perspective taking" draws from standing in a certain position and then seeing from that "point of view." This is one way that painters, photographers, writers, and other artists gain new perspectives and represent insights in everyday life. And, as we will see in this book, our students gain insight into their own worlds when they begin to apply visual tools, look up, and say: "I see what you mean."

In sum, visual tools are for constructing representations of knowledge. In educational terms, visual tools are for constructing and remembering, communicating and negotiating meanings, and assessing and reforming the shifting terrain of interrelated knowledge. We even use maps to rediscover information, ideas, and experiences lost in the recesses of our minds. We use maps to find our way to new information, much like an evolving treasure map of the mind for seeking new meaning in texts and other materials.

This book is about visual tools, which show patterns of thinking, and how they help us and our students make sense of the world, communicate better, and become life span learners. The richness of the mapping metaphor for the 21st century may have a central role in helping us understand how visual tools and technologies support learners in their ancient human capacity to take static information from the modern world of ideas and transform it into active maps of knowledge.

Figure 1.3   Everyday Uses of the "Seeing" Metaphor

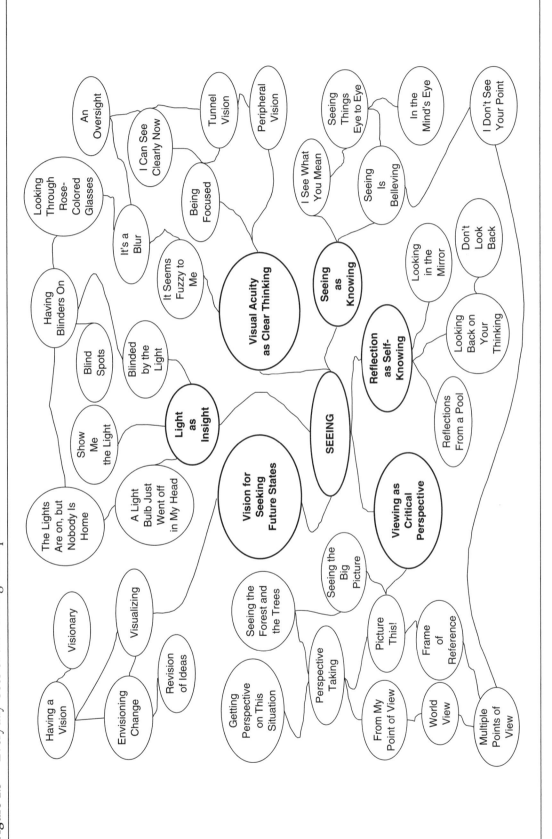

2

Facilitating the Networking Brain and the Patterning Mind

Leonardo da Vinci's Principles for the Development of a Complete Mind

1. Study the science of art.

2. Study the art of science.

3. Develop your senses— especially learn how to see.

4. Realize that everything connects to everything else.

—Buzan, 1996, p. 26

The "mapping metaphor" offered in the last chapter effectively conveys the big-picture influence of visual tools for transforming isolated, static information into actively mapped knowledge. This chapter goes to the heart of the detailed, conclusive research base that documents how visual tools facilitate learners' capacities to move fluently from the internal, unconscious networking brain to the external, conscious patterning mind through visual representations of thinking. Leonardo da Vinci offers guidance for this chapter as we see that students need to study analytically (scientifically) and creatively (artistically) and to develop their senses, but especially to *see* and to realize how everything is connected. Maybe da Vinci gives us the best definition of visual tools! Brainstorming webs directly facilitate creativity, graphic organizers help in more analytical processes, while conceptual mapping offers a rich synthesis of creative, analytical, and connective conceptual processes.

We will look through multiple frames in this chapter to see how visual tools facilitate the dynamic, evolving, lifelong development of the neural networking brain and the schematic patterning mind through nonlinguistic and linguistic representations of mental models. Before we delve into the implications for the use of visual tools as they are seen through the lens of brain research, schema theory, multiple intelligences, emotional intelligences, and habits of mind, let's first look at the most relevant research to classroom practice: the use of *nonlinguistic representations* and the significant area within that research that shows the high degree of effectiveness of graphic organizers.

NONLINGUISTIC AND LINGUISTIC REPRESENTATIONS

In what has become a landmark research study cited in many journals and by word of mouth in many schools around the country—*Classroom Instruction That Works: Research-Based Strategies for Increasing Student Achievement*—Robert Marzano, Debra Pickering, and Jane Pollock identify nine strategies that directly impact student achievement (Marzano et al., 2001):

1. Identifying similarities and differences

2. Summarizing and note taking

3. Reinforcing effort

4. Homework and practice

5. Nonlinguistic representations

6. Cooperative learning

7. Setting objectives and providing feedback

8. Generating and testing hypotheses

9. Cues, questions, and advance organizers

The authors, with the Mid-continent Research for Education and Learning Institute (McREL), used a meta-analysis process for analyzing and synthesizing classroom-based research studies to make key generalizations about what works. (For a discussion of the meta-analysis process, which combines results from studies to find "average effects," refer to pp. 4–6 of their book.) One of the top nine instructional strategies they identified is nonlinguistic representations. Following is the authors' background theory and definition of this instructional strategy:

> Many psychologists adhere to what has been called the "dual-coding" theory of information storage. This theory postulates that knowledge is stored in two forms—a linguistic form and an imagery form. . . . The imagery mode of representation is referred to as a nonlinguistic representation. The more we use both systems of representation—linguistic and

nonlinguistic—the better we are able to think about and recall knowledge. (p. 73)

This *integration and direct use by students* of linguistic and nonlinguistic forms is the essence of visual tools. Integrating drawings or pictures in a visual map along with words creates a rich mental bond within the brain and mind for remembering information. This bond is constructed by the learner and thus offers a process for conceptualizing and transforming information into a meaningful visual display of the knowledge base of the learner on paper or computer screen. The maps become an external memory for the brain and mirror for mental reflection and self-assessment for the learner.

The authors continue to both distinguish between linguistic and nonlinguistic forms and link the forms, as they represent a range of graphic organizers that represent how to effectively translate research and theory into classroom practice:

Graphic organizers are perhaps the most common way to help students generate nonlinguistic representations. . . . Graphic organizers combine the linguistic mode in that they use words and phrases, and the nonlinguistic mode in that they use symbols and arrows to represent relationships. (p. 75)

The "symbols and arrows" and other graphic representations such as boxes, ovals, and lines used for linking information in brainstorming webs, graphic organizers, and concept mapping may be the macroscale visual links shown on paper that mirror the microscale *neural* connections the brain is making. The isolated words held in the web of a visual map—the vocabulary we wish students to acquire related to content knowledge—are the bits of distributed information that the brain is connecting together from across its neural pathways. As Pat Wolfe says, "One of the most important things we have learned is that the brain is primarily visual. . . . The brain does not outline. You form networks or maps of neurons and information is held within these maps" (Wolfe, 2006). The traditional linear outlines and linear sentences and paragraphs found on a "wall of text" are not representative of how the brain stores and links information. Visual tools are much more attuned to the natural networking of the brain, as we shall see in more depth in the following sections, and this is one of the reasons why linguistic/nonlinguistic visual tools work in classrooms.

Authors Marzano and Pickering extended their research on these nine strategies, with particular emphasis on graphic organizers, into an approach to *Building Academic Vocabulary* (Marzano & Pickering, 2005). What is of particular interest here is that the authors propose six instructional steps for typical classrooms that includes nonlinguistic representations as a key, including an adapted sequence for second-language learners. The reason for emphasizing visual tools in this sequence may be that, as we see throughout this book, visual tools are so supportive of and easily integrated with many of the other eight strategies that work. The authors refer to several visual tools, including the explicit use of several graphics that form Thinking Maps as a common visual language for learning (see Chapters 7 and 8).

For example, the strategy of "comparing and contrasting" is most easily accomplished by students when they graphically detail similarities of and differences between two concepts rather than only verbalizing their thinking. Marzano and Pickering suggest that the Thinking Map called the "Double-Bubble Map" is an effective tool for this process. Consider that it is very difficult for students to generate, organize, synthesize, and then evaluate all the information required for a comparison while holding this information in short-term memory or attempting to scan a page of linearly organized notes. They never transform the information into active and accessible knowledge. This is particularly important when students are using another of the nine strategies, *cooperative learning*. Students in cooperative groups—or adults working together in collaborative groups—need to be able to pull together the thinking of the group as a product that also represents their process. So often, the wide-ranging and rich patterns of learning generated during cooperative interactions are lost in the experience of the group and not represented in a form that really honors the depth of the group's thinking and conceptual growth. Oftentimes these rich patterns are just noted as static information in linear-list form. They are not *transformed* from bits of static information into rich, active patterns of knowledge.

This holds true for another of the nine effective strategies, "summarizing," as students are asked to summarize and to take notes from linear text. Often what students end up doing, without a visual tool, is merely to copy down ideas in static linear form even though the information is, for example, hierarchical, causal, or comparative in *form*. They have not *transformed* the information into rich patterns of knowledge. They then do not internalize this *static* information as *active* knowledge but instead as a disconnected list. What *does not* show up in students' notes is their thinking patterns and processes of active knowledge. Additionally, as related to the nine strategies, visual tools offer "advanced organizers" or "cues" for beginning a lesson related to "setting objectives": when the teacher draws out a visual representation on a chalkboard or projected image on a screen, then students *see* the structure of thinking they are going to be asked to per*form* to most effectively meet a standard or objective. Obviously, my wordplay with the root "form" is important for understanding the power of visual tools related to learning: if we believe that learning is in the minds of the students, then they must be empowered to transform information into active, meaningful knowledge and deeper learning.

RESEARCH STUDIES ON GRAPHIC ORGANIZERS

The meta-analysis conducted by the McCREL authors identifies nine effective instructional strategies and is derived from reviewing research across a wide array of educational research designs and topics. When we look closely at the specific research on graphic organizers, it becomes obvious why these tools surface in the Marzano, Pickering, and Pollock study. A study recently released by the Institute for the Advancement of Research in Education (IARE) was generated from an analysis of 29 scientifically based research studies using academic databases to locate research on the instructional effectiveness of graphic organizers. Using the definitions set forth by Section 9101 of the No Child Left Behind Act (NCLB) of 2001, IARE selected studies that applied "rigorous, systematic, and objective procedures to obtain reliable and valid knowledge relevant to education activities and programs." The resulting summary that is excerpted below shows conclusively that *visual learning strategies improve student performance.*

The scientifically based research cited in the literature review demonstrates that a research base exists to support the use of graphic organizers for improving student learning and performance across grade levels, with diverse students, and in a broad range of content areas. IARE conclusions, taken verbatim from this review include the following:

Reading comprehension. Use of graphic organizers is effective in improving students' reading comprehension.

Student achievement. Students using graphic organizers show achievement benefits across content areas and grade levels. Achievement benefits are also seen with students with learning disabilities.

Thinking and learning skills. The process of developing and using a graphic organizer enhances skills such as developing and organizing ideas, seeing relationships, and categorizing concepts.

Retention. Use of graphic organizers aids students in retention and recall of information.

Cognitive learning theory. The use of graphic organizers supports implementation of cognitive learning theories: dual coding theory, schema theory, and cognitive load theory.

The evidence offered in this research and throughout this book shows that the outcomes with the use of graphic organizers include retention and recall of basic information as well as facilitation of conceptual development and higher-order thinking. The analysis showed that visual tools help students across a range of processes required in classrooms. Here is an (unorganized) summary list detailed in the study:

- Brainstorm ideas
- Develop, organize, and communicate ideas
- See connections, patterns, and relationships
- Assess and share prior knowledge
- Develop vocabulary
- Outline for writing process activities
- Highlight important ideas
- Classify or categorize concepts, ideas, and information
- Comprehend the events in a story or book
- Improve social interaction between students, and facilitate group work and collaboration among peers
- Guide review and study
- Improve reading comprehension skills and strategies
- Facilitate recall and retention

It is interesting to note the wide range of effects on student performance from these studies. Unfortunately, because the term *graphic organizer* has become common and ubiquitous, many educators assume that the use of linguistic/nonlinguistic graphics are constrained to the analytical processes under the heading "organize." The wide range of types of visual tools in this book attests to the flexible uses of these forms beyond supporting only the organization of information. Although it is true that most visual tools support organizational processes to some degree, many tools, as the research shows, are used for generative brainstorming, comprehension, synthesis, and evaluation as well as communication of ideas in classrooms.

READING COMPREHENSION
AND READING FIRST RESEARCH

Instruction supporting early reading comprehension is now perceived as crucial to all learning and so it is essential that we go one step deeper into the research, beyond broad instructional strategies as defined by Marzano et al., and specific research on graphic organizers. In a document that was widely distributed by the U.S. Department of Education, *Put Reading First* (Armbruster et al., 2001), the use of graphic organizers is established as a central strategy for text comprehension. Developed by the Center for Improvement of Early Reading Achievement, this publication focused on five areas of early reading instruction: phonemic awareness, phonics, fluency, vocabulary, and text comprehension. Although debate on *the degree* of focus on phonics has intensified, the report's section on text comprehension meshes with the two meta-analysis studies reviewed earlier. Graphic organizers and a range of semantic maps are identified as central to reading text comprehension:

> Graphic organizers illustrate concepts and interrelationships among concepts in a text, using diagrams or other pictorial devices, . . . and can help readers focus on concepts and how they are related to other concepts. Graphic organizers help students to learn from informational text in the content areas, such as science and social studies textbooks and trade books. Used with informational text, graphic organizers can help students see how concepts fit common text structures. Graphic organizers are also used with narrative text, or stories, as story maps.
>
> Graphic organizers can:
>
> Help students focus on text structure as they read;
>
> Provide students with tools they can use to examine and visually represent relationships in a text; and
>
> Help students write well organized summaries of a text. (Armbruster et al., 2001, pp. 50–51)

If we look at the three meta-analyses reviewed previously—*Classroom Instruction That Works*, specific graphic organizer research, and the *Put Reading First* publication—a clear picture emerges: visual tools are concrete tools that enable all students to visually organize information, generate ideas and summaries of what they are reading and learning, and transform information into *active forms of* knowledge beyond the traditional linear structures teachers most often use.

Visual tools also offer graphic structures for content vocabulary development as well as visual bridges from basic information to improved thinking, metacognition, and self-monitoring practices by students. The *Put Reading First* document states that "metacognition can be defined as 'thinking about thinking.' Good readers use metacognitive strategies to think about and have control over their reading. . . . Comprehension monitoring, a critical part of metacognition, has received a great deal of attention in the reading research" (p. 49). So, despite the recurring "reading wars" that produce battle lines and philosophical/political swings between phonics-centered and meaning-centered activity at the early grades, *visual tools* provide a foundational bridge between the two. Visual tools, used with care, coherence, and deliberation, support content-specific vocabulary development *and* concept development. The capacity of our students to use visual tools for seeking isolated definitions in context while also consciously seeking the form in text structures across whole passages and books takes the learner to a higher-order level of understanding and awareness.

Although all of this research is crucial to a new level of awareness of the implications for using visual tools, let's contextualize this discussion by stepping back from specific classroom instruction and student-centered strategies to look at the broader context of educational research. Given what the detailed research shows about the processes of teaching, learning, and reading comprehension, let's consider the following questions:

How are visual tools supported by research across wider fields beyond education?

How do our brains and minds interact in this world to generate, remember, organize, and make sense of the information we take in from our body?

As we shall see, the links between the research on mapping information in classrooms for tasks such as vocabulary development, reading comprehension, and writing—across all content areas—dovetails with what we know about how the brain-mind-body system works in the "natural" world.

MAPPING LIVING SYSTEMS

Though obvious, it is important to recognize that the brain, mind, and body thrive within the natural systems that influence how we come to be human. Shifts in scientific theories of the structures and processes of life systems, brain research, schema theory of the mind, and intelligences all frame what is now becoming much clearer in educational practice: the use of visual tools for visual patterning and thus transforming information into knowledge may have a far greater impact on student learning than any other set of tools. It is very easy for us as educators to focus on the refined research in areas such as ever-expanding brain research, intelligences, cognition, and even reading comprehension without even starting with the world in which we swim, or *living systems*. A brief discussion of new theories of living systems may give us a wider context for seeing why visual tools are needed in the midst of shifting scientific paradigms for perceiving and understanding the world around us.

Over the past 50 years, a dramatic shift has occurred in the scientific and philosophical underpinnings of our understandings of life forms. In *The Web of Life* (Capra, 1996), Fritjof Capra brings together quantum physics, information theory, systems thinking, and theories linking the brain, mind, and cognition into a viewpoint of life processes. Briefly, Capra defines a living system as a system that "has a *pattern of organization* that is physically structured and activated by a life process that embodies these" (Capra, 1996, p. 161). The key characteristic of this definition of a living system is the *pattern of organization* of an organism and how we make sense of these patterns. Capra states:

In the study of structure we measure and weigh things. Patterns, however, cannot be measured or weighed; they must be mapped. To understand a pattern we must map a configuration of relationships. (p. 81)

This underlying principle is what is now guiding brain researchers and educational leaders to use tools and techniques that support students in seeking, constructing, and, ultimately, understanding the *patterns* of information that ground every discipline we teach, and that support connecting all disciplines together. I believe that visual tools may have surfaced as tools for learning directly out of the need at this time in history to cope with a fundamental shift in our understanding of life systems. In times gone by, we were plenty satisfied by linear text and spoken language alone because these are primarily representation systems for expressing and coding a linear, structural understanding of the world.

If a new paradigm for understanding life forms is based on a dynamic systems view, rather than a mechanistic view of life, then tools that help us schematically *map* these networks become paramount. Of course, our perceptions of the natural world also influence our present conceptions of the human brain.

> "Mind is not a thing but a process—the process of cognition, which is identified with the process of life. The brain is a specific structure through which this process operates. The relationship between mind and brain, therefore, is one between process and structure" (Capra, 1996, p. 175).

As we will see in the remainder of this book, a rich array of visual tools provides a way for students to discover what they know as they creatively weave static bits and linear strands of information from paper texts and electronic screens into active, meaningful knowledge. Students are seeking patterns in nature and in their neighborhood. Their brains are actively detecting patterns, and through a range of habits of mind and their multiplicity of "intelligences," they are organizing the raw data into schemata and attempting to surface these relationships. They are inductively generating new mental models of knowledge as networks of interconnected information.

> "Maps are frames of reference. In them, a student must find a way to relate new information to other information. . . . Teachers often have not been exposed to creative map-teaching models or forfeit map learning to accommodate the mandate for higher test scores" (Caine & Caine, 1994, p. 46).

THE BRAIN IS A PATTERN DETECTOR

If we believe nature exists as patterns, then it is no wonder that the experts in brain-based learning all agree on one thing: the brain makes sense of the world by *constructing or mapping* patterns of the world. The focus on "patterning" is thus the entry point to understanding the connection between brain functioning and visual tools:

> The overwhelming need of learners is for meaningfulness. . . . We do not come to understand a subject or master a skill by sticking bits of information to each other. Understanding a subject results from perceiving relationships.

The brain is designed as a pattern detector. Our function as educators is to provide students with the sorts of experiences that enable them to perceive "the patterns that connect." (Caine & Caine, 1994, p. 7)

The array of linked patterns in the brain is *always* more complex than the linear form in which we normally communicate these ideas in classrooms. Too often, students are returning to us linear lists of information or quick responses without having to organize the information into patterns. Or, they do *all* of this patterning in their mind without the memory capacity to fully *see* the patterns. Unlike the repetitive listing of information so often found in textbooks and classrooms, the brain is unconsciously reconstructing bits, shreds, and strands of related information from all over its physical frame while integrating sensory inputs into a multitude of overlapping patterns. As educators, we know that students have much more going on "in there" than we "get out" of them. Why? Many say that the brain is being underutilized. Less obvious is that what is actually "going on in there" has few pathways for "getting out of there" other than on the lined paper of schooled, linear representations. The brain's structural capacity for constructing patterns and the mind's cognitive processing capacity for expressing complex interrelationships in networks of knowledge is being dramatically underrepresented in linear strings of words, numbers, and other traditional symbol systems.

For example, when we ask students complex, higher-order questions, we are activating an unbelievable network of patterned firings of neural networks in the brain. But then we ask them to answer in linear terms: verbally, in writing, or by strings of numbers on the page. Often, many students respond by looking dumbfounded. Could it be that they do not have the tools to think and express their ideas holistically? Or is it that their rapidly patterned ideas are being condensed into short answers and exclusively in linear terms? The true mismatch is between the brain's capacity to pattern and the weak representation systems we provide students to represent their thinking. This situation creates an overload, or overly stressed cognitive load.

> "Visual tools are effective as learning aids. I want to find out what others have learned and how they connect it to prior learning. One end-of-course strategy is to cover a wall with flip chart or butcher paper. Then let small teams design a huge visual representation of what was learned. Either they can cooperate to create a synergistic visual map, or they can split up the content and each team makes their material as part of the whole. When it's done, it's a mural that creates common, unifying thinking—and it opens up new possibilities where gaps exist or connections are open" (E. Jensen, personal communication, August 1998).

THE VISUAL BRAIN

The mismatch stated in the preceding section is apparent because of the brain's structure. Remarkably, unbelievably, the brain is capable of absorbing 36,000 visual images every hour. How can this imponderable ability be true? It is because the sophisticated visual capacity of our brain system is beyond the conscious processing of our mind: research approximates that between 70 and 90% of the information received by the brain is through visual channels. Though our auditory and kinesthetic modes of "sensing" are complex, the brain's *dominant* and most efficient sensory filter for most information is our eyes. As Pat Wolfe states, "The brain is dominantly visual," partially because of the survival mechanism that was developed and evolved: we must remember what we see to survive. In a dramatic reversal of the view of many educators that auditory, visual, and kinesthetic approaches to teaching and learning must be balanced, we now know that the human brain has evolved into an *imbalanced* visual-spatial imager/processor. As Sylwester (1995) describes:

> The site of 70 percent of our body's sensory receptors, our eyes begin the cognitive process of transforming reflected light into a mental image of the objects that reflected the light. Light rays (photons) enter an eye through the system of the cornea, iris, and lens, which focuses the image on the thin retina sheet at the rear of the eyeball. The rays are absorbed by the retina's 120 million rods and 7 million cones, with each rod or cone focusing on a small, specific segment of the visual field. (p. 61)

Though most memory is constructed from activations all over the brain and all modalities must be reinforced, the brain has been evolving over time toward visual dominance. Even if we each believe that we are strongly "kinesthetic" or "auditory" or "visual," consider that each of us is still taking in *much* more information "visually" than through other modalities. We need to understand, and thus teach and learn with, this imbalanced strength in mind: most of our students and most of us, as we read this page, are strong visual learners.

> "The impact of visualization on memory and recall has been demonstrated in numerous studies. In one, subjects were shown as many as 10,000 pictures, and then later shown some of these same pictures along with other pictures they had not seen. Under these conditions, they were able to recognize more than 90 percent of the pictures they had already seen" (Standing, 1973).
>
> "It appears that not only are visual tools extremely effective in assisting students to initially process and make sense out of abstract information, they are also taking advantage of our brain's almost unlimited capacity for images" (Wolfe & Sorgen, 1990, p. 8).

Current brain research has provided many insights into how the brain unconsciously takes in and simultaneously and consciously processes information. Pat Wolfe represents three major stages of information processing within the dynamic system of the brain: paying attention, building meaning, and extending meaning (Wolfe & Sorgen, 1990). Most visual tools provide flexible cognitive patterns to students and teachers that are congruent with and facilitate each of these stages.

> "The one million fibers in the optic nerve of each eye carry a summary of the vast amount of data that the [retina's] 127 million rods and cones receive. . . . Further processing (forward in the cortex) combines line segments into shapes, colors them, combines them, locates them in space, names them, and contemplates their meanings. At this point, sensory processes are being transformed into thought processes" (Sylwester, 1995, pp. 61–62).

THE MIND ORGANIZES
INTO SCHEMATIC PATTERNS

The tantalizing details of recent brain research supports decades of cognitive science research drawn from behavioral studies focused on the mind at work. The dovetailing of brain and cognitive science research is grist for many books, but one of the most important links is between the networking structure of the brain and the "schematic" processing of the mind. Schema theory—which has been used as a foundation for brain research—brings the networking structure of the brain and the schema-generating mind together. The physical structure and actions of the brain are networking information, physically chunking and storing bits of information in certain regions. When these are "called up" from all over the brain, these isolated bits are integrated.

On a micro level, this integration supports the moment-to-moment, instinctual, unconscious, and repetitive processes of life. When larger chunks are called up to a more conscious level, the process of building or constructing cognitive structures from experience occurs. Schemas are not patterns available to the conscious human mind, but the building blocks of cognition and conscious mental modeling. As Daniel Goleman pointed out in his first book over 20 years ago, schemas are the transitional, ghostlike forms that carry raw experience to an organizational level:

> The packets that organize information and make sense of experience are "schemas," the building blocks of cognition. Schemas embody the rules and categories that order raw experience into coherent meaning. All knowledge and experience is packaged in schemas. Schemas are the ghost in the machine, the intelligence that guides information as it flows through the mind. (Goleman, 1985, p. 75)

Goleman's early work linked brain research with cognitive science and the beginnings of the concept of emotional intelligence in the book *Vital Lies, Simple Truths: The Psychology of Self-Deception* (1985). Here he shows the connection between brain research on attention and research on schemas:

> Schemas and attention interact in an intricate dance. Active attention arouses relevant schemas; schemas in turn guide the focus of attention. The vast repertoire of schemas lies dormant in memory, quiescent until activated by attention. Once active, they determine what aspects of the situation attention will track. . . . They also determine what we do not notice. It is here where the structure of brain and the processes of mind unite: the neural networking as a growing structure and the mindful attention and/or inattention to the organization of experiences. (Goleman, 1985, pp. 79–89)

Because schemas are often but not exclusively networks of categories, visual tools may complement a range of structural patterns of neural networks and schematic structures of concepts. Piaget and many others since have conferred great importance on the capacity of a learner to assimilate and accommodate new information and concepts into a previously held schema. The mental schema and the actual neural, *physical* structure of the brain then shift and re*form* into a new structure. If schemas are the bridge between the structure of the brain and the processing mind, visual tools may be a bridge between the patterning mind and the outward representation of the *form of thinking*.

MULTIPLE INTELLIGENCES AS ACTIVE PATTERNS

When we understand the brain as a pattern detector, we begin to see that the intelligences described by Howard Gardner are really about how the multiplicity of patterns is expressed—or represented in different ways. The eight intelligences (and possibly a ninth) are then more easily understood as different ways of re-presenting knowledge. In Gardner's fascinating early book on cognitive science, *The Mind's New Science*, he brings forth the idea that this new science traffics in representations:

> The cognitive scientist rests his discipline on the assumption that, for scientific purposes, human cognitive activity must be described in terms of symbols, schemas, images, ideas, and other forms of mental representations. (Gardner, 1985, p. 39)

Symbols and symbol systems thus are the translators or medium of the brain-mind-body connection into the realm of intrapersonal and interpersonal communications. What Gardner has done is ask us as an educational community—and as a larger community encompassing work, family, and personal leisure time—to expand our awareness and appreciation of different representation systems. The full expression is in products of mind:

> Symbols and symbol systems gain their greatest utility as they enter into the fashioning of full-fledged symbolic products: stories and sonnets, plays and poetry, mathematical proofs and problem solutions, rituals and reviews. (Gardner, 1985, p. 301)

Here we can make some correlations between the eight intelligences (representation systems) and visual tools. Linguistic, logical-mathematical, visual-spatial, interpersonal, and intrapersonal intelligences are directly supported by brainstorming webs, graphic organizers, and conceptual maps. These visual symbols support the construction of networks of language and logical processing and are based on a spatial patterning of information. These tools also provide a means of communicating frames of mind, perspectives, emotional patterns, and mental models among people. These visual maps become mirrors of the mind at work, thus facilitating an internal dialogue and self-assessment. Most important, visual tools act as *synthesizers of ideas* from across the multiplicity of intelligences.

Yet something deeper is at hand with visual tools than surface-level links to various intelligences: the brain-mind is a structure-process organism that detects and constructs patterns, and visual tools are foundational for sensing, thinking, and feeling across all these intelligences. Interpersonal and intrapersonal intelligences and communication are frames for action and emotional-intellectual responses in the world. As basic patterning tools, visual tools support learners as they seek patterns across all symbolic systems, since these symbolic systems are bound up in schemas. As Daniel Goleman (1985) points out,

> Schemas are intelligence in action. They guide the analysis of sensory input. . . . Schemas determine which focus attention seeks, and hence what will enter awareness. When driven by emotions like anxiety, schemas impose themselves with special force. (pp. 82–83)

Given these overlapping views, I am suggesting that what integrates different intelligences, and what also makes them distinct, is the brain-mind schemas, or webs of relationships, patterns, and interdependence.

HABITS OF MIND

So how do we understand and respond "intelligently" to the patterns that are before us? How do our habits of mind attend to all these patterns that the brain has detected and the mind has organized?

Capra and many critics of Western philosophy and education point out that the traditional paradigm for studying living systems has been based primarily on the study of structures; therefore, our educational system has as well. Translated into classroom life, students have been asked, "What are the parts?" rather than "How do all these parts work interactively together in a system?" We are beginning to shift from asking students to regurgitate discrete parts of topics toward a different way of perceiving the world—one requiring that they show *how* these discrete parts integrate into dynamic patterns. The idea of seeing the interconnected nature of things in the world is not new, but the idea that we need a representation system of visual tools outside of our existing forms is.

Educators are now shifting toward more process questions, and with this shift from the study of structures to an integrated study of patterns and processes, we will also change or add to our basic tools for understanding, constructing, and communicating knowledge. In a sense, we are in a transitional time of habituating our students to thinking in patterns.

How our minds respond to stimuli is bound up by the storehouse of overlapping, interconnected schema, yet our minds are not passive, and we make decisions—often unconsciously—about how we respond. These decisions are guided by habits of mind fully described and researched by Dr. Arthur Costa. Consider a few of these behaviors and habits of mind:

- Are we *impulsive* when confronted with an overload of information?
- Are we *empathic* when listening to another point of view?
- Are we *flexible* when we are in unfamiliar contexts?
- Are we *systematic* when working through a problem?

These habits of mind are among 16 Costa identified, which are used as an explicit framework in classrooms and across whole schools by students, teachers, and administrators as powerful facilitators of thinking.

- Persisting
- Managing impulsivity
- Listening with understanding and empathy
- Thinking flexibly
- Thinking about thinking (metacognition)

- Striving for accuracy
- Questioning and posing problems
- Applying past knowledge to new situations
- Thinking and communicating with clarity and precision
- Gathering data through all senses
- Creating, imaging, innovating
- Responding with wonderment and awe
- Taking responsible risks
- Finding humor
- Thinking interdependently
- Remaining open to continuous learning

Art Costa and Bena Kallick, in *Activating and Engaging Habits of Mind* (2000), offer this guidance as we consider the importance of facilitating mindfulness:

> In teaching for the habits of mind, we are interested in not only how many answers students know but also how students behave when they don't know an answer. We are interested in observing how students produce knowledge rather than how they merely reproduce it. A critical attribute of intelligent human beings is not only having information but also knowing how to act on it. By definition, a problem is any stimulus, question, task, phenomenon, or discrepancy, the explanation for which is not immediately known. Intelligent behavior is performed in response to such questions and problems. Thus, we are interested in focusing on student performance under those challenging conditions—dichotomies, dilemmas, paradoxes, ambiguities and enigmas— that demand strategic reasoning, insightfulness, perseverance, creativity and craftsmanship to resolve them. (p. xv)

This vision and the 16 habits of mind are often facilitated when visual tools are in practice. It is also clear that different types of visual tools—with varying purposes and outcomes—actively facilitate and trigger different habits of mind through the design and use of the tools. As we look at classroom practices of each type of visual tool— brainstorming webs, graphic organizers, and conceptual mapping—it becomes clear that there is a general correlation between each type of visual tool and clusters of habits of mind. (For a more detailed description, see Hyerle in Costa & Kallick, in press.)

Generally speaking and through specific examples shown in the following chapters, I have found that brainstorming webs focus more on the facilitation of creative thinking, graphic organizers on analytical thinking, and conceptual mapping on a synthesis of creative and analytical thinking while also directly framed by a metacognitive stance. Figure 2.1 shows these relationships in three categories I have created in a Tree Map. This view of the 16 habits of mind, as related to visual tools, is certainly not "set in stone," but is offered merely as a way of thinking about the purpose of the tools and beginning to distinguish between different types of visual tools, how they were created by their authors, and how they are typically used in classrooms. This view of the interplay of habits of mind and visual tools will be discussed more closely as we begin to also evaluate the strengths and weaknesses of each form in the following chapters.

Bringing forth Costa's habits of mind also gives us greater clarity about how and why visual tools are important and effective in classrooms. In this chapter, we have seen that there is conclusive evidence of the effectiveness of the tools for improving teacher instruction and thus student performance across disciplines and grade levels. But we must ask ourselves: Is there something more for us to learn as educators about visual tools beyond the constrained focus on testable outcomes and student achievement, as documented in these concrete results and as evaluated in schools? I believe there is something more, and I believe it is in the heart and mind of every educator and parent of the children in our schools. The goal of education must be to have our students exit our schools with capacities not presently explicitly taught or tested: to think creatively, analytically, and conceptually beyond the assignments, writing prompts, and tests of the factual information found in content-area texts. It is the facilitation of these kinds of habits of mind.

We now turn to the more practical applications of different types of visual tools with this question in mind: How do we support students to creatively, analytically, and reflectively transform information in every content area into active knowledge using visual tools?

Figure 2.1   Tree Map for Habits of Mind

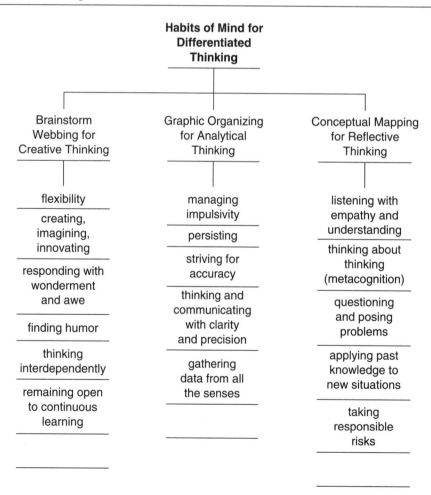

3

Using Visual Tools

CLARIFYING A CONFUSION
OF TERMS AND TOOLS

The exciting variety and successful uses of visual tools now available in classrooms across the states and around the world has also brought about a confusion of terms and definitions for educators. The following terms are often used synonymously: webs, spider maps, clusters, mind maps, semantic maps, cognitive maps, story maps, diagrams, templates, and graphic organizers. Adding to the confusion is that some approaches are used in coherent and consistent ways, whereas other tools are downloaded off of Web sites for duplication and have highly circumscribed, simple applications.

Some visual tools are delivered only through software programs, such as Inspiration® Software, OmniGraffle®, and STELLA Software. Some approaches such as Concept Mapping, Mind Mapping, Thinking Maps, and "Teaching with Unit Visual Frameworks" have evolved into powerful and comprehensive visual models that require professional development. These models may be fully researched and become a foundation for learning across whole schools and school systems. In a nutshell, many of the models described in the chapters to follow have evolved through research and practice and significantly improve student performance, whereas other graphics are used merely as worksheets for students to fill in, requiring little thought and often adding little value to classroom performance. Oftentimes, from just looking at a graphic, one cannot tell the degree of complexity, meaningfulness, or effectiveness of the visual tool: you must see it in action!

Many educators, having been saturated with simple brainstorming web processes as "warm-ups" during professional development workshops over the years or with repetitive graphics presented in textbooks, may look at new visual tools and models and say, "Oh, we've done that before." This attitude is understandable because at first glance, many of these visual forms *look* like any other. But the range of uses and distinctions among different visual tools can be profound. The true definition of each visual tool or model of visual tools is usually found in how it is explained and introduced to teachers and students and its subsequent interactive use and *not in how it looks on a static page.*

This chapter offers an introduction to visual tools and discussion of common concerns about the uses of these tools as presented in the Summary Definition of Visual Tools at the beginning of this book. Take a moment and reread the text and review the Tree Map presented in the summary (see Summary Figure 1). This general introduction is followed by practical concerns and questions about general guidelines on how to introduce visual tools into a classroom or whole school. This includes steps for reviewing visual tools in your learning environment, suggestions on how to introduce the tools to students, guiding questions for choosing appropriate tools, and an overview for using visual tools in cooperative learning. The questions raised in this chapter are offered as guides to active reading of the remainder of the book. Thus, this chapter is a taking-off point for a deeper discussion and more comprehensive view of each of the three types of visual tools we explore.

CONTENT-SPECIFIC VISUAL TOOLS

One reason for bringing some clarity and definition to different types of visual tools in the next three chapters is that their long-term potential and significance may be eroded if students, teachers, and administrators—along with publishers and researchers—do not begin discussing their common benefits and best uses. These tools are being used successfully and differently across disciplines, deepening content-specific and interdisciplinary understandings, but mostly they are used in isolated situations. For example, in the field of science, students may use hierarchical *conceptual mapping* to develop visual mental models of how they perceive scientific concepts. Teachers use those mental models to assess the development of students' concepts and misconceptions. Teachers of mathematics, having long ago gone beyond the Venn diagram, have become leaders in promoting students' use of visual modeling such as flow charts and diagrams for problem solving and concept development. For reading comprehension across disciplines, students practice with visual scaffolds—story maps—to analyze and synthesize meaningful patterns of ideas not readily apparent in page after page of text. And, increasingly, brainstorming webs, or *mind mapping*, have become basics in some schools for writing process prompts. Finally, maps based on thinking processes have been used extensively, enabling students to transfer complex thinking skills in the form of tools across disciplines. Though the uses of these tools overlap, there is rarely a coordinated effort to help students make sense of *all* of them.

Of course, some successes with these tools happen without coordination, but even a limited effort in a school or district to identify and share best uses, and agree on some common visual tools, could exponentially expand their quality use by students. A nearly universal response from teachers who have experimented with visual tools reveals an often undervalued and ungraded change in performance: enjoyment of an intellectual challenge. There is also evidence of these tools being used for students with special needs, especially when all students in a classroom and school are using common visual tools (see Thinking Maps, Chapters 7 and 8). Students are motivated by using tools for actively and visually *constructing* "whole" ideas independently and in cooperative learning groups. The use of visual tools creates a shift in classroom dynamics from passive to active and interactive learning for all to see.

DEFINING VISUAL TOOLS

Historically, the most commonly used term for visual tools has been either *semantic maps* or, more recently, *graphic organizers*. A succinct definition of graphic organizers is found in one of the most comprehensive theoretical and practical investigations of these tools, a text written by John Clarke titled *Patterns of Thinking* (Clarke, 1991). This text is required reading for educators interested in studying a comprehensive research base on visual tools. Clarke defines graphic organizers as

> Words on paper, arranged to represent an individual's understanding or the relationship between words. Whereas conventions or sentence structure make most writing linear in form, graphic organizers take their form from the presumed structure of relationships among ideas. (p. 30)

Whereas this definition clearly and simply expresses the open, generative quality of some graphic forms, the term *organizer* may not fully represent the many types and uses of these tools. The term implies that these graphics are used *only* for organizing information. Yet many visual tools that might be called graphic organizers are used for brainstorming, seeking open-ended associations, and consciously delaying organization. Other visual tools have been designed for moving well beyond brainstorming and organizing ideas to specifically facilitate dialogue, perspective taking, mediation of students' thinking, metacognition, *theory* development, and self-assessment. Unfortunately, the worst-case scenario for the use of graphic organizers is students' repetitive use of preformed organization charts as merely "fill-in" boxes on activity sheets. Most publishers now offer packets of fill-in graphic forms that have simple and intellectually limiting use. These activities, though helpful in some special cases, are not far removed from filling in empty spaces on worksheets, a commonplace activity since the creation of workbooks, blackline masters, and copying machines.

Another term, *semantic maps*, has also been used to represent the field of graphic representations. But historically, the term has been used predominantly for describing brainstorming webs for writing process and language arts instruction. Visual tools are now used well beyond the field of semantics. Neither of these terms, *graphic organizers* nor *semantic maps*, satisfactorily represents the dynamic quality and wide range of uses that the phrase *visual tools* offers. The term *tool* conveys the essential quality of these visuals: they are dynamic and constructive in the hands of students.

The term *tool* is crucial to this definition, and clarifies what this book *is not* investigating. Many valuable graphic representations are used primarily for storing, graphing, or displaying information, often after much of the thinking about a problem has been completed. These forms include matrix diagrams, tables, basic charts, axis diagrams, bar graphs, and pie diagrams. These types of graphics may be used for analysis and to facilitate evaluation and other complex tasks. But they are often used as *placeholders* and displays for information and not specifically as constructive *tools*.

One way to think about the tool-like quality of these representations is to consider an underlying metaphor for the tool concept. The meaning of the term *tool* as used here comes from the philosophical and psychological stance of constructivism, which is based on several metaphors. One central metaphor is that of a student building knowledge, much like a carpenter building a house with materials such as wood, nails, concrete, and glass. These are the contents of the work. A carpenter comes to a job with the practical abilities to mold and structure these materials. Those abilities—both discrete skills and general strategies—have been learned through years of experience at different jobs. At most work sites, carpenters apprentice and work in teams under the guidance and supervision of a mentor who is a knowledgeable, expert, responsible, licensed contractor. One of the first things a carpenter does on arriving at the work site is to put on a tool belt that holds a hammer, screwdriver, tape measure, and other necessary tools. These are the basics of the trade, skillfully used to directly form materials and construct a final product. So, too, a student entering the classroom needs a "tool belt" of sorts, filled with a variety of visual tools that are well defined, developmentally appropriate, and flexibly used to construct meanings.

THEORY-EMBEDDED TOOLS

Each visual tool *explicitly* embodies, in its development, definition, and use, one or several processes, just as a hammer explicitly embodies the process of hammering. This explicitness of process, in turn, implies an underlying theory for the tool, or what have been called *theory-embedded tools* (McTighe & Lyman, 1988). In their introduction to several kinds of learning tools, including what they call *cognitive maps*, McTighe and Lyman draw from the research of Nathanial Gage (1974), who proposed four requirements for teaching/learning tools:

- *psychological validity*—it reflects what is known about teaching and learning;
- *concreteness*—it embodies knowledge in materials and equipment;
- *relevance to teachers*—it has practical value in the classroom; and
- *differentiation by type of learning*—a relationship exists between the type of tool and the way in which a skill, concept, process, or attitude is best learned.

This set of four attributes creates a helpful filter for thinking about the difference between a visual tool and content knowledge as well as the difference between a visual tool and a skill or process.

Using this filter, the visual tools investigated in this book are

- *psychologically valid* given our present knowledge about the processes of teaching and learning, especially schema theory, various learning theories, and brain research;
- *concretely* linked to how knowledge is formed, because they tangibly represent and thus embody this knowledge;
- *relevant for teachers* because students are able to use the tools on a daily basis to learn content and improve thinking processes; and
- *differentiated* by way of the various types of visual tools that relate directly to different ways of perceiving, conceiving of, and patterning knowledge.

So what is the difference between a tool and a skill or a strategy? Visual tools are neither contents nor processes but offer a third way: the *form* of contents and processes combined. They are tools of the learner's trade for concretely transforming information into active knowledge structures. Specifically, visual tools are not, in and of themselves, skills or strategies, in the same way that one does not say that a hammer, saw, or screwdriver is a carpentry "skill." It takes a skillful hand to use a jigsaw to cut a delicate pattern in wood, just as it takes a skillful thinker to create a multidirectional feedback flow chart of an ecosystem. Thus, visual tools are *instruments* used skillfully and strategically by teachers and students to construct content knowledge.

TYPES OF VISUAL TOOLS

We could categorize examples of visual tools in many ways: how they are used, the rules for constructing the graphic, degree of flexibility in use, the theoretical foundation, and, more practically, how each approach is integrated into classroom use for specific objectives. The categories established for this book are based on concrete, practical purposes: the form of the visual tool often follows its function. The three relatively distinct yet sometimes overlapping purposes of these tools are for, respectively, brainstorming ideas, graphic organization, and conceptual development.

The Tree Map (see Summary Figure 1) shows the three types of visual tools and examples of each. Interestingly, each of the three purposes could be easily construed to reflect certain philosophies of educating:

- brainstorming webs for fostering individual and group creativity;
- graphic organizers for fostering basic skills and content learning; and
- conceptual mapping for fostering cognitive development and critical thinking.

To these three branches is added the Thinking Maps language, which is a synthesis of the three kinds of visual tools. Thinking Maps consist of eight graphic primitives that integrate brainstorming, organizing, and conceptualizing into a unique language for learning.

These broad philosophical descriptions will come into focus in the following three chapters reflecting, respectively, the three basic types of tools. These categories are offered as a way of distinguishing these tools so that each type can be used with greater clarity and purpose and used together when it is appropriate for the classroom activities. Several of the developers of the examples described in the following three chapters might argue that their ultimate goal is for their graphic to be used to support two or all three of these purposes. This may be a valid criticism of this category structure. Keep in mind, then, that these categories were constructed so as not to be mutually exclusive. In addition, there is absolutely no "most appropriate" sequence of hierarchical design for using these tools. A student may begin a learning activity by using a graphic organizer, shift to a brainstorming web, and finally use a conceptual map to focus. Students who have learned how to use Thinking Maps as a language of visual tools may fluidly move among an array of different forms as independent tools users.

REVIEWING YOUR TOOLKIT

Before looking at each of these types of tools, teachers in a school or curriculum coordinators across a whole school system may want to consider their own learning environment and past experiences to identify visual tools that are already being used. It is also essential, before beginning this discussion, for practitioners to consider some essential questions about using different tools:

How do I introduce visual tools to students?

How do I choose appropriate tools?

How are these tools used with cooperative learning?

These concerns, questions, and suggestions provide a framework for exploring the remainder of this chapter.

The first step in introducing visual tools into a classroom or whole school is to identify those situations where visual tools are already being used. Take these experiences and successes as the starting point for focusing deeply on tools you have found or believe to be successful. This kind of analysis and collection of examples will support you through this reading. Consider this set of reflective questions:

How do you already use visual tools or other graphics such as charts, pie diagrams, Venn diagrams, and flow charts?

Which of these are most successful? Why?

If you and your colleagues are already using visual tools, what type are you using (brainstorming webs, graphic organizers, concept mapping)?

Are you using one type more than another? Why?

Do your students enjoy using these tools?

Are the tools being used in paired and cooperative learning settings?

Ask your students: "How are these visual tools helping you learn?"

Are students learning to use visual tools on their own and in flexible ways and for interdisciplinary learning?

Can students use these tools without your guidance?

Is there any common use of the same visual tools across the whole school?

Is the lack of consistency in the use of visual tools from previous classes confusing your students?

What types of visual tools are suggested in student textbooks? Are these tools used meaningfully, or are they just add-on activities?

Is there consistency in the definition and use of the tool, or is the same visual used for different processes?

Which of the published materials and professional development resources focused on visual tools would best support your students, classroom, and whole school?

Has your district, county, or state office of education integrated visual tools into curriculum guides and assessment instruments?

Embedded in each of these questions are some obvious assumptions. The issues they bring up include the use of visual tools: breadth in the type and number, interactiveness, flexibility, consistency, independence, meaningfulness, and integration with assessment. As we investigate different types of visual tools, these issues will surface. Though the questions have no absolute answers, some commonsense responses and research show the best practices in classrooms and schools.

CHOOSING APPROPRIATE VISUAL TOOLS

The pleasurable dilemma of choosing the most appropriate tool becomes more interesting as a classroom adds more tools to its intellectual toolkit. But this is only a short-term problem as students practice and become fluent with each new form. Choosing the appropriate visual tool, or a set of visual tools, compares to the challenge a carpenter faces when considering what to use to build a structure. The carpenter must first think about the needed tool as related to the ultimate objective or outcome—what is being built. As we look ahead to the following chapters, here are some essential questions and comment you may reflect on as you consider introducing visual tools to students:

1. **Which type of visual tool best supports the purpose or learning objective of this study?** Identifying the purpose of an activity and the expectations for students is key to choosing a visual tool. For example, if you want students to generate ideas for a project or piece of writing, a brainstorming web may be used. If you want students to organize information in a highly specific way, such as a defined order of operations for solving an equation, then a graphic organizer may work. And if you want students to independently apply a thinking process such as comparison to a reading selection about two characters, then a conceptual map may fit the need. As mentioned previously, there is no generalizable sequence for using visual tools.

2. **What form of the tool is developmentally appropriate?** Once you have clarified the visual tool(s) that fit your purpose, you will need to consider the form of the tool. For lower elementary students, the graphic must be large enough to draw pictures, and instructions must be given verbally. Coloring crayons and pens also will help give form to these graphics. The fewer types of visual forms (circles, rectangles, triangles), the better for all elementary students. Highly complex and densely packed visual tools actually lose their usefulness at any level. For upper elementary and secondary students, clear guidance in the reason and steps for using the visual tools independently is important, so that students can make meaningful use of the tool.

3. **How will we, as a class, interactively use this tool?** It is important to decide how the tool will be used: individually, in pairs, or in cooperative groups? As a whole class through teacher direction and facilitation? Or with a combination of these methods, such as using the Think-Pair-Share format?

4. **How will we assess the effectiveness of this tool?** After you and your students have practiced using a visual tool, it is important to reflect on its usefulness. You and your students may want to evaluate whether or not, and how, the tool furthered learning and thinking.

5. Is this tool going to be used throughout the year and in coordination with other visual tools? If you are committed to using particular visual tools consistently throughout the year, the processes by which the tool is introduced, improved, and integrated into teaching, learning, and assessment are important. If you take this step, you are telling students that you want them to gain ownership of the tool so they will use it independently. Make this clear to students by telling them you want them to take control of their own learning by using the tool regularly, without prompting.

THE IMPORTANCE OF STUDENT OWNERSHIP OF VISUAL TOOLS

One of the most common areas of agreement among those who have used visual tools is that what distinguishes them from static graphic displays is that students use them to become independent, flexible, and interdependent builders of knowledge. As students gain ownership of these tools for active meaning making, the experience is intrinsically rewarding.

As you read the chapters ahead, consider how you might introduce visual tools to students so that they become fluent graphically representing their ideas. If you want students to gain full ownership of a tool, some form of a systematic introduction is necessary, followed by modeling, practice, and coaching.

The following sequence of steps for introducing a visual tool was provided in an article about using graphic organizers for reading comprehension across disciplines. Remember, all of the practical documents presented in this book are models and not blackline masters. This process works well for a graphic in any content area:

1. Present at least one good example of a completed graphic outline.

2. Model how to construct either the same graphic outline or the one to be introduced.

3. Provide procedural knowledge.

4. Coach the students.

5. Give the students opportunities to practice. (Jones, Pierce, & Hunter, 1989, p. 24)

Notice that Jones et al. are not describing a "graphic organizer" that is printed on a page for students to work through or fill in like a worksheet. Initially, students are learning how to draw, change, expand, and manipulate a visual tool so that they construct knowledge on their own in response to the structure of the text or other learning resources. Students should also be asked to review, reflect on, and assess their evolving capacities to use visual tools.

The example provided in Figure 3.1 shows how a fourth-grade teacher might introduce a graphic organizer to students over several days. The task, common from kindergarten through college literature courses, requires students to examine the rising action of a story as a specific dimension of plot analysis. The Rising Action Organizer is first introduced using a story students have already finished reading. Notice the focus during the procedures, coaching, and practice steps on students being able to use the tools individually, in cooperative pairs and groups, and for homework. Students also are asked to use the organizer to verbalize how they perceive the pattern of information and to compare interpretations.

Figure 3.1   Introducing a Visual Tool: Task-Specific Organizer—"Rising Action"

Purpose: Use the "Rising Action" organization for identifying and analyzing the significant events leading up to the climax of a story and ending (or denouement).

1. **Example:** Distribute this completed example of the organizer, using a story students have recently read.

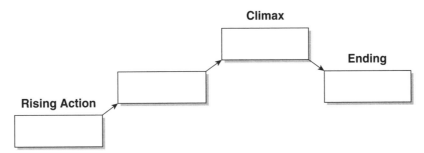

Introduce the vocabulary for each box (important events, climax, ending) and state the purpose for using the organizers and how this tool will help students organize the plot of a story in a meaningful way.

2. **Modeling:** Read a new story with students, and ask them about this organizer as they read. After completion of the story, slowly create the "Rising Action" organizer on the chalkboard without student input. Start with the climax "box," explaining your interpretation of the climax of the story. (This models your metacognitive processes with the tool.) Then proceed to show and explain the rising action of events and ending. Ask for clarifying questions.

3. **Procedures:** After completion of the modeling, ask students to create a "Rising Action" organizer on a sheet of paper. Have students draw their own organizers so that they immediately take responsibility for using and owning the tool. Discuss the need for starting at the top, using only rectangles, and linking the literature-based vocabulary to the visual tool. Discuss possible variations, such as adding more boxes, if necessary.

4. **Coaching:** On the next day, ask students to read a new story and structure students in a "Think-Pair-Share" format for creating a "Rising Action" organizer. As the pairs are constructing the organizers, move around the classroom and coach students as they work. Ask several pairs of students to share their organizers with the class and discuss the different interpretations and how they have used the tool.

5. **Practice:** Reinforce the use of the organizer with each reading selection. Assign the organizer for homework so that students have time to practice on their own.

6. **Reflection:** Ask students to discuss the effectiveness of the visual tool and how this tool could be used in other subject areas, such as in history.

Some adaptations of this process are made for lower elementary students. For example, teachers may first want to distribute a partially predrawn organizer to all students and have them draw pictures and write a few words in each box. The content task vocabulary may be simplified to "beginning, middle, and end" rather than "rising action, climax, and denouement." In addition, the modeling stage of introduction may go on for several weeks before students—even kindergartners—begin drawing their own boxes and start down the road to independent use of visual tools.

Once this visual tool is fully introduced to students, what does this change mean for teachers? First, students have a concrete way of seeing the key relationships built into the task and directly linked with related vocabulary (in this case, rising action, climax, ending or denouement). Second, as students use the tool, teachers are able to assess their view of the pattern of the story efficiently and effectively by viewing the completed organizers. In a typical classroom without visual tools, a teacher is often dependent on direct questioning or students' written responses. Most of the time, teachers will have time for only one or two students to respond. Third, discussion and dialogue between students is supported because students have their visual representation displayed in front of them and thus can visually and verbally share their ideas. Fourth, the teacher can facilitate a discussion using the same graphic on the chalkboard or overhead projector.

SAVING TIME

Once students learn how to use a visual tool, the teacher and students save the most precious resource of any given school day: *time.* Time is saved in three basic ways:

- First, students are able to do more independent, meaningful work, enabling the teacher to spend less time explaining terms and concepts.
- Second, during instruction, teachers may quickly assess students' patterns of thinking about content, thus enabling more effective, focused instruction.
- Third, over the school year, more formal assessment is supported as students collect samples of applications in a portfolio that provides the teacher with an effective, time-saving means of reviewing individual growth and group progress.

Possibly the greatest area of time saving is in assessment. Visual tools provide teachers with a picture of student thinking in the same display that students can use for self-assessment. One of the main reasons we have difficulty assessing students is not that we don't realize the depth and importance of the task; rather, it is because the task is extremely time consuming and students' verbal or written abilities may not match their thinking abilities. As we look at different visual tools in the following chapter, it will become clear that each form has unique dimensions that foster effective and deep levels of reflectiveness and self-assessment.

CONSTRUCTING KNOWLEDGE IN COOPERATIVE GROUPS

A last area to consider before looking closely at practical examples of each type of visual tool is their effectiveness for cooperative learning, or, more specifically, how these tools facilitate the sharing and building of knowledge in a group setting. Following is a brief summary of the implications for using visual tools in an interactive, inclusive classroom that constantly shifts among individual, paired, cooperative, and whole-class learning structures.

Individual Sharing

Given visual tools, students can individually generate ideas apart from the group and then share their ideas. This action promotes visual dialogue: students have the means to convey the holism of their thinking to peers rather than rely exclusively on linear speech or writing. For those students who are not strong at verbalizing their ideas, visual tools become the platform from which they can more fully express their thinking in a paired problem-solving format or group setting. Visual tools also provide an emotionally and intellectually "safe haven" for every student—across all ability levels for a certain task—to generate and show their thinking.

Negotiating Meanings

In pairs or cooperative learning groups, students use visual tools to negotiate meanings and not merely mimic existing knowledge provided by the teacher. Visual tools become a vehicle for deepening and expressing individual views of how information is connected, for sharing multiple perspectives and opinions, and for rigorously discussing different cultural perceptions and frames of reference. It is much easier for a peer group, or a single dominant voice, to dismiss alternative points that are stated in a few sentences than to dismiss a display of interconnected ideas supporting a different perspective. In an inclusive classroom, all students can share their ideas with others, incorporating new information from other students' maps, while developing their own understandings of contents and processes.

Staying Focused

As the old saying goes, talk is cheap, and this may be particularly true in some cooperative learning groups where students stray from the task at hand. Visual tools give students alternative, concrete structures for focusing and persevering in long work sessions, for extensive interdisciplinary projects, and for working together with information as they form a final product.

Teacher Facilitation of Groups

Teachers may support and guide the construction of knowledge in the group by suggesting certain tools that may be most helpful. This may be followed by the teacher moving from table to table, *seeing* the progression of ideas and offering reflective questions, and coaching students' thinking and conceptual development. This also enables the teacher to review the group's work much less intrusively by *seeing how the thinking is progressing* rather than verbally interrupting to *ask* how things are progressing.

Group Presentations

Students are often asked to make group presentations of ideas to classmates. If everyone in the class has access to and regularly uses visual tools, an oral presentation supported by such visuals means that a classroom discussion or dialogue may be richer. This is because the organization of the main and supporting ideas is available for all to see and interpret.

Group Self-Assessment

Once a view of knowledge has been constructed in the group, students may look on the map of their work and be able to evaluate both the holistic view of their understanding and the supporting connections. As different groups present their constructed views of knowledge, students and teachers alike are able to compare alternative structures that have been created and thus evaluate with greater depth not only the product of learning but also the otherwise hidden processes and forms of knowing.

BEYOND BLUEPRINTS, TEMPLATES, AND BLACKLINE MASTERS

Teachers, curriculum authors, and test creators must ask themselves an essential question: Who holds the blueprint for knowledge? Consider carpenters, who work together with a blueprint for a structure given to them by the contractor. During the construction process, the carpenters may choose to use certain techniques and make minor changes in detailing, but each carpenter is constructing a building with a *predetermined outcome*. For most carpenters, this is not a problem, but the issue of outcomes remains a conundrum in the teacher-student relationship.

As curriculum standards are tightened—and standardized tests remain important—the quality and use of visual tools force the issue of outcomes to the surface. Many visual tools, by definition, embody the value of students actively constructing knowledge and building theory. This highlights an unresolved problem of constructivism: Are educators interested in giving students their own tools for critically analyzing accepted "truths" and for constructing new knowledge, or are we giving students only enough skills and tools to "frame" knowledge within the boundaries of old paradigms?

Visual tools provide only one of many answers to this dilemma. By learning and using visual tools, students are given the opportunity and responsibility to actively and rigorously construct and show how they have transformed content information into conceptual knowledge. Teachers who use visual tools are explicitly showing the relationships that they deem essential for learning. Together, teachers and students are able to use visual tools to actively compare and negotiate meanings they espouse in the classroom in a clear display. The process of this negotiation is the heart of the educational experience.

Many of these issues presented in general terms in this chapter are addressed in the next chapters as we look very closely at three types of tools. As you continue reading, consider that, in fact, visual tools are not blueprints for students to follow, but the tools they can use to transform information into knowledge.

4

Brainstorming Webs for Facilitating the Creative Mind

Highly developed cave drawings have existed since the beginning of humankind as groups visually displayed their world for future generations. Now, as a literate culture with written language, we are slowly coming to a new integration of visual representations with verbal forms as an essential means for learners to show their thinking and to build mental models: colorful, pictorial, often idiosyncratic and collaborative, rich in detail, and complex in the interconnections of symbols and meaning.

As this chapter shows, brainstorming webs and colorful graphic representations of many kinds, often spreading from the center of a paper or electronic page, derive from a synthesis of creative drawings *and* language. Of the range of techniques and examples in this chapter, most include the use of sketches, drawings, icons, graphic figures (ovals, boxes, linking lines)—all integrated with key words. Although there may be general guidelines for creating brainstorming webs in groups and for classroom use, the overarching vision is for these visual tools to become *idiosyncratic, highly generative, and creative* representations of thinking. This approach has benefits for the differentiation of learning as individual students become fluent with generating ideas, and serves as a macro lens for teachers to focus on unique representations of their thinking. Brainstorming webs have tremendous generative power, though as noted in the following text, the lack of common graphic structures can also make this form of visual tool problematic for classroom communication between teachers and students.

Drawing is the key to webs of creativity, and once this door is opened, mental fluency is facilitated. For example, Lana Israel, a self-described "13-year-old kid living in Miami, Florida," conducted a two-part experiment that became the central thread of her book on Mind Mapping, *Brain Power for Kids* (Israel, 1991). As a school science project investigating mapping and links to the brain, Lana asked her peers to write a draft of a speech on the topic "My Ideal Day." Later, after introducing Tony Buzan's Mind Mapping techniques to these students, she asked them to do the same exercise with specific mapping processes. Here are some of the responses Lana recorded from the two events:

Statements After Writing a Draft:

- I was more concerned about spelling than my ideas.
- I could not write fast enough.
- I was unable to go back and add ideas or expand.
- I was worried about neatness.

Statements After Mapping a Draft:

- My ideas flowed faster, and I felt more creative.
- I could see connections between ideas easily.
- I could always build up all ideas.
- I got an amazing amount down.

It is clear even from this informal experiment that writing often gets in the way of the natural networking capacity of the brain to think, create, and even construct logical connections. Brainstorming webs offer a representation system for facilitating an unfettered flow of the mind.

FLOW OF INFORMATION AND KNOWLEDGE

In this new century, the technological worlds of school, work, and work-at-home overlap to require a different set of tools—mental knowledge tools—beyond those for craftspeople and industry from generations gone by. From cave dwellers to Webmasters, we have come to a different place requiring new capacities and representation systems for the shift from hunting to put food on the table to capturing information and creating knowledge. As Tom Friedman details in *The World Is Flat* (2005), technological advances have created knowledge work that has flattened and transformed the world in fundamental ways, requiring new mental tools.

In the workplace and in schools, the theories and realities of our knowledge and practical affairs are now slowly being translated into these new forms of tools such as brainstorming webs. Unfortunately, we really have not yet become fluent tool users in this new information age, as were hunters fluent with the bow, farmers with the plow, and line workers in shaping metal. We now attempt to shape information into knowledge as we once so fluently transformed a rocky field into furrowed crops and ore into folded metal. We now need to become much more fluent with mapping tools for our thinking, so that we can transform information into knowledge.

In his book *Flow* (1991), Mihaly Csikszentmihalyi takes us back to another time when the daily job experience was more fluid: "Hunting, for instance, is a good example of 'work' that by its very nature had all the characteristics of flow. For hundreds of years chasing down game was the main productive activity in which humans were involved" (p. 152). Csikszentmihalyi guides us from hunting to farming to the crafts and cottage industries, including weaving—which were based in home "work"—from the industrial to the postindustrial age when

> such cozy arrangements conducive to flow were brutally disrupted by the invention of the first power looms, and the centralized factory system they spawned. . . . Families were broken up, workers had to leave their cottages, and move en masse into ugly and unwholesome plants, rigid schedules lasting from dawn to dusk were enforced.
>
> Now we have entered a new post-industrial age, and work is said to becoming benign again: the typical laborer now sits in front of a bank of dials, supervising a computer screen in a pleasant control room, while a band of savvy robots down the line do whatever "real work" needs to be done. (pp. 153–154)

As a postindustrial society, we have not yet adapted to "information" work, much as workers in the past century attempted to adapt to factory work. Much like the inadequate working conditions of early factories, our schools and workplaces are equipped with crude "information" tools. Yes, many of us have become computer literate, but this does not mean that our human thinking capacities are fully adapted or that we have become expert at generating high-quality knowledge from information.

Actually, our students are facing information overload, which is to say that we and they do not now know how to deal with massive amounts of information efficiently, effectively, or wisely. Students are somehow expected to know more, learn more, do more, share more, collaborate more, create more, and be more independent with information than ever before. Teachers, many of whom were trained long ago and find new technologies somewhat daunting, attempt to "work harder" with the same mental tools and representations they were taught with, and are not given the training required to "work smarter" with new tools for generating knowledge.

History of Visual Brainstorming

Far from the cave dweller's time, in the late 1930s, Alex Osborn initiated the first visual brainstorming sessions in his advertising company. He later wrote a text outlining rules for the group process, which included making no judgments, welcoming "wildness," eliciting quantity, and seeking improvement (Wycoff, with Richardson, 1991). Today, the focused use of brainstorming sessions plays a prominent role in many corporate cultures—often using Tony Buzan's techniques of Mind Mapping—where there is, oddly enough, a deeper history of group problem solving and the need for quick generation of ideas than in school cultures. Brainstorming techniques can be used to efficiently and effectively access the best thinking about a new idea or marketing concept or to develop new products and services, and they can become the reference point for whole work projects from beginning to end.

As a surface indicator of the corporate uses of visual tools, if you look at advertisements across any media these days—newspapers, magazines, television, or the Web—you will often see graphics linking ideas with images to give the viewer a big-picture view of the ideas and the highly detailed information within. Rarely do you see a bland page of text. Recently I saw an advertisement for an "all-in-one" printer that looked exactly like a brainstorming web, with clusters of ovals extending from the printer in the center. The lively and large fonts described the five or six key characteristics of the printer, while the fine print below added extensive and important factual, technical-numerical information for the viewer. There was more information on the page than could have been presented in linear text; the information was not just more "flashy" than a wall of text but also *much more accessible*, visually showing the big-picture concepts *in relationship* to the finer details. This is a clear example of how visual tools may be more effective, complex, and representative of the actual structure of the information being presented than traditional text. Of course, this also shows how the visual-spatial-verbal-numerical information may be richly integrated on a single page.

Historically, schools have focused much less on group work and more on the long-term goals of individual learning, growth, and achievement, and thus group brainstorming has been of limited use. Additionally, schools have not granted higher status to the generation of novel, out-of-the-box concepts by students or challenges to the knowledge being presented. Student work is often evaluated in highly constrained formats based on the retention and synthesis of information provided by text and/or teacher. More recently, both school and corporate cultures are beginning to reward those who think independently and "outside the box," work in teams, co-generate new ways of doing work, and, to a certain degree, challenge the system of prescribed knowledge and acceptable truths.

Since the late 1970s, a range of brainstorming techniques called webbing, clustering, semantic mapping, mindscaping, and Mind Mapping have become more popular in many schools. Though we often think of brainstorming and webbing techniques as being highly creative and idiosyncratic, remarkably, almost all of these processes use similar techniques: usually generating from a central point on a page to the outward perimeters to fully capture a concept, much like a spider spinning a web to trap flies. Most of these techniques inspire a unique blend of intellectual curiosity and artistic expression that contributes to the construction of knowledge, as presented most vividly in the applications of brainstorming webs for educators by Nancy Margulies (Margulies, 1991; Margulies & Valenza, 2005).

The first systematic use of webbing in schools was to facilitate students' fluency of ideas during prewriting activities. When I was pursuing my teaching credentials in the early 1980s through the *Bay Area Writing Project* at the University of California at Berkeley, the use of brainstorming webs was just beginning to be accepted as a technique for prewriting. The process of writing has always depended on generating and recombining ideas, but the "process writing" approaches have highlighted the need for students to generate and connect a large quantity of ideas before sitting down to a first draft. Unfortunately, few teachers have been thoroughly trained in these techniques, which may be used throughout the writing and revision process, so teachers and students often leave the brainstorm web behind after the first draft is complete and the refining and editing steps begin, a mere remnant of the creative beginning of the paper.

But brainstorming webs now are used across disciplines for more than seeking out the initial kernel of an idea. They are used to develop students' fluency with thinking. Fluent nonlinear, organic, open-ended thinking is a critical dimension of learning, as critical as fluency with speaking and writing, which are both primarily represented in linear forms. This concept—*fluency with thinking*—is the capacity to *flow* flexibly within one's mind from idea to idea, within and across disciplines, and easily make interconnections among ideas. It is also the capacity to sustain open inquiry over time, pursue alternative points of view, question and possibly discard hardened opinions, and get "unblocked" when faced with a difficult task.

By gaining fluency with thinking, students become aware of their own generative thinking patterns, the unspoken linkages between thoughts and feelings, and the more subtle metaphorical understandings derived from connecting and bridging usually unconnected ideas in a holistic meeting of one mind, or many. The by-product for teachers is that they, as coaches, gain precious, authentic insights into the interior designs of students' thinking. This enables greater differentiation of teaching and thinking in the classroom.

Many of the initial brainstorming techniques used in schools were based on the translation of early brain research showing that the mind does not process information solely in linear patterns. Tony Buzan, developer of the Mind Mapping process, grounded his work in the brain specialization research conducted by Roger Sperry, Robert Ornstein, and others. Summarizing this research in the field that has dramatically evolved in the neurosciences, Buzan said about some early concepts of brain hemispherisity:

> In most people the left side of the brain deals with logic, language, reasoning, number, linearity, and analysis; . . . right side of the brain deals with rhythm, music, images and imagination, color, parallel processing, daydreaming, face recognition, and *pattern or map recognition*. (1979, p. 14)

A foundation of brainstorming webs is that the integrated facilitation of the "whole brain" is essential to the learning process. A second foundation is the visual dimension. We all daydream and make free associations on a moment-to-moment basis in our minds. It is a part of the human condition. Yet when these associations become more grounded by the individual and are put into visual form, there is an added capacity for seeing the ideas holistically, making more associations, reorganizing concepts and details *as images,* and then communicating these *ideas as images* to others. This is when brainstorming in the mind moves outward to others and becomes a useful tool for collaborative work.

THINKING IN PICTURES

An extreme case of the power of mental fluency and visual thinking is expressed in a unique book, *Thinking in Pictures,* by Temple Grandin (1996). Grandin has a PhD in animal science and has created numerous unique and highly successful inventions for use in the cattle industry. Grandin is also severely autistic. She has, as she described, a remarkable capacity to form a virtual visual library in her mind:

> I store information in my head as if it were on a CD-ROM disc. When I recall something I have learned, I replay the video in my imagination. The videos in my memory are always specific. . . . I can run these images over and over and study them to solve design problems. . . . Each video memory triggers another in this associative fashion, and my daydreams may wander far from

the design problem. . . . This process of association is a good example of how my mind can wander off the subject. (Grandin, 1996, pp. 24–25)

While this is an extraordinary example—certainly outside the scope of a typical student—this individual's experience gives us insight into basic human capacities. The use of extraordinary examples is actually a foundation in the process of discovery whereby Howard Gardner developed his theory of multiple intelligences. He looked at the far reaches of human capacities and extrapolated from these cases to reveal these capacities within all of us.

"Think of your eyes as the projector lens, and your visual cortex as the screen that registers the rapid sequence of sunlight-to-starlight still pictures it has received from your retina—still pictures that it translates into a continuous mental motion picture that functions magnificently beyond mere flickering shadows on the wall at the back of a cave" (Sylwester, 1995, p. 62).

In the case of visual association, retention, and generation of ideas, we know as practitioners that many if not most of our students are strong visual learners. As mentioned in Chapter 2, brain researchers believe that between 70 and 90% of the information received by the brain is visual. Grandin's rich descriptions of her thinking processes are a magnification of what most of our students are able to do, given the practice and right tools. Yet most students after kindergarten are given a vertical lined page on which to record their thinking. It's important that we also give them a horizontal blank page for developing pictures of their thinking (Figure 4.1).

THE BRAIN AND BRAINSTORMING

Brainstorming webs are *natural bridges* between the neural networking of the brain and the conscious mapping by the mind. Webs are a bridge between the "radiant" capacities of our thinking and the typical linear form of representing knowledge in classrooms. The associative power of the human brain is facilitated through and ignited by a high degree of open-ended brain networking. It is understandable and somewhat haunting that many "webs" look similar to the newest pictures we have of neural networks, neurons being the building blocks of the brain that communicate with one another. Axons send information to other neurons; dendrites (Greek for "tree") branch out with the cell body to receive information—networking neuron to neuron at a rate of 10 billion transmissions per second. Figure 4.2 shows the complex, treelike branching forms created by neural networks.

Brainstorming webs are mostly open systems for thinking "outside the box." This means that the students creating webs often share no formal or common representation system. Often private graphic languages develop in classrooms, each related to the personality, primary and secondary discourses of language, and the cognitive style and cultural background of the thinker. But to believe that brainstorming webs should not or cannot evolve into more formal, holistic structures is to

Figure 4.1   Experiment! A Picture of One's Thinking

Before you ask students to take notes on a chapter, write a draft of a story, or do a prewriting activity, ask them to take out a blank piece of paper and place it horizontally before them. Ask them to draw their thinking by first sketching a picture or using words in the center of the page. They may sketch a picture, use words, or just doodle. As they proceed through the chapter, or collection of information, ask them to continually add to the picture. After the session is over, tell them to scan their page. Then ask them to close their eyes. Ask: How many of you can see your drawing as a picture in your mind? You will be surprised, and your students will be on their way to using webs in a more systematic way in your classroom.

deny the great depth of these visual tools. Clustering, Mind Mapping, and Mindscaping, as we see in this chapter, are all forms that the developers of these tools see as a process of moving from generation to organization to transformation of ideas into active knowledge. With advanced development of a graphic, these visual representations may also be final products for presentation in a classroom or boardroom.

"Radiant Thinking (from 'to radiate,' meaning 'to spread or move in directions, or from a given centre') refers to associative thought processes that proceed from or connect to a central point. The other meanings of 'radiant' are also relevant: 'shining brightly,' 'the look of bright eyes beaming with joy and hope' and 'the focal point of a meteoric shower'—similar to the 'burst of thought'" (Buzan, 1996, p. 15).

Figure 4.2 Schematic Side View of Cortex Shows Treelike Branching of Neural Networks

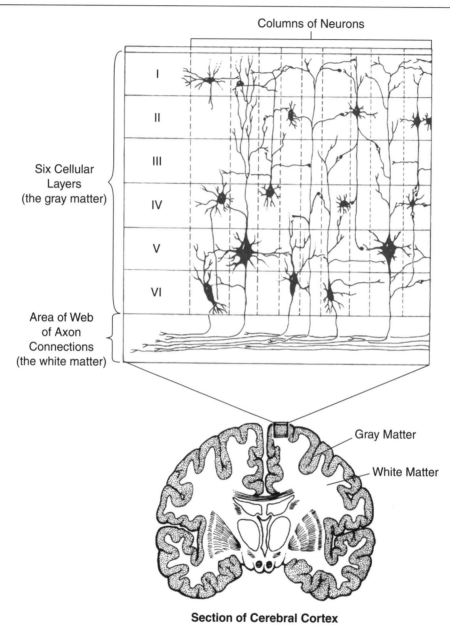

Source: Sylwester, R. (1995). *A celebration of neurons: An educator's guide to the human brain* (p. 46). Alexandria, VA: Association for Supervision and Curriculum Development. Reprinted with permission.

THE MISCONCEPTIONS ABOUT BRAINSTORMING WEBS

One of the most prevalent misconceptions about brainstorming webs is that they involve simple, one-step processes of visually linking free associations without a special technique. As noted earlier, another misconception is that brainstorming is used only at the beginning of a process, then left to the side after the initial brainstorm. Many educators mistakenly believe that brainstorming webs are merely a first step rather than a continuing process that extends even beyond a final product. I have even heard some teachers say that students brainstorm information and then don't even refer to the document during the later processes of completing a project. Often, then, brainstorming webs are perceived as static visual pictures—snapshots of creative energy—somewhat disconnected from further creative and analytical work, rather than a running video, or flow of evolving mental models. Moving too quickly from brainstorming, before deeper processing and revision of the web occurs, prematurely closes this open state of the brain. Students may grow a web outward but never seek the interdependencies lying at deeper reaches in their neural networks and in their conscious perceptions of an idea.

Unfortunately, few educators have had more than a cursory introduction to these techniques, thus they use webs as superficial "warm-ups" to a lesson or unit. Some educators may even associate brainstorming with a lack of intellectual rigor. Practiced with depth, brainstorming webs offer students the opportunity to break the stiff intellectual molds of the "behavioralist" classroom and to spin new interpretations and construct new forms of knowledge at any point of a lesson or unit of study. Webs may also be expanded during a unit of study as new information is drawn together and to use as a document for assessment and self-assessment at unit's end.

Importantly, brainstorming webs are usually guided by focus questions or a defined objective, such as "What is my topic?" or "What do I need to produce?" Several webbing techniques promote the retention of details and lead to the further organization and analysis of ideas. Brainstorming webs are not just starting points, but can evolve in sophistication in relationship to any task. If there is a "mistake" in using this type of visual tool it is that we ask students to stop the webbing process too soon and immediately move on to revision and structuring of a product instead of motivating students to deepen and strengthen the conceptual linkages of their first vision.

WEBS FOR FACILITATING HABITS OF MIND

During the short time it takes for students to become comfortable and then fluent with brainstorming webs, or Tony Buzan's more specific techniques of Mind Mapping, it becomes clear that a cluster of habits of mind centered on creative thinking are actively engaged and facilitated. Although educators have found it easy to identify verbal and written fluency as key objectives, we have not been activating mental fluency, which matches the holistic networking capacity of the human brain.

Art Costa (Costa & Kallic, 2000) refers to this process of mental fluency with such words as *ingenuity*, *originality*, and *insightfulness*. By continuously probing and adding ideas via branching techniques, we can use all the different types of brainstorming webs as tools for seeking the edge of our thinking, and thinking beyond the edge. In the world of business, this has been called "thinking outside the box." This process also opens up other habits of mind that Costa identifies: flexible thinking, thinking independently, and remaining open (Figure 4.3).

Figure 4.3   Thinking Outside the Box

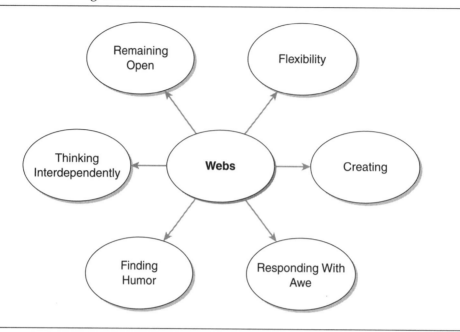

Use of visual branching and linking of ideas to become more flexible and curious also interacts with the habit we wish to develop in students: their capacity to transfer experiences between and among personal, work-related, and academic learning contexts. Webbing supports students in stretching their thinking beyond the standardized frames of mind that usually constrain thinking to the immediate context of learning. Each of these habits of mind—flexibility, creating, and thinking interdependently—are key habits for developing the more general quality of creative thinking. All the types of brainstorming webs shown in this chapter center on openness to continuous learning while also providing a "safety net" for seeing how generative ideas link together to form more coherent pictures of thinking and feeling.

An excellent starting point for developing mental fluency in visual form is to use very simple "clustering" techniques with students and adults of all ages. Figure 4.4 describes clustering and provides a guide for using the technique. As the figure shows, this form requires no special drawing ability, nor does it focus on more advanced uses of brainstorming techniques.

Importantly, a first cluster may evolve into a graphic that is overburdened with information. When a cluster becomes unmanageable with too much information and too many links, ask learners to revise it into a more organized cluster by pruning bits of information, much as the brain naturally prunes away unused dendrites. As the learner focuses on later stages of the process—on the way to a final product—he or she may need to delete or reform whole portions of the cluster that have become irrelevant. It is important, however, for learners not to discard the various revisions, as they become a cumulative assessment of the emerging ideas.

These techniques resonate with most artists, as artists must generate excessive, redundant, and irrelevant expressions and concepts before focusing on the evolving

Figure 4.4   Clustering Overview

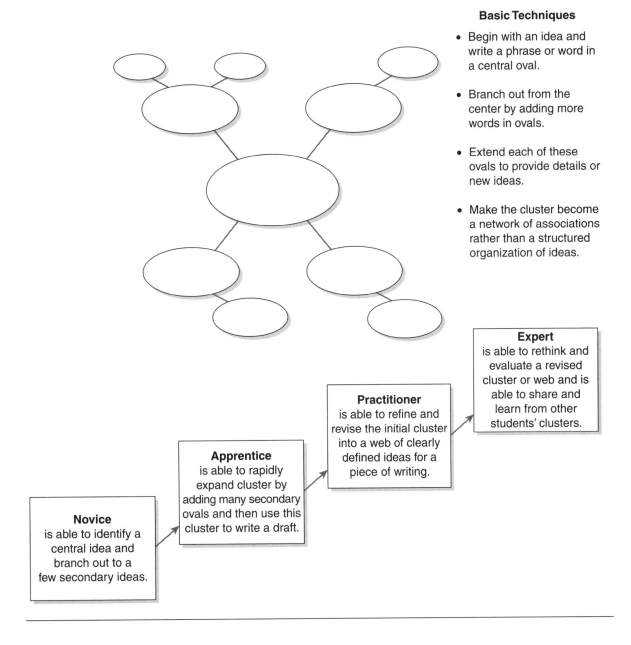

Background The "clustering" of ideas using simple ovals and words was first highlighted for educational use by Gabriel Rico. She established a strong link between associative thinking, creativity, drawing, and fluency of thinking and emphasized clustering as a prewriting strategy. The simplicity of the techniques for clustering enables all learners to begin the process of being in touch with their own holistic flow of ideas. Rico suggests that after creating initial "clusters" students revise their drawings into more focused "webs," thus leading to greater clarity of thinking and writing.

Basic Techniques

- Begin with an idea and write a phrase or word in a central oval.

- Branch out from the center by adding more words in ovals.

- Extend each of these ovals to provide details or new ideas.

- Make the cluster become a network of associations rather than a structured organization of ideas.

Expert
is able to rethink and evaluate a revised cluster or web and is able to share and learn from other students' clusters.

Practitioner
is able to refine and revise the initial cluster into a web of clearly defined ideas for a piece of writing.

Apprentice
is able to rapidly expand cluster by adding many secondary ovals and then use this cluster to write a draft.

Novice
is able to identify a central idea and branch out to a few secondary ideas.

piece of work. Then comes the process of discarding the unusable drafts, brush strokes, doodles, and shards that are absolutely necessary for the creative process, but not for the final product.

SOFTWARE FOR BRAINSTORMING WEBS

In times gone by, we have isolated mental fluency and the facilitation of habits of mind within the framework of spoken language and written text. No more. We must now also open this frame to see that fluency of mind is essential within the environment and influence of a range of new technologies *and* access to an infinitely growing supply of unfiltered information. As students become learners in the world of work, they will be required to weave information together from different sources as they work at a computer station, laptop, palm computer, or nimbly use graphics with projection units to facilitate working groups. With "nano" technologies, the micro scale of computers will enable greater speed, easier mobility, and expanded use of graphic forms for communicating information.

Interestingly, one of the greatest needs we now all recognize students must have is the ability to filter vast amounts of information from the Internet. This need is partially met by well-designed software programs based on webbing and other types of visual tools. A high-quality and flexible software program for creating graphic representations that is used in many schools is Inspiration. Inspiration Software, Inc., has upgraded its earlier versions and added a version for early elementary students called *Kidspiration*.

The two-page example provided in Figure 4.5 is excerpted from a guide showing how the software can be adapted and easily integrated into classroom use. In this sample lesson, the teacher would bring this brainstorming software into the flow of an interactive classroom focused on the topic "The Impact of Exploration" to support students working together in teams and using research techniques for accessing information, as well as analyzing and synthesizing the information. As you review this two-page document, notice the basic technique of brainstorming webs being used: starting from the center and then webbing out to other ideas. But the integration of other visual tools, such as the Venn diagram, sequencing with a flow chart, and simple cause-effect reasoning are also used as extensions from the center. The best examples of visual tools in use rise to the surface when multiple patterns of thinking are engaged, as this example shows, and when the visuals are explicitly used by students and correlated to essential questions, existing standards, and production beyond the graphic such as a piece of writing.

With Inspiration Software, students and teachers have a user-friendly visual technology tool that provides the bridge between raw data (preprocessed information) and a unique document. They can return to their web and add information, include immediately available clip art, move it around, color it in, or delete it. They may also press a key to transform the whole web into a traditional outline. Additionally, many other software programs now offer preformed templates based on typical graphic organizer structures that can be expanded. This is a huge step beyond some of the graphic organizers that show up as blackline masters in classrooms, which we look at in the next chapter. All these functions provide students with the capacity to move from initial vision, to revision, to final concepts and pieces of writing.

Many graphics programs are now readily available on the Web and through almost any "draw" program. These programs are what I call "open palette" tool sets. This means that students using Inspiration and other programs can create unlimited designs. This is the creative upside, but there is a significant downside unless teachers and administrators have evaluated these programs' purpose and ultimate effectiveness. An advantage is certainly gained if a teacher is focused on

Figure 4.5   Brainstorming Lesson: The Impact of Exploration

The Impact of Exploration

Overview

Exploration and colonization have built and destroyed cultures around the globe. In this lesson, students compare cultures and learn about the effects of a historical encounter.

Standards

- Students know famous explorers and what happened as a result of their travels.
- Students understand the people, events, problems, and ideas that were significant in creating the United States of America.

Preparation

Gather informational material on the two cultures to be studied. For example:

- the Native American people of the Chesapeake and Captain John Smith's Europe
- the Celtic people of the British Isles and the Roman Empire
- the native people of Central America and the Spanish culture of Hernando Cortez

Lesson

1. Discuss exploration and explorers with your students. Ask them to speculate about what prompts exploration now compared to long ago.

2. Divide students into teams of two and assign each team to research either the indigenous culture or that of the explorer. Instruct teams to use the informational materials on cultures to study beliefs, economy, government, and relationships with neighboring cultures.

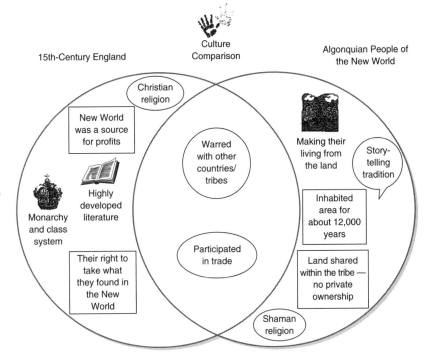

3. Have each student pair with a student who studied the other culture. Ask them to open the Social Studies—Culture Comparison activity and record similarities and differences between the cultures.

4. Guide students to use their Culture Comparison diagram to predict what happened when the cultures made contact. For example, if the commonalities between cultures are warfare or trade, what are the possible outcomes?

5. Share the history of the initial encounters between the cultures. Open the Social Studies—Historical Event activity and use it to demonstrate flow of events, causes and effects, and people involved.

(Continued)

Figure 4.5 (Continued)

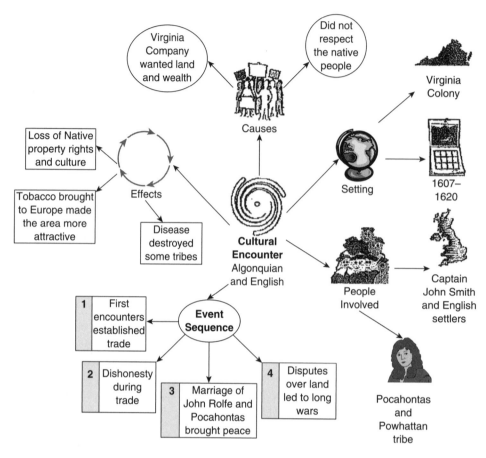

Extension

Challenge students to write a short monologue from the point of view of one of the participants looking back on the effects of this encounter. Suggest they open a new Social Studies—Historical Event activity and use it to organize their ideas.

Source: © Kidspiration in the classroom, by Inspiration Software, Inc. Diagram created in Kidspiration by Inspiration Software, Inc. Used with permission.

facilitating students' creative, open-ended graphics. Yet sometimes this open-ended approach is a disadvantage when students spend an inordinate amount of time generating highly idiosyncratic visuals that may lack coherence and clarity of purpose related to the instructional objectives set out by a teacher as related to concepts being taught or standards being met. Unfortunately, these types of programs are often sold in bulk to schools and systems without professional development training, do not have any published and well-documented results, and thus may become just another underutilized software application taking up space but no time on school computers. There is no educational framework, theory, or practical design to guide teachers and students when they use these programs. An additional concern is that, as isolated programs bound to computers at the back of the room or in a computer lab, these programs may not allow students to use the webbing techniques regularly in other classroom practices or allow teachers to use them as instructional tools. For the greatest effectiveness, these open-palette software programs should be used within clearly defined lesson plans laid out by the teacher, and the techniques used on the machine should be mirrored in classroom practice. If teachers helped students become fluent with foundational techniques for brainstorming webs and Mind Mapping and then introduced "open-palette" graphical software programs, this concern may be resolved.

In summary, it is important for students to become fluent with "open-palette" software programs so that they are facile with generating graphics, but at the same time they need to receive guidance, structure, and, most important, feedback from teachers for the graphics they create to be used meaningfully and successfully over the course of their years in school and work. Visual tools that are based on educational theory, research, and extensive practice in schools, such as those we investigate in the next few chapters (concept mapping, connection circles, Unit Visual Frameworks, and Thinking Maps Software), integrate the generative side of brainstorming webs while also offering coherent "languages" that allow students and teachers to communicate conceptual patterns and common patterns of thinking with greater ease and focus.

Open-palette graphics programs are also used by teachers and administrators in schools, not by just students. Workers regularly research information using online sources and need to amass and synthesize information into meaningful, useful knowledge. They must then deliver it in written or spoken form to others in the working group or to administrators. This process is demonstrated quite well by David Schumaker, superintendent of schools in Hayfork, California, and former teacher, principal, and director of the State of California Central Coast Consortium Professional Development Division. Here is a rich description of how iterations of a brainstorming web become a means both for generating and communicating ideas and for transforming information into useful knowledge.

Brainstorming Webs for Collaborative Reflection, by David Schumaker

My father once told me that while he was working at General Electric in Schenectady, a memo was circulated asking for people to think of a new way to "dehydrate bread." From that question came the idea for the GE Toaster Oven, one of GE's bestselling appliances. He went on to explain that if the question had been, "How can we build a better toaster," the image of a square box with slots in the top would have clouded people's thinking and the idea for the toaster oven may never have come.

When I am looking for input on an idea or to understand a process, I like to start with a very primitive diagram of my thinking. I do not want to "poison the well" with too much stuff so that I can get other people's thinking instead of mine. I usually start with my Inspiration program and map out a few points to illustrate my question and, then, with copies in hand, ask people I respect to go to lunch or meet for breakfast. During the meeting I give them a copy of the graphic, and we discuss the question and I take notes on my copy of the diagram.

(Continued)

(Continued)

Figure 4.6a   Student Outcomes Idea Map: Beginning

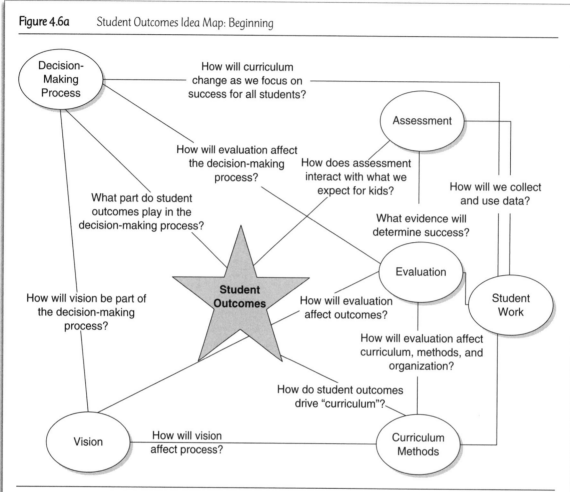

Source: Created by David Schumaker.

In one example (Figure 4.6a and b) the questions I asked were "How does the concept of student outcomes fit into the restructuring of schools? How do we decide what the outcomes should be and determine student progress toward meeting them?"

After one or two meetings, I go back to my computer and "flesh out" my diagram with ideas gained from the meetings. After doing some further research, I then print out a new diagram. I send this to the people who had input into the process for feedback. I also ask others to meet with me to give input on the more detailed idea. Finally, after several stages I produce the complete map and then use it in my writing or decision making.

Figure 4.6b Student Outcomes Idea Map

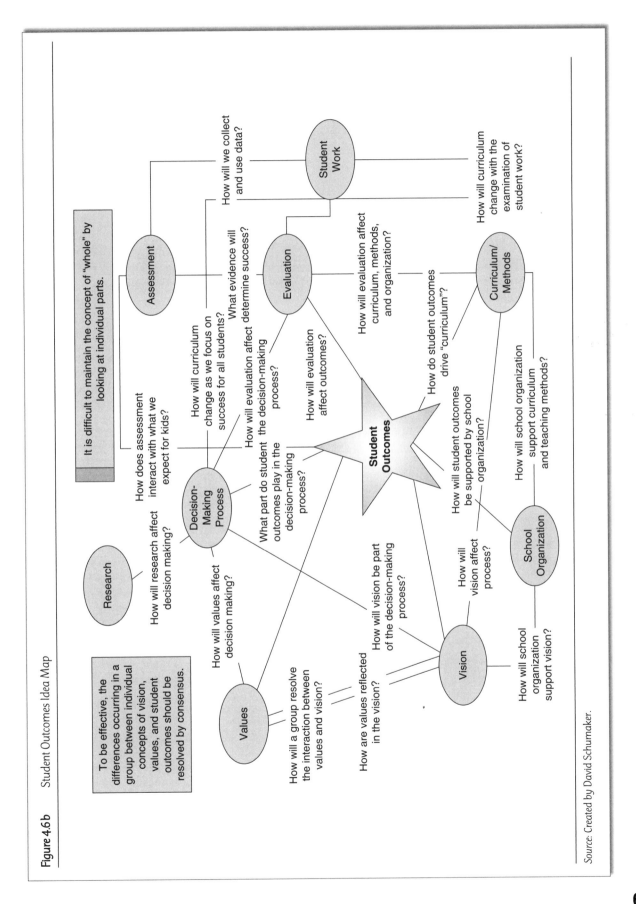

Source: Created by David Schumaker.

Fluency with Inspiration Software, as with webbing itself, comes remarkably quickly. This fluency, at the click of a button, does not replace the power and personal touch of hand-drawn webs. It simply provides another avenue for expressing holistic understanding of mental models, models networking constantly in the human mind. David Schumaker's example is well taken: the software may be used as layers of new information are learned and integrated into a changing structure.

MIND MAPPING

Brainstorming webs come in infinite forms, though most of these processes start in the center of a blank page, as we have seen with "clustering," and then branch out according to the idiosyncratic designs created as an idea expands. This idea came from the revolutionary work of Tony Buzan decades ago (Buzan, 1979) and is captured with new vigor and depth in what may be considered his culminating text, *The Mind Map Book.*

> A Mind Map always radiates from a central image. Every word and image becomes in itself a subcentre of association, the whole proceeding in a potentially infinite chain of branching patterns away from or toward the common center. Although the Mind Map is drawn on a two-dimensional page it represents a multi-dimensional reality, encompassing space, time, and color. (Buzan, 1996, p. 57)

The open form and purpose of brainstorming webs preceding from a key concept in the center promote creative generation of ideas without blinders. The basic techniques of Mind Mapping (Figure 4.7) evolve to reveal personal styles, especially with the addition of colors, drawings, depth, and multidimensions.

While most educators think of Mind Mapping as focused on the "generative" beginning point for entering a new subject, even greater implications for learning exist when students use Mind Mapping over time to concretely "draw" from their past knowledge everything they know about a topic and then link newly accessed information to their Mind Map. Drawing on past knowledge is a habit of mind essential for transfer of information and skills to new contexts. So often in school we talk about finding out what students already know (facts and conceptual understandings). Yet in concrete, practical terms, there are few efficient and effective ways to assess their knowledge base.

Mind Mapping and other visual tools offer students "think time" for showing what they know in an interrelated form so that teachers can quickly review their webs. New information may be introduced that fills in the factual or conceptual gaps in students' thinking, thus saving teachers and students a great deal of time.

VIEWING BOOK REVIEWS

One practical example of Mind Mapping is found in *Mapping Inner Space* (Margulies, 1991), a simple format for reviewing books or textbooks. Notice the emphasis on the metaphor of "viewing" rather than "reporting," as a student can uncover all the pertinent details and conceptual linkages on a single page. This document thus becomes

Figure 4.7 Mind Mapping Overview

Background Mind Mapping is based on early research showing left- and right-brain dominance for linear and holistic operations, respectively. Tony Buzan created the techniques of Mind Mapping® to support creativity and memory, and to deepen these links of creative functions to logical operations. Buzan's model has specific graphic techniques for Mind Mapping that support memory, expansion, and depth of concepts, and for readability so that collaborative problem solvers may more easily share their maps. Although Buzan suggests that learners share common techniques, he also emphasizes the development of personal style in mapping.

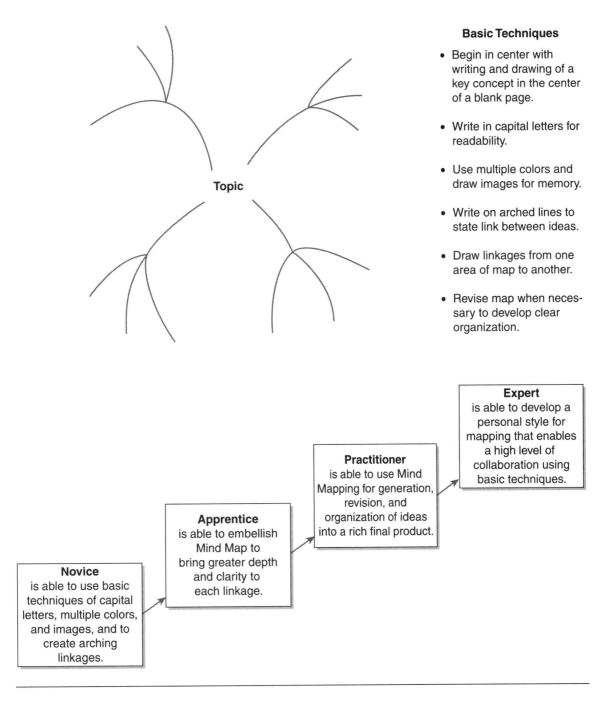

Basic Techniques

- Begin in center with writing and drawing of a key concept in the center of a blank page.

- Write in capital letters for readability.

- Use multiple colors and draw images for memory.

- Write on arched lines to state link between ideas.

- Draw linkages from one area of map to another.

- Revise map when necessary to develop clear organization.

Topic

Novice
is able to use basic techniques of capital letters, multiple colors, and images, and to create arching linkages.

Apprentice
is able to embellish Mind Map to bring greater depth and clarity to each linkage.

Practitioner
is able to use Mind Mapping for generation, revision, and organization of ideas into a rich final product.

Expert
is able to develop a personal style for mapping that enables a high level of collaboration using basic techniques.

a guide that could be used as a supporting graphic for an oral or written presentation of the book (Figure 4.8). As students create their own catalog of book reviews, they can begin to compare different books with greater ease simply by scanning their webs. They can see both the big picture and details for each book. The information is much more accessible and interesting in visual form compared to wading through pages of text to find links between books.

Students can also use this type of book review for studying content-area textbooks. So often when students take notes on chapters of a history, science, or mathematics book, they have difficulty seeing the interrelationships among all the concepts that accumulate or evolve over the course of a text, or a text for a course.

These webbing techniques support students in *making* notes. By making a drawing of each chapter of a textbook, they can synthesize the information from multiple webs into a big-picture view of the subject matter at the end of a term. This big-picture web helps students construct and see both the forest and the trees, thus assimilating new knowledge with prior knowledge.

MINDSCAPES FROM METAPHORS

More than a few educational and corporate trainers are using clustering, Buzan's Mind Mapping techniques, and generic brainstorming tools. Many teachers and students are also beginning to use Inspiration and other mapping tools in classrooms. Although they facilitate open-mindedness, often these tools do not reach into the rich area of metaphorical reasoning. A technique developed by Nancy Margulies (1991) called Mindscaping provides learners from classrooms to boardrooms with a fun and rigorous approach to constructing a metaphorical picture of complex information. Here is a unique insight into Nancy's thinking as she formed the idea of Mindscaping from Buzan's early work on Mind Mapping:

> I found myself moving away from the rules and creating maps that had no central image (gasp!), more than one word on a line, and other rebellious inventions. . . . The name I decided to use is MINDSCAPES . . . landscapes of inner terrain. (p. 118)

There are unlimited forms of Mindscaping, though one model seems most productive for learners, site-based decision teams, and management purposes. The example given in Figure 4.9 was created by corporate trainer and expert in Mind Mapping Joyce Wycoff and teams of workers from four divisions of the DuPont plant in La Port, Texas. Here Wycoff describes the outcomes desired from the management teams:

> They wanted the divisions to recognize that they had many issues in common . . . such as safety and quality . . . as well as their beliefs and values. I was invited to help them brainstorm ways to develop, visually represent, and communicate a shared vision. In searching for a visual metaphor, we considered an underwater treasure hunt, a trip through outer space, a hike through the woods, and running along a race track. (Wycoff, with Richardson, 1991, p. 171)

Figure 4.8 A "Mapping Inner Space" Book Review

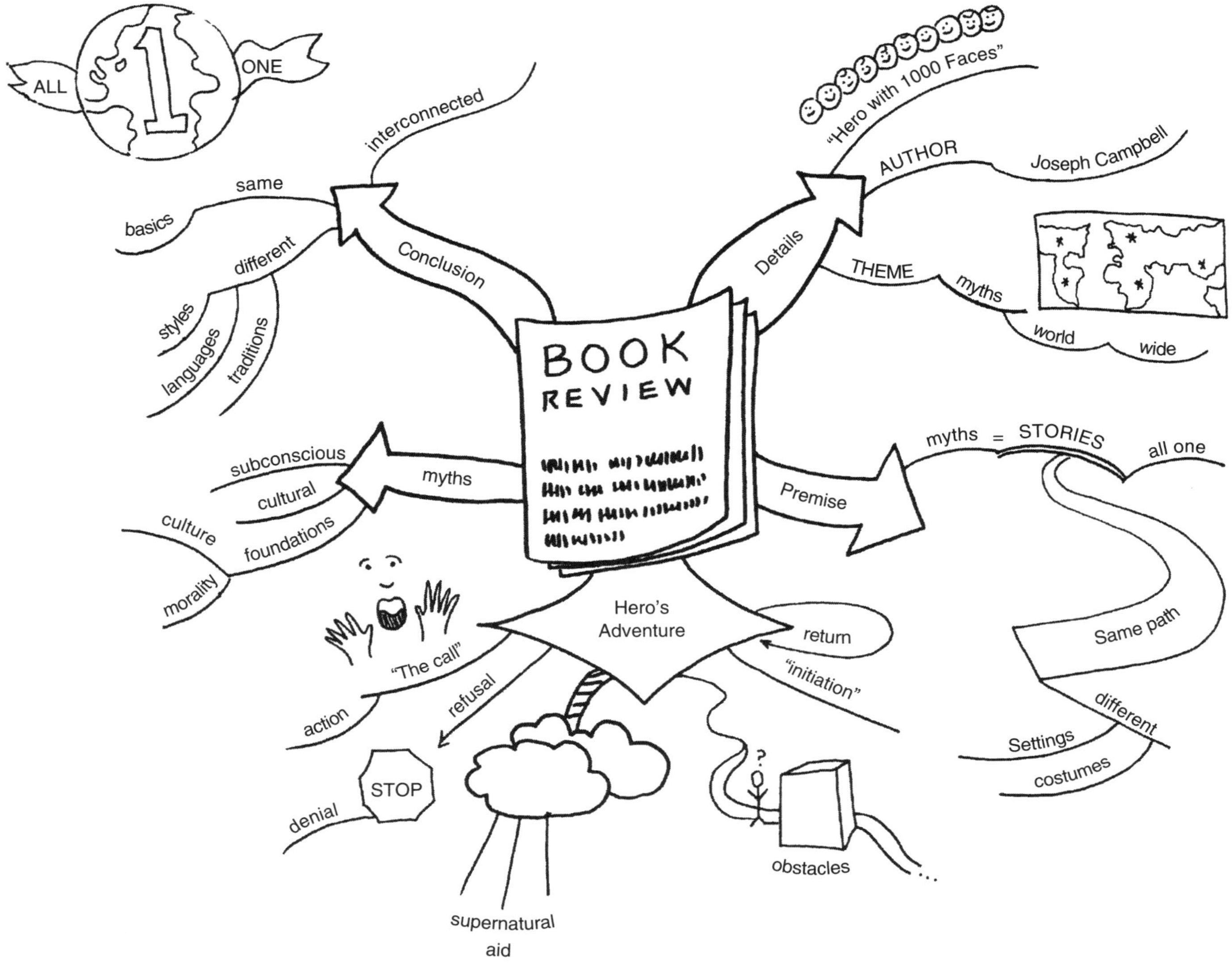

Permission to publish granted by Zephyr Press, PO Box 66006, Tucson, AZ 85728-6006.

As shown in the figure, the management teams chose a "trek map," with each symbol on the page representing key elements of this DuPont plant: four people for the four groups, boxes for the initial barriers to climb out of, a strong foundation at the bottom from which to begin, roadblocks as barriers and obstacles along the way, and a banner, trophy, and balloons signaling the final destination in the clouds.

This fundamental metaphor of everyday life—the journey—is especially rich and useful, as most people conceive of "life as a journey" (Lakoff & Johnson, 1999, pp. 193–194). This visual metaphor surfaces and makes concrete the interdependencies of a complex organism (the organization), and provides a way to synthesize overlapping ideals, belief systems, varying problem definitions, and solutions. It also helps teams literally work together to draw out a *common* vision.

SEEKING PERSONAL GROWTH

As we close this chapter and turn the page to open another, a key lesson may be learned from reviewing the webs of creativity presented in these pages: very simple graphics help learners and groups of learners represent and share evolving complexity, and through this complexity, seek a common vision. These tools also support inner understandings and open us to reflection. This reflection is prompted by looking down on clusters, webs, mind maps, and mindscapes of our own holistic making, much as we look at ourselves in the mirror or see our likeness on the surface of a pond.

This lesson has been revealed to me through the use of a brainstorming tool called the Circle Map, which I developed as one of eight Thinking Maps (see Chapter 7). I devised this tool to support learners in seeking the surrounding context to give definition to an idea or concept. The Circle Map purposefully prompts learners to not immediately connect everything. Things may simmer a bit before connections occur. For example, the Circle Map in Figure 4.10 was created by a student who was learning how to use Thinking Maps through a self-concept activity called MY STORY (Hyerle, 1995; Hyerle & Yeager, 2007). The information surrounding the student's name is information from her life, and the information within the outside "frame" are the influences on her life. The Circle Map supports seeking and deepening associations and reflective, metacognitive habits of mind.

After I drew a first version of the Circle Map—two concentric circles within a square—I looked down and realized it was, in fact, a simple extension of an ancient visual tool for self-reflection and personal growth: a mandala.

This simple map is one of the most powerful symbolic and spiritual representations for humankind—from mandalas used for centuries in India to the forms found on Native American shields. C. G. Jung used mandalas with his patients, asking them to draw out their thoughts, feelings, and intuitions in this format. Jung also spent many years experimenting with this form by waking every morning and creating a new mandala, expressively representing his own changes and transformations—as each of us has in our daily lives—as a kaleidoscope turning with every waking day into evening.

Jung goes on to identify the square (surrounding the concentric circles) as having four quadrants representing thinking, feeling, sensing, and intuition (Fincher, 1991, p. 134). From a Western perspective, Jung states: "The self, I thought, was like the monad which I am, and which is my world. The mandala represents the monda, and corresponds to the microcosmic nature of the psyche" (1973, p. 198). It is through the mandala that Jung also gained insight into a Western view of the "self."

Figure 4.9   Mindscaping Overview

Background Techniques for Mindscaping have come from many sources including Nancy Margulies, Joyce Wycoff, and Suzanne Bailey. The foundation for Mindscaping is in the metaphorical drawing of ideas and is most useful when attempting to see the big picture of an idea, vision, or outcome. Much as an artist has an image in mind for an idea, a learner identifies a concrete image in everyday life—such as a path, a building, or a plate of food—to represent both the conceptual basis and detailed interrelationships for an idea. Like any rich metaphor, it is important that the image is a clear metaphoric reflection of the idea rather than merely a placeholder for information.

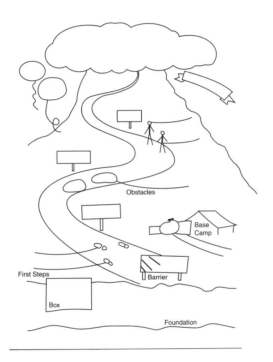

Basic Techniques

- Begin with an idea and identify a concrete image of the idea that seems to represent the topic.

- As you begin to sketch the image, think about how each part of the object may represent different concepts or aspects of the idea.

- After making an outline of the major parts of the object and linking them to the concept, begin adding details to the picture.

- Add colors and words to the picture and return to the picture to revise.

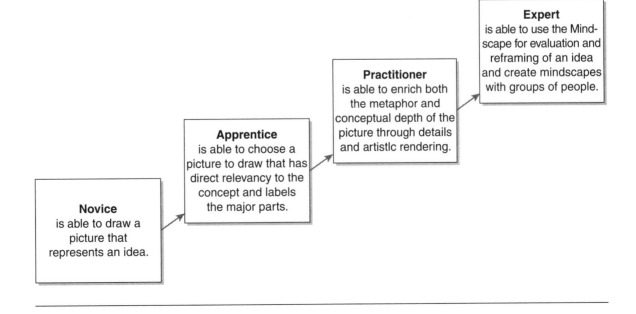

Novice
is able to draw a picture that represents an idea.

Apprentice
is able to choose a picture to draw that has direct relevancy to the concept and labels the major parts.

Practitioner
is able to enrich both the metaphor and conceptual depth of the picture through details and artistlc rendering.

Expert
is able to use the Mindscape for evaluation and reframing of an idea and create mindscapes with groups of people.

Figure 4.10 A Student's Circle Map About Her Life

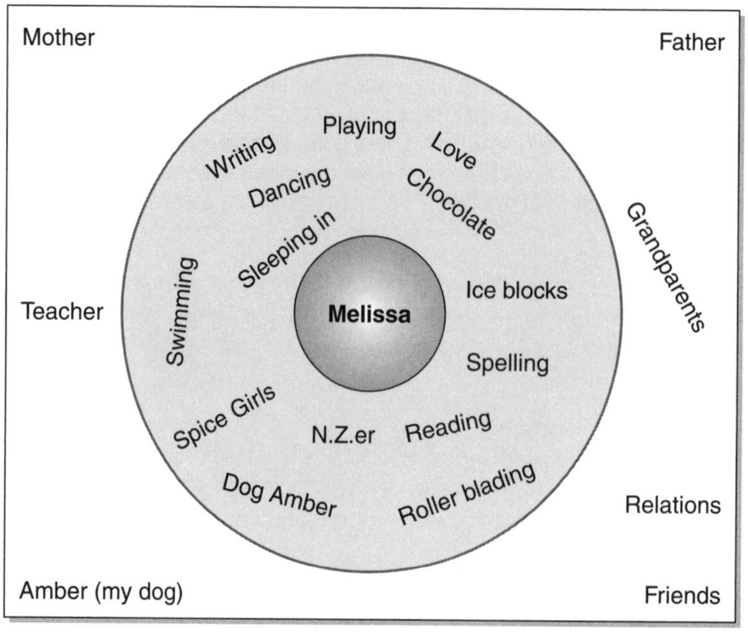

Created by Melissa Eades.

In traditional Indian culture, *mandala* means center and circumference, a microcosm and connection to an ideal reality. This idea of connections from the center, or what Tony Buzan calls "radiance" from the center, is central to how we may see that the visual tools that we use today—and the uses of brainstorming webs as we have seen in this chapter—pull from the core of what makes us human and even links us back to our cave-dwelling ancestors who painted pictures of their lives: creative, open, interdependent, and deeply important as reflections of self in culture.

5

Graphic Organizers for Analytical Tasks

No good teacher ever wants to control the contour of another's mind. That would not be teaching; . . . but no good teacher wants the contour of another's mind to be blurred. Somehow the line between encouraging a design and imposing a specific stamp must be found and clarified, . . . all so that the student may turn himself not into you but into himself.

—Giamatti, 1980, pp. 28–29

If teachers from across the grades, disciplines, and range of teaching styles can agree on one thing, it is that lack of analytical, organizing abilities is *the* ultimate academic downfall of many students. Teachers' desperation echoes in the hallways of elementary schools and colleges like parents' desperate calling out for their children to clean up their rooms: "If only my students could organize their ideas!" This need for organization is the major reason why graphic organizers have spread so rapidly through schools at every grade level and across all disciplines. A second major reason for the spread is that, as shown in Chapter 2, the published research on graphic organizers and practical use of these types of visual tools is extensive, with significant statistical influences on improving students' performance. A third reason is that new electronic-computerized technologies developed over the past 20 years enable fluid use of graphic representations and explicitly show students *visually* how to climb to higher levels of organizational structure.

Here is a very rich description of the intersection of graphic organizers and technologies from a former teacher, Greg Freeman, who has worked extensively with graphic organizers and new technologies.

An Overview of Graphic Organizers, by Greg Freeman

A graphic organizer is a visual representation of concepts, knowledge, or information that can incorporate both text and pictures. The true value of such organizers is in the mind seeing visual patterns and relationships and deriving new insights from the patterning of the information. The pieces of a graphic organizer are much like the pieces of a jigsaw puzzle. When the strange pieces are put together, they form a familiar picture. The individual pieces have no meaning, but the constructed puzzle does.

They have been used for many years as a visual tool for gathering, sifting, sorting, and sharing information in many disciplines. Early childhood teachers use Venn diagrams to teach comparing and contrasting objects, and engineers use complex organizers to develop new processes and simulations. They are easier for humans to understand than other representations such as pure text. They allowed the mind "to see" and to construct meaningful patterns to create new insights.

The research and power of graphic organizers is well documented in education. However, they were difficult to develop and time consuming to produce and edit. Most were templates, workbook-generated versions more often than teacher-generated ones. Until now, graphic organizers such as concept maps, radial diagrams, and note-taking matrices required careful planning and editing to avoid being cluttered, confusing, and consequently—unusable. They became unwieldy and not very user-friendly. The generation of a new idea or an unanticipated change necessitated a complete remake of the map, diagram, or matrix. Furthermore, the map was often limited to the size of the paper and time allocated to generate the organizer. Think about your personal calendar!

Consequently, the organizer and the developer lost their creative power to collect and generate ideas and information—bogged down by erasers, space limitations, and capabilities to edit. Graphic organizers were bound by a "typewriter mentality" and cumbersome paper, pencil, and eraser. These problems kept the applications limited in scope and use to all but the most sophisticated user. Recent development of software to produce and edit graphic organizers has opened up new vistas for uses in gathering, sifting, sorting, and sharing information in visual forms, yet unexplored. Barriers have been removed.

Newly developed electronic organizers and multiple windows ease designing, gathering, and rearranging information. They allow the developer to cut, clip, paste, move, and rearrange information at will. Not having to preplan, draft, and remake brings into being the free flow of creativity and information in a natural manner. In view of the wealth of information (info glut?) and continued development of the Internet, a new and powerful tool, the electronic graphic organizer, can help plan, gather, sift, and sort the vast amount of information generated in cyberspace.

The use of hierarchical graphic organizers as a Web site navigation tool is appearing more frequently in Web site development. Internet search engines are incorporating graphic organizers as a tool to lead info seekers in their quests for information.

As Greg Freeman points out, the interplay of electronic media and traditional paper-pencil are helping our students of this information age grapple with the problem of transforming information into knowledge. But what do students think? Here are some of their opinions.

Words of Wisdom About Graphic Organizers

Students in Suzanne Dobbs's history classes at Brethren Christian Junior and Senior High School in Huntington Beach, California, find graphic organizers (G.O.'s) to be welcome tools through which they can wrap their minds around the daily dynamic work of schooling. After reviewing their Web site on graphic organizers, I asked for their words of wisdom. Here are a few:

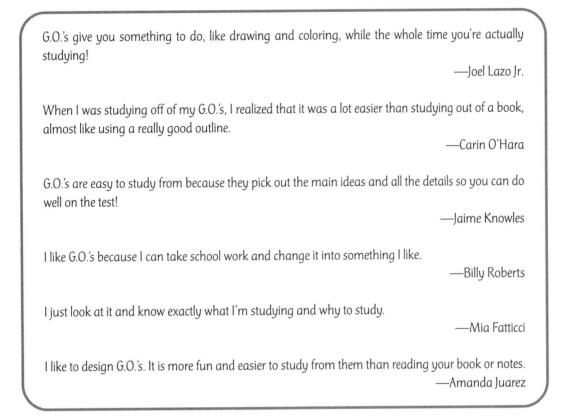

G.O.'s give you something to do, like drawing and coloring, while the whole time you're actually studying!

—Joel Lazo Jr.

When I was studying off of my G.O.'s, I realized that it was a lot easier than studying out of a book, almost like using a really good outline.

—Carin O'Hara

G.O.'s are easy to study from because they pick out the main ideas and all the details so you can do well on the test!

—Jaime Knowles

I like G.O.'s because I can take school work and change it into something I like.

—Billy Roberts

I just look at it and know exactly what I'm studying and why to study.

—Mia Fatticci

I like to design G.O.'s. It is more fun and easier to study from them than reading your book or notes.

—Amanda Juarez

COMPARING GRAPHIC ORGANIZERS AND BRAINSTORMING WEBS

Graphic organizers are a type of visual tool often designed for the purposes of analytically structuring and displaying information. Most of these visual tools are created for content-specific tasks and for defined process skills reflecting particular content patterns within a body of knowledge. What is the difference between brainstorming webs and graphic organizers? Figure 5.1 gives you a visual overview using a Thinking Map called the Double-Bubble Map generated with Thinking Maps Software. As the information shows, graphic organizers are often teacher centered and distributed in the form of a worksheet or blackline master for students, whereas the brainstorming webs are open-ended and require students to generate their own visual structuring of knowledge. Unlike brainstorming webs, these graphics are formalized, teacher created, refined, and rule governed to fit a specific content learning process. Students are given a certain visual design and systematic process for using the graphics and text to guide them through a task. Flexible use is sometimes encouraged, but *within the boundary of the task*, as it is difficult, on most of these graphic organizer worksheets, to actually expand the graphic.

Some graphic organizers, though they border on rote processing of information, may be extensions of traditional organizing charts and templates and thus are effective for the content or process purpose. These include charts, matrices, and axis

Figure 5.1   Comparing Organizers and Webs

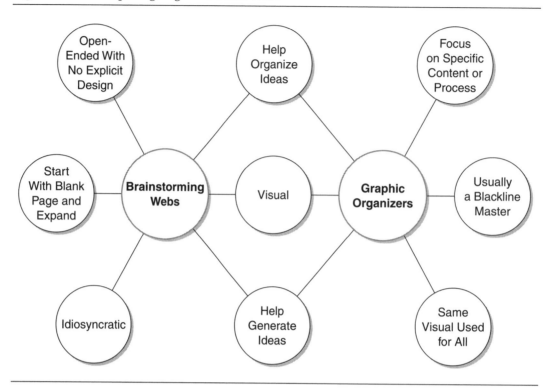

diagrams, all of which are used mostly for charting preformed information for presentation. Most important, with a brainstorming web (or concept mapping and Thinking Maps), students gain ownership of the visual tools, whereas traditional graphic organizers are often not student centered. Although brainstorming webs and graphic organizers may seem worlds apart, both draw on the ever-present power of visual representations to show interrelationships, though in a different way and with a different purpose. Webbing primarily facilitates the unbridled generation of ideas with idiosyncratic graphics and secondarily promotes organizational, analytical structuring of information. Whereas creativity may be a by-product of some graphic organizers, each design is primarily a supportive guide for organizing ideas toward a specific outcome.

Karen Bromley and colleagues (Bromley, Irwin-De Vitis, & Modlo, 1995) offer a very helpful set of seven basic filters, or steps, for evaluating the usefulness and meaningfulness of graphic organizers in their book *Graphic Organizers* (Figure 5.2). These seven guides suggest that teachers should actually learn from the generative qualities of brainstorming webs and make sure that students are using graphic organizers more dynamically in practice. If school leadership teams, and then teachers from across whole schools, adopted this filter as a starting point for reviewing the use of graphic organizers as described in this chapter, the common blackline master and duplication of these visual tools would soon fade and students would elevate their uses of these tools to the highest levels. Bromley is offering a vision of the use of graphic organizers that is significantly different from the common uses in classrooms: ultimately, organizers should be student developed, flexible, and used as reflective tools.

Figure 5.2   Seven Filters for Graphic Organizers

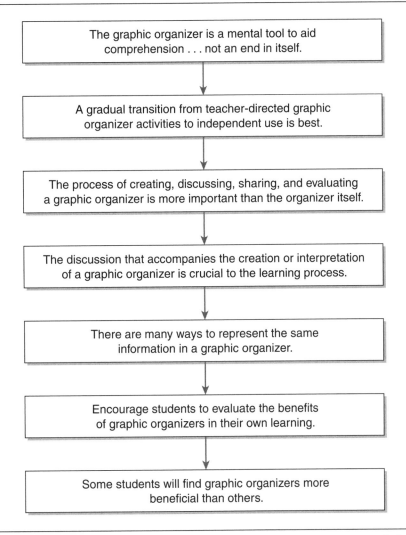

Source: K. Bromley, L. Irwin-De Vitis, & M. Modlo. (1995). *Graphic organizers.* New York: Scholastic.

This view resonates with the need for students to move toward higher-order thinking as independent learners. In terms of Benjamin Bloom's Taxonomy of Educational Objectives (see Bloom's revised taxonomy in Anderson et al., 2001), the cognitive capacities to analyze and synthesize information (organize, break down, and reformulate) are the steps toward evaluative thinking. Yet even the lowest level of Bloom's taxonomy—knowledge—is defined as the basic *organization* of content. It is no wonder, then, that most students have difficulty with complex tasks. They have the intellectual *capacity* but do not have the intellectual *tools* for constructing, patterning, and reforming information into meaningful, organized knowledge. Importantly, *even the most basic level of organization of information is inherently conceptual.* Unfortunately, retention of isolated content knowledge by rote memorization is over emphasized in classrooms instead of retention through the development of organizational designs *and* conceptual understandings. The general processes of organizing information require that learners go well beyond the retention of isolated bits of information. Students must have the know-how to analytically *construct* interrelationships so they can *evaluate* knowledge. This process takes mental energy, perseverance, and much more: it also takes the support of focused linear and non-linear organizational tools that reflect different content-specific patterns of knowledge and conceptual structures.

In this chapter, we investigate a wide range of graphic organizers and their uses, from useful starting points, or *templates,* to more "dynamic graphics." Graphic organizers begin with a relatively clear structure on a page or in the mind and are expanded according to the established pattern. This different type of visual tool thus becomes a focal point for facilitating a different array of habits of mind.

ORGANIZERS FOR HABITS OF MIND

Unlike brainstorming webs, which facilitate creatively "thinking *outside* the box," most graphic organizers are often structured to support students in analytically "thinking *inside* the box." A teacher may create or find in a teacher's guide a specific visual structure that students follow and "fill in" to proceed through a complex series of steps. This scaffolding is sometimes *essential* for some students. Often teachers match specific patterns of content (plot in a story) with the development of process skills (a sequencing organizer). I often call graphic organizers "task-specific" visual tools because of their focus on using a single graphic that is clearly designed to help students achieve a certain objective, outcome, or standard.

These highly structured graphics may seem constraining at times, yet they are fruitful for many students who have trouble systematically approaching a task, organizing their ideas, and staying focused (especially when the task is complex). For example, many organizers are sequential, showing the guiding steps for solving a word problem, organizing content information for a research report, learning a specific process for a certain kind of writing prompt, or for a "story board" highlighting essential skills and patterns for comprehending a story. Because these types of visual tools are highly structured, they directly facilitate several habits of mind, as defined by Art Costa, such as managing impulsivity, persistence, striving for accuracy, and precision of language and thinking. Return to the Tree Map for Habits of Mind presented in Chapter 2 for a graphic view of these specific attributes of thinking.

Review almost any graphic organizer—found in a textbook or teacher created—and you will find that the visual/spatial structure guides students through the steps, box by box, or oval by oval. Teachers report that one of the main advantages of using graphic organizers is that they provide a concrete system and model for proceeding through a problem that students would otherwise give up on because they have not developed their own organizational structures to persevere in completing the task. An obvious reason is that the visual structure reveals a whole view of the process and, importantly, an end point.

This kind of structuring also provides some visual "guidelines," much like a safety rope learners can hang on to—and a structure to hang on to information—rather than impulsively jumping outside the problem to what Benjamin Bloom called "one-shot thinking." The visual modeling thereby shows students that they can decrease their impulsivity, persist, and stay "in the box" when they need to focus on following through to a solution.

This kind of modeling also lends itself to greater accuracy and precision of language and thinking. Oftentimes students don't have a record of their thinking—the steps and missteps along the way—and have a hard time differentiating one idea from the next. By capturing their ideas along a visual train of thought to a solution, students can look back on their ideas, refine them, and share them with others for feedback. These habits of mind are facilitated by most graphic organizers in large part because of the visual dimension, but also because the brain both needs and loves to organize!

CHUNKING, MEMORY, AND THE ORGANIZING BRAIN

In the previous chapter on brainstorming webs, we saw that webs and mind maps almost always start in the center of the page and flow outward, radially, drawing out and linking associations guided by few rules. Obviously, these relatively conscious associations being made are actually quite sluggish compared to the linkages each association is making deep in the unconscious, internal functioning of the brain. Whereas brainstorming webs are commonly understood to be based on associative logic, most graphic organizers are often derived from formalized processes. These organizers build students' abilities to consciously "chunk" information.

From the mid-1950s on, we have believed that the brain automatically associates bits of information into "seven plus or minus two" *chunks* (Miller, 1955). This chunking is now getting a tremendous amount of attention, with brain research reinforcing behavioral research, especially regarding how it supports the transfer of information from short- to long-term memory. Chunking happens unconsciously as the brain grapples with new information and pulls up information from long-term memory. Chunking may also be consciously engaged and may be improved when teachers introduce graphic organizers into the classroom in a *meaningful* way.

It is only through the chunking of information that we can get hold of infinitesimal and infinite actions of the brain, the stream of consciousness. When students chunk information, they are transforming it into a formalized array of information. Graphic organizers have been successful because these tools allow students to create a logical *and spatial* arrangement of the chunks of information bit on the page rather than having to do all the chunking in their minds.

The active chunking of information onto a page is much like constructing a constellation from a sky full of stars. Students can scan information, make sense of it, and see the pattern that the teacher is helping them connect. They can remember the visually chunked information better this way *along with* the auditory chunking that occurs when a teacher delivers information through a lecture or in lines of text written on the front board.

Robert Sylwester makes this point as he relates chunking to the curriculum:

The curriculum enhances this remarkable brain capability when it focuses on the development of classification and language skills that force students to quickly identify the most important elements in a large unit of information. (Sylwester, 1995, p. 93)

In designing curriculum, publishers, curriculum directors, and teachers usually "chunk down" the content. We normally start with the big themes and break them down into manageable, smaller chunks. Heidi Hayes Jacobs's work with mapping curriculum is a good example of this process (Jacobs, 1997). Much like a tree, the concepts are at the top, with the details organized into a foundation or a branch and root system of smaller chunks, and then coordinated in a sequential flow over the course of the year. The delivery of information—often through textbooks—is led by this kind of design. What Jacobs and others are attempting with curriculum mapping is to link the relatively independent content sequences into a big picture for teachers across a whole school or district.

Unfortunately, many concepts and ideas are presented to students in a deductive, preprocessed fashion with no clarity about how it all fits together. The organizing has already been done by the textbook, the teacher, or the computer program. By and large, students are supposed to see the big picture on their own and are rarely given the tools to put it all together other than through tests of their discrete knowledge. The students are asked to "learn" the information in a deductive way: taking notes, memorizing the information as organized, and giving back the information in written or verbal, that is, linear, form.

So where do graphic organizers fit into this discussion? Many of the early and present graphic organizers are highly structured *advanced organizers* and *templates* into which students fit information. These preformed graphics have been successful because they match the capacity and needs of the brain to pattern information, to move the information from short- to long-term memory, and to make the information more meaningful. Although some students may find prestructured graphics helpful when confronted with complex tasks or concepts, they *may* sometimes be just a more sophisticated tool for replication, not the transformation or construction of new knowledge.

In these cases, I believe that graphic organizers act much like training wheels for a child learning to ride a bike—useful in the beginning but downright clumsy and embarrassingly extraneous in a very short time. We would not ask a 6-year-old who could ride a bike to keep the training wheels on, yet unfortunately textbook publishers and graphic organizer books continue to suggest that teachers have handfuls of duplicated graphics for students to fill in. In many schools I have worked in as an outside consultant, more than a few teachers have stated that their students are bored by graphic organizers.

When students become fluent with using preformed graphic organizers, they want to begin to control their own patterns of information and knowledge generation, and not have their minds controlled, as Giamatti warns in the quotation at the head of this chapter. They have the capacity to construct their own processes and visual tools for chunking information—and thus constructing knowledge. They want to move from strictly top-down, deductive reasoning to bottom-up, inductive reasoning. They want to begin chunking content and developing concepts on their own.

From all the preceding perspectives—words of wisdom from students, brain research, and Costa's habits of mind—the mantra that may come to your mind about graphic organizers is that these are *tools* and should not remain *templates*. We now look at some of the best ways of systematically bringing these frameworks into classrooms so that not only are students not bored by staying within the lines, but they are guided to seek key relationships on which they will be evaluated. To summarize this general introduction to graphic organizers, I have created a list of seven warning signs that you can use as a reflective framework for previewing these graphics in basal programs and textbooks, and for using graphics in your classroom, school, or district (Figure 5.3).

Figure 5.3   Seven Warning Signs That Graphics Aren't Working

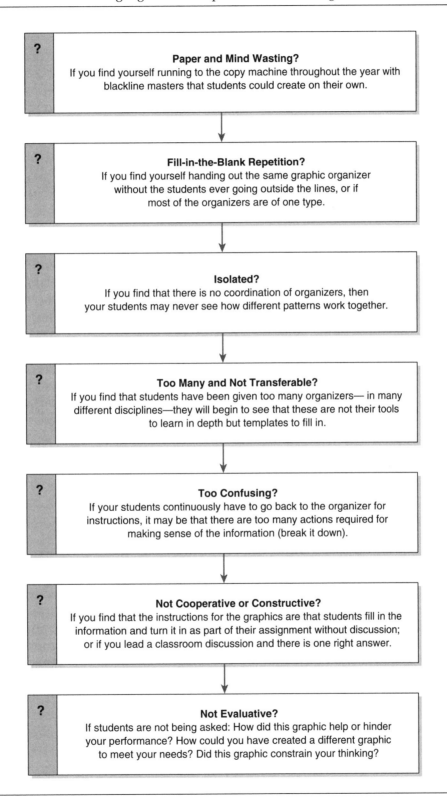

?   **Paper and Mind Wasting?**
If you find yourself running to the copy machine throughout the year with blackline masters that students could create on their own.

?   **Fill-in-the-Blank Repetition?**
If you find yourself handing out the same graphic organizer without the students ever going outside the lines, or if most of the organizers are of one type.

?   **Isolated?**
If you find that there is no coordination of organizers, then your students may never see how different patterns work together.

?   **Too Many and Not Transferable?**
If you find that students have been given too many organizers— in many different disciplines—they will begin to see that these are not their tools to learn in depth but templates to fill in.

?   **Too Confusing?**
If your students continuously have to go back to the organizer for instructions, it may be that there are too many actions required for making sense of the information (break it down).

?   **Not Cooperative or Constructive?**
If you find that the instructions for the graphics are that students fill in the information and turn it in as part of their assignment without discussion; or if you lead a classroom discussion and there is one right answer.

?   **Not Evaluative?**
If students are not being asked: How did this graphic help or hinder your performance? How could you have created a different graphic to meet your needs? Did this graphic constrain your thinking?

CONTENT-SPECIFIC GRAPHICS AS ADVANCED ORGANIZERS

For the remainder of this chapter, we turn to a range of types of graphic organizers, beginning with their use as advanced organizers for students and moving to their use in curriculum mapping by teachers. In the 1960s, David Ausubel (1968) introduced the idea of *advanced organizers* into educational practice. These organizers, as identified by Marzano et al. (1997) and described in Chapter 2 as an instructional strategy that works in classrooms, do not need to be graphic. An advanced organizer could be merely a guiding question to help students organize ideas as they read through a text. Some of these advanced organizers are note-taking guides or well developed like Donna Ogle's concept of the K-W-L process used by students as they list what they want to know and reflect on what they have learned after reviewing their completed graphic.

A *story organizer* is a form of advanced organizer used in a content area: communication skills and English classes for studying literature. It is content specific in that it is designed specifically for the content and is not transferable to other content areas, unlike process graphic organizers, which we will look at later. This story organizer supports students before they begin to read a story so they can think about the big-picture patterns of development of the story, characters, and themes as they read the story (Figure 5.4). This graphic, which may be used in many ways from individual to group to whole-classroom discussion, leads to a rich structuring of information that also provides a bridge for a follow-up piece of writing. It is an example of how a graphic representation lays out a teacher's verbal flow of questions and literary points of analysis much more clearly for the student:

- How would you describe the setting?
- What is a summary plot (beginning, middle, and end) of the story?
- Compare and contrast two main characters.
- What is the major theme and what are at least three supporting ideas or minor themes?

In this case, students are actually given the "road map" of questions through which they can see the whole process. They can see where the questioning is going, jot down responses, and see how the parallel questions about two characters come together to form a rich analysis. More students per classroom will be able to follow discussions, stay on task, and be able to move to a higher level of comprehension with this road map in hand. What is most important here is that students soon move from this advanced organizer for story analysis to being able to organize their own thinking without having to fill in the boxes and ovals on a preprinted page. For an example of how this is done, you may wish to look ahead to the student work using Thinking Maps in Chapter 8.

An infinite array of these advanced organizers can be produced. They are used in every discipline: from time lines in history to matrices in mathematics. Enough has been stated about the limitations of these tools, yet it should be restated, for comparative purposes, that these are static tools focused on a particular structure of information or flow of questions. This advanced organizer actually acts as a tool for

Figure 5.4   Story Organizer

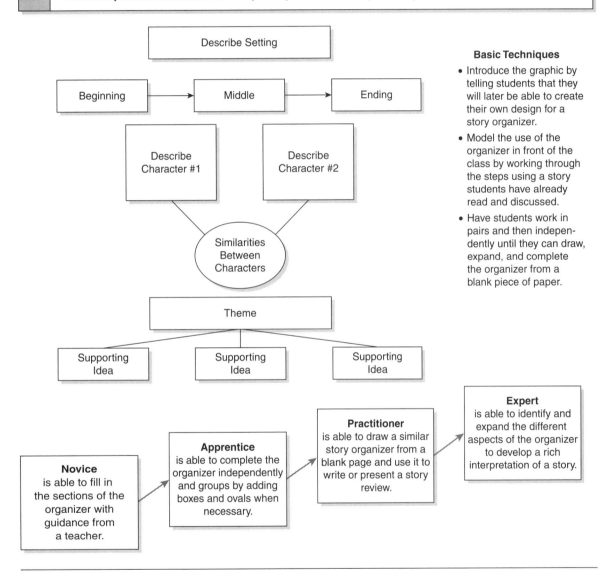

Background The story organizer or map is a generic tool used specifically for interpretation of fiction. Other organizers have been developed for analyzing specific tasks for reading a story, such as plot analysis and rising action, and character description, comparison of characters, and for identifying thematic structures. Story organizers such as the one shown below are used to support students in bringing as many of these aspects of the story analysis together on a single page. It reinforces for students that most of these dimensions of the story must be included in the interpretive process for a complete analysis.

Describe Setting

Beginning → Middle → Ending

Describe Character #1

Describe Character #2

Similarities Between Characters

Theme

Supporting Idea

Supporting Idea

Supporting Idea

Basic Techniques

- Introduce the graphic by telling students that they will later be able to create their own design for a story organizer.
- Model the use of the organizer in front of the class by working through the steps using a story students have already read and discussed.
- Have students work in pairs and then independently until they can draw, expand, and complete the organizer from a blank piece of paper.

Novice is able to fill in the sections of the organizer with guidance from a teacher. →

Apprentice is able to complete the organizer independently and groups by adding boxes and ovals when necessary. →

Practitioner is able to draw a similar story organizer from a blank page and use it to write or present a story review. →

Expert is able to identify and expand the different aspects of the organizer to develop a rich interpretation of a story.

advanced planning, as a focus during reading, and as a reflective and writing plan for after reading. But this multiple-organizer approach also does not provide much depth of thinking about each of the four literary dimensions listed above. This is a common problem with many graphic organizers: too many different patterns being integrated on a page without depth. One of these macro organizers could be deepened by shifting to another organizer, such as one designed especially for analyzing the theme of the story (Figure 5.5). Students and teachers can move from a macro view of various dimensions of the story to looking specifically at the themes, secondary themes, and details that draw from the macro view. Combining organizers of different types from the story organizer, each with depth in one area, enriches the quality of instruction and learning.

Figure 5.5a   Theme Organizer

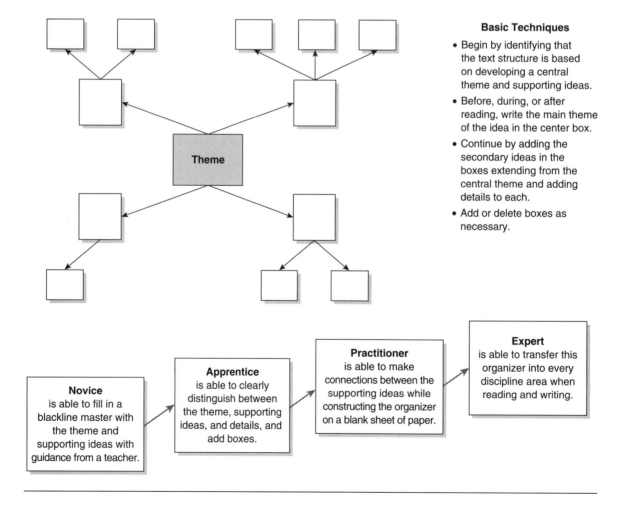

Background The theme organizer is a generic form that has been developed and used by many teachers and curriculum developers. It is a key tool in Richard Sinatra's collection of text structures in the Thinking Networks approach and Sandra Parks's "Graphic Organizer" books. It is used as an organizer for reading comprehension across disciplines for supporting students in identifying a main theme, supporting ideas, and details. In this way, it is based on the cognitive skill of categorization, or the grouping of information. Students identify the main theme of a piece of writing and then group the key supporting ideas and details together into smaller boxes. Most often this organizer is presented to students as a blackline master.

Theme

Basic Techniques

- Begin by identifying that the text structure is based on developing a central theme and supporting ideas.
- Before, during, or after reading, write the main theme of the idea in the center box.
- Continue by adding the secondary ideas in the boxes extending from the central theme and adding details to each.
- Add or delete boxes as necessary.

Novice is able to fill in a blackline master with the theme and supporting ideas with guidance from a teacher.

Apprentice is able to clearly distinguish between the theme, supporting ideas, and details, and add boxes.

Practitioner is able to make connections between the supporting ideas while constructing the organizer on a blank sheet of paper.

Expert is able to transfer this organizer into every discipline area when reading and writing.

Figure 5.5b   Overview for Creating Your Own Theme Organizer

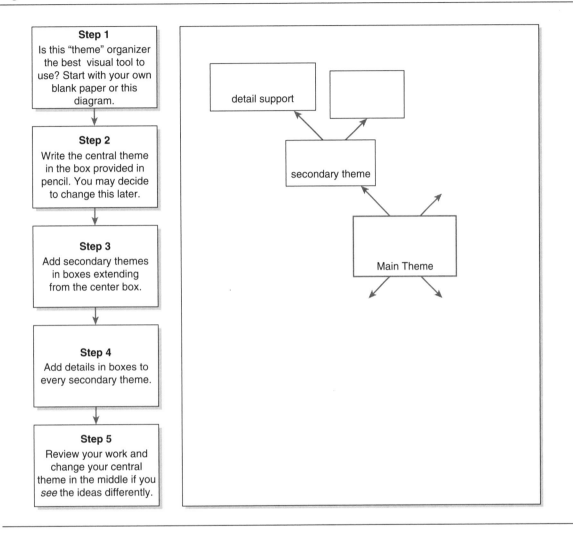

PROCESS-SPECIFIC MAPS

There are many clear examples of basic process organizers based on facilitating thinking skills that, unlike the preceding examples, can be easily transferred by students across disciplines. The most commonly used organizer is the Venn diagram, developed in 1898 by John Venn as a logic tool for showing category structure. It is important to note confusion arising from teachers using Venn diagrams differently across disciplines for two different cognitive skills: categorizing and comparing. This is unfortunate because students will need to use this tool in mathematics to show overlapping categories.

Influential books in this area date back to the early 1990s, full of graphic organizers with a range of visual tools for categorizing, comparing, sequencing, and cause-effect reasoning. The repeated use of these forms—often suggested as blackline masters—has developed a specific way to apply these process/thinking skill organizers. This is a positive beginning because students develop automaticity in the skill, but the blackline masters should be used for introductory purposes and then quickly discarded so that students may create their own graphic structure and gain independent control over their own thinking.

There are many other examples of these basic cognitive organizers. James Bellanca collected two dozen of these graphics in *Cooperative Think Tank, I and II* (Bellanca, 1991). He shows in very explicit terms how to develop process organizers. Working with individuals and cooperative learning groups, he models the dynamism of the tool linked with interactive classroom thinking. For example, the "Fish Bone" is a long-used tool for collecting, organizing, and then linking causes to a single effect. Figure 5.6 shows the steps involved in using this technique.

Figure 5.6   Fish Bone Organizer

Eight Steps for Using the Fish Bone and an Example
1. Identify the effect.
2. Identify the category names.
3. Use a round robin to suggest possible causes.
4. Discuss the suggested causes.
5. Privately rank the causes.
6. Use a round robin to make an unduplicated list of the causes.
7. Vote for rank order.
8. Prepare an explanation of the choices.

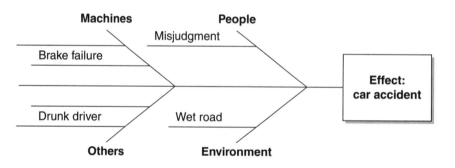

Source: From James Bellanca, *The cooperative think tank: Graphic organizers to teaching thinking in the cooperative classroom,* © 1990 by IRI/SkyLight Training and Publishing, Inc. Reprinted by permission of SkyLight Professional Development, Arlington Heights, IL.

In summary, the difference between process graphic organizers and content or "task-specific" graphic organizers is this: students are learning and practicing a thinking process in visual form *in depth* that can be applied to and transferred into other disciplines (with extensive practice and whole-school involvement), rather than using a graphic handed out by a teacher just a few times to learn a content skill, only to discard the tool and never use it again.

THE BIG-PICTURE ORGANIZERS

In the dimensions of learning approach (Marzano et al., 1997), graphic organizers may be used across dimensions for acquiring and integrating knowledge (Dimension 2), extending and refining knowledge (Dimension 3), and using knowledge meaningfully

(Dimension 4). When used systematically, organizers are also keys to creating positive attitudes and perceptions (Dimension 1), because there is a greater clarity of processes, tools for collaborative learning, and high expectations for working with information. And, as highlighted in this book, graphic organizers have a direct impact on productive habits of mind (Dimension 5), as identified by Art Costa.

In the discussion of Dimension 4, "use knowledge meaningfully," several process organizers are presented for macro processing, such as for general problem-solving steps. Using organizers in this way gives students a flow of possible solutions and pathways back when a solution is not immediately apparent. This graphic is much like the process organizers just discussed and most effective when brought to life through active teacher modeling.

General problem solving leads us into the larger concern of how to support students in moving from being able to follow a discrete problem and solve it to being able to deal with the executive functions needed to work at the macro level of solving larger problems, such as how to organize and follow through on a research project. An example of a big-picture graphic organizer is the Pathfinder Research Template developed by Gwen Gawith (1987) from New Zealand (Figure 5.7). It is amazing that on just one page so much graphic support holds together such a normally overwhelming process for students. There are only five steps, but along the way students receive facilitative questions, alternative pathways, sources to reference, suggestions for capturing information, and hints to get help when stuck within the process. Notice that at each step a question, rather than a to-do list, is offered.

Within this macro organizer you can also see full integration of different types of visual tools. Before step 1, the students are asked to brainstorm ideas about the topic using webbing and to focus a broad topic "chunked down" by revising their web. Within steps 4 and 5, students are asked how they will organize and present the information, with sketches, diagrams, and charts. This research template, or Pathfinder, is a synthesis of a whole process, which includes diagramming templates, Mind Mapping, keywording templates to categorize information, and presentation templates. Although Gawith's *Information Alive!* booklet (1987) is out of print, her updated version, *Learning Alive!* (Gawith, 1996), for teachers of secondary students, is a rich extension and deepening of her first text on action learning. In the next chapter, the Unit Visual Frameworks design, created by Christine Ewy and based on conceptual mapping, takes this macro view of transforming information into knowledge to the center of the teaching, learning, and assessing cycle of classrooms.

MAPPING LESSON PLANS

The research template shown earlier could well be used by students, teachers, administrators, and planners in the workplace. We already have examples of graphic organizers used in schools for organizing, analyzing, and evaluating classroom planning and larger organizational structures called curriculum. Many examples exist of lesson plan design tools that are graphically structured.

More recently, with the greater emphasis on complex integrated, thematic, or interdisciplinary curriculum designs, the need for graphic representations has increased. The "Planning Sheet" shown in Figure 5.8 begins with the identified theme in the center. The teacher then uses the template subject-specific applications and detailed language investigations to expand and link the theme through the disciplines. Whereas teachers usually use such graphic templates, students can also use

Figure 5.7 Pathfinder Research Template

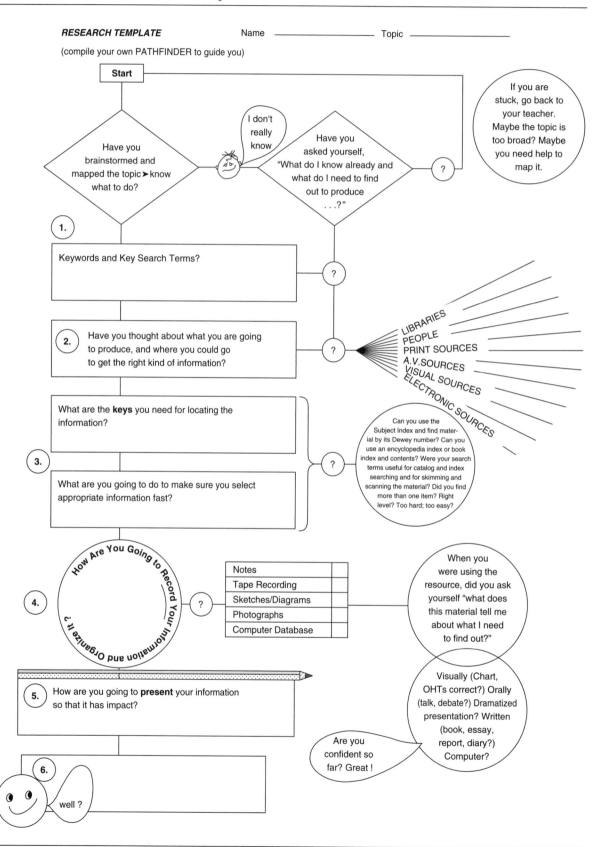

Source: From Gwen Gawith, *Information Alive!* © 1987. Reprinted with permission.

Figure 5.8 Interdisciplinary Planning Sheet

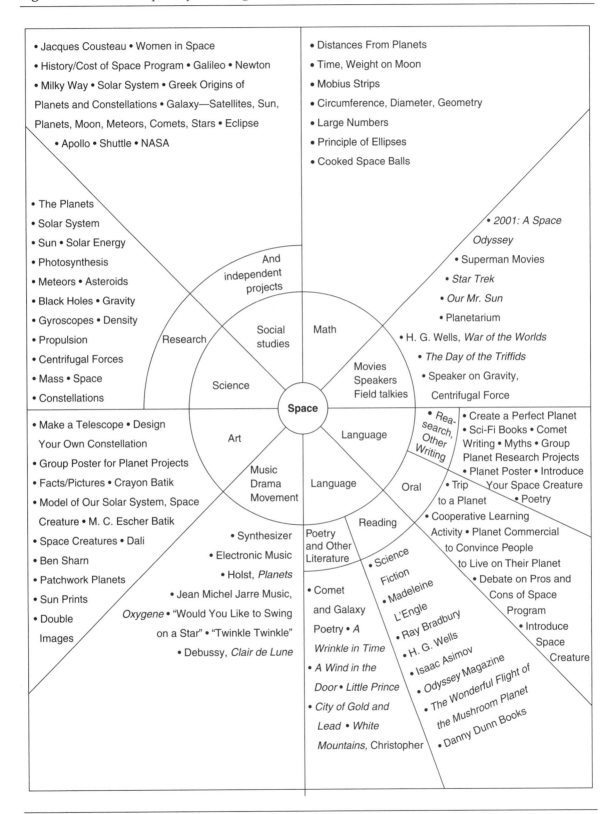

them to record the array of activities surrounding the topics of "Change" and "Space." Students often need powerful tools like these because they reduce abstract, complex activities to a concrete and simpler representation. After going through a series of enlightening activities in an interdisciplinary unit, students are often left with no road map to show where they are going, how they are faring along the way, and how they can reflect on the trip they have taken.

To organize the big picture, students can use a research template, teachers (and students) can use an interdisciplinary design wheel, and teachers and administrators together can use detailed matrices for mapping the complex flow of curriculum from classroom to classroom, school to school in a district. In *Mapping the Big Picture*, Heidi Hayes Jacobs (1997) uses a graphic charting of curriculum as the central tool and organizing form for

- collecting evidence of the existing state of what is being taught and when in a school or district;
- analyzing the flow, connections, and gaps in the existing curriculum; and
- constructing new forms to systematically link curriculum and instruction.

This approach brings a high level of organizational consistency and efficiency that otherwise would not be possible for taking on a complex systems problem. No doubt this work is challenging, time consuming, and an adventure into the politics of districtwide structures, especially when all the stakeholders are included in the process. And it is hard to imagine being able to conduct this process without a graphic template and the software program that provides ease of entry, revision, and speed toward completion before participants bog down in details of the process.

What are the implications of this example for present students and for lifelong learning? If we want students to understand and express their conceptual and theoretical understandings within knowledge domains—and if we understand that these concepts are fundamentally nonlinear—then we need to give them the graphic tools to show these models. Larry Lowery (1991), a leader in science education and stage development of thinking, provides a description and graphic example of an advanced stage (that all learners can attain) of flexible thinking (Figure 5.9). Here, the learner takes an organization structure such as a taxonomy and

> becomes able to develop a framework based on a logical rationale about the relationships among the objects or ideas in the taxonomy, while at the same time realizing that the arrangement is one of many possible ones that eventually may be changed based on fresh insights. This stage of thinking can deal very flexibly with complex situations. Each field of endeavor produces new knowledge and further insights. Resolutions to problems and knowledge generation often take many forms. (Lowery, 1991, p. 113)

The emphasis here on "arrangement," complexity, and forms of knowledge reveal that to think flexibly and gain new insights, students must be able to go well beyond textbook information to arrange (spatially) complex (linear and nonlinear) information into different (graphic) forms. Without graphic representations, most students' mental models will be stunted by a linear mass of information, a bare taxonomy chart memorized for the next exam.

Figure 5.9   Flexible Thinking

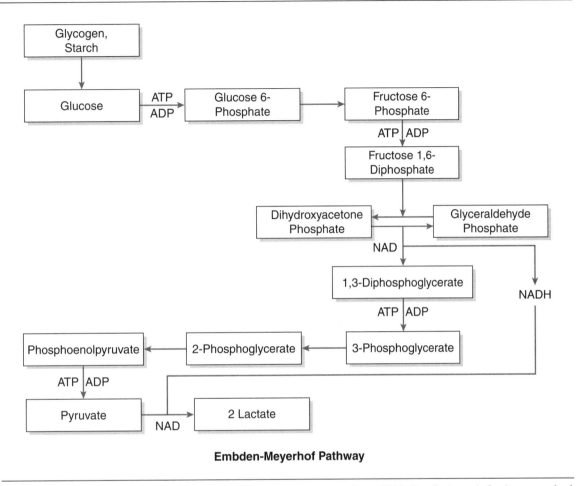

Embden-Meyerhof Pathway

Source: L. Lowery. (1991). The biological basis for thinking. In A. L. Costa (Ed.). *Developing minds: A resource book for teaching thinking* (p. 113). Alexandria, VA: Association for Supervision and Curriculum Development. Reprinted with permission.

DESIGN AND UNDERSTANDING

As this chapter shows, from micrographics for reading comprehension of stories to macrographics for interdisciplinary and districtwide curriculum alignment, the design of graphic organizers is becoming an essential element to the successful representation of ideas. These are all "intelligent" tools. This chapter is no better summarized than by Grant Wiggins and Jay McTighe in their approach, *Understanding by Design*. The graphic design templates that are key for applying this approach are tools for learning a process, and process tools for deeper understanding:

> Why do we refer to the template, design standards, and corresponding design tools as "intelligent"? Just as a physical tool (e.g., telescope, automobile, or hearing aid) extends human capabilities, an intelligent tool enhances performance on cognitive tasks, such as the design of learning units. For example,

an effective graphic organizer, such as a story map, helps students internalize the elements of a story in ways that enhance their reading and writing of stories. Likewise, by routinely using the template and design tools, it is likely that users will develop a *mental* template of the key ideas presented in this book: the logic of backward design, thinking like an assessor, the facets of understanding, . . . and design standards. (Wiggins & McTighe, 1998, p. 180)

In any learning organization, ideas need to be organized, yet *too much organization* isn't necessarily the solution. We have all worked with some students and coworkers who cannot live outside the box of some preordained organizational structure. They are trapped, and trap others, in a static world when in fact the world is often messy, ambiguous, and dynamic. This is the conundrum of the use of graphic organizers: sometimes too many organizers are handed out as fill-in-the-blank worksheets that actually may confuse students' thinking.

Our natural world has complex and stable organizational structures that are also in a state of transformation. This is best reflected by chaos theory, which posits that even within seemingly chaotic systems there are relatively stable structures and patterns. And this is reflected in our lives. Both the unique organizing structures and sensory systems of our brain and our conscious capacities of mind enable us as human beings to slow the world down so we can make organizational sense of it. The organizing minds of our students are constantly learning new ways of both seeing and organizing the information taken in by the senses. Yet this process takes time—a lifetime! This is because as we mature and shift from job to job, or across content areas, we are learning about new and ever more complex organizational structures. Graphic organizers, especially when used dynamically, offer students a wide array of analytical visual structures that they can draw on lifelong.

In the following three chapters on conceptual mapping and Thinking Maps, we investigate how the analytical organizing capacity of graphic organizers and the creative brainstorming in webs can be synthesized into highly creative analytical forms, and an evolved, third generation of visual tools.

6

Conceptual Mapping for Integrating Creative and Analytical Thinking

THINKING *ABOUT* THE BOX

As we saw in Chapter 4, brainstorming webs are used for thinking creatively "outside the box" of the daily classroom and workplace *mental* routines. These open webs help us to break mental and emotional barriers, reflecting the millions of rapid-firing associations that occur in the brain. These are highly generative tools and don't often lead to a range of organizing structures that focus on specific designs. In Chapter 5, we saw that the diagrams and templates that frame many graphic organizers help students think analytically "inside the box." These tools, while often highly structured, help students see a big picture by analytically organizing information. Though graphic organizers may be the teacher's framework and not the students' "big picture" or organizational structure, this graphic modeling within particular content units or specific processes supports the drafting of high-quality, and very specific, content outcomes. These graphics supply a mental safety net for many students, leading them into success and future independent applications.

There is a third tool that joins these creative webs and analytical organizers. This third type of visual tool—what I call *conceptual maps*—is in many ways an outgrowth and synthesis of brainstorming webs and graphic organizers. Conceptual maps sometimes look like some graphic organizers we see in classrooms, but the differences in the purpose, introduction, application, and outcomes are highly significant.

Different conceptual maps are emerging in classrooms and the workplace for *simultaneously* supporting thinking "inside and outside the box." Most important, these tools explicitly focus students' attention on thinking *about the box* itself: they ask us to question what is influencing the creation of the graphic and the actual design as it unfolds on the page or computer screen. Conceptual mapping techniques are often used across disciplines and systematically support teachers and students through recurring thinking patterns and reflective questioning. Conceptual maps:

1. *Define* fundamental and specific thinking processes as recurring patterns

2. *Support* expanding, applying, and transferring these patterns across disciplines

3. *Guide* building simple to complex mental models individually and in collaborative working groups

4. *Focus* on evaluating your own and others' thinking and models of concepts

5. *Reflect* how your frame of reference influences your meaning-making, thinking patterns, and understandings

As we will see in this chapter, these practical and conceptually elegant tools are often designed to reflect hierarchical structures such as in Concept Mapping and inductive towers, and logical argumentation through Reason!Able Software. They may also represent dynamic systems approaches with feedback loops such as "Connection Circles" and STELLA software for systems diagramming. We will look at the approaches and then close with an integrated visual tools approach developed by Christine Ewy called Teaching With Unit Visual Frameworks.

HABITS OF MIND AND CONCEPTUAL MAPS

Although conceptual maps scaffold many habits of minds that relate to brainstorming webs and organizers, they focus explicitly on different forms of concept development and reflection such as listening with empathy, thinking about thinking or metacognition, consciously applying past knowledge to new situations, and questioning and posing problems. For a view of the range of habits of mind heightened by each type of visual tool, refer to the Tree Map in Chapter 2, Figure 2.1. Unlike with brainstorming webs or most graphic organizers, through the designs and uses of conceptual mapping of different kinds, students are being guided to consciously ask themselves these reflective questions:

- How am I perceiving and thus making sense of this system?
- What senses, inputs, and data am I using?
- What kinds of thinking patterns and processes am I using?
- What frame of reference, or mental model, is influencing how I am patterning this information?
- What are some other ways of seeing these patterns?
- Where are my blind spots?

These metacognitive questions lead quite naturally and consciously to empathic understanding. Preeminent within the processes of concept maps is the practical understanding that every person may create a different mental model based on his or her prior knowledge, multiple frames of reference, and conceptual understandings.

Empathic understanding—as a reciprocal process—engages not only a selfless recapitulation of another's thinking and feeling but a deeper sense of linkage and interpretation between the mental model in one's mind and the map being expressed by another within the multiple frames of reference influencing these maps. Engaging students' capacities to think outside and inside the box, as well as *about* how the box is constructed, brings students to a critical perspective on how information is transformed into meaningful, active knowledge and is essential to the thinking-process skills required for 21st-century thinking and learning in schools and workplaces around the globe.

WHEN THINKING BECAME POPULAR

Making sense of conceptual maps requires context building so they are understood as significantly different from brainstorming webs and graphic organizers. During the mid-1980s, "thinking" became *popular* in schools. While this sounds odd, an early history of education in the Americas and most other countries around the world shows quite conclusively that the overlapping acceptance of behaviorism and theories of static "intelligence" shaped an educational paradigm based on a "banking" system of learning, not the facilitation of thinking as we now understand it. It was well accepted that during the week, teachers deposited pieces of concepts, like pieces of silver, in discrete chunks, and students made withdrawals through quizzes and tests. If the deposit was not learned, lessons were often repeated in the same format independent of learners' individual cognitive styles or the complexity of their unique capacities (Freire, 1970).

Of course, educators in schools should not be singled out as having a limited view of learning, because pedagogy is often framed by social and scientific paradigms of the past and not emerging ideas and theories. And education has often been perceived as transmitting existing knowledge rather than transforming information into knowledge and providing students with the tools for these transformations. Change processes are slow; so many remnants of the old paradigms (positive and negative) still inhabit classrooms of today. Educators are often constrained by the societal pressures of educating students for today's world and not educating based on prognostications of future needs. Now changes are happening quickly, so we must respond expeditiously and with greater care as well.

Before and during the early stages of the thinking skills movement of the past 20 to 30 years, the "brain-mind" was often called a "black box," an unknown and unknowable mystery. Breaking through the existing paradigm was the slow integration of process writing, problem-based learning, cooperative learning, and thinking skills instruction. An emphasis on thinking processes and conceptual learning led to a wide array of thinking skills programs in the 1980s, gave rise to a focus on higher-order questioning, and opened doorways to a constructivist view of learning and pedagogy. A very wide panorama of this movement—and the programs and approaches that embodied the ideas—can be viewed in the multiple editions of *Developing Minds* (Costa, 1991a).

Howard Gardner's theory of multiple intelligences was one of the waves of change that broke open the static view of intelligence and gave voice and vision to different ways of thinking. Brain research has been a second wave, carrying us toward a new understanding of the complexity of cognition, learning, and human development. With brain research showing the emotional gatekeeping and filtering of the brain comes the third wave, in the form of emotional-interpersonal intelligence (Goleman, 1995). As these waves of change influence classroom interactions, we can look back and see that the black box of brain functioning was central to how we underestimated human capacities and learning.

One foundation for the thinking skills movement was being built by cognitive scientists and developmental psychologists. One of the most influential of these pioneers was David Ausubel, whose research in concept development deeply influenced Joseph Novak's applications of concept mapping that we will look at in the following text. In a book on Concept Mapping for schools and corporations, Novak describes Ausubel's view of primary and secondary concepts. The distinction between primary and secondary concepts, by Ausubel's definition, is the difference between being able to actually touch and see concrete "ideas" and concepts that are abstract or invisible "ideas." Importantly, *these secondary concepts necessarily require model building*. Models are representations of concepts that otherwise cannot be held in the hand for whatever reason. In a classroom, when a child creates a papier-mâché elephant, a sugar-cube model of an early California mission, or a Styrofoam model of a molecular structure, a physical model is being built. As much as we all talk about having such hands-on experiences for students, in practical terms, the physical creation of these models on a regular basis is impossible and ineffective.

> "Ausubel (1968) distinguished between primary concepts and secondary concepts. . . . Dog, mom, growing, and eating are examples of primary concepts formed by young children. As the child builds cognitive structure, he or she can acquire secondary concepts by the process of concept assimilation. Here concepts and propositions in the child's cognitive structure function to acquire new concept meanings including concepts that have no visible exemplars such as molecule, love, and history. By school age, almost all concept learning is concept assimilation" (Novak, 1998, p. 41).

Visual tools, and particularly conceptual maps, are dynamically created *schematic mental models* of concepts often negotiated between students and with teachers. Students are able to draw the secondary concepts that they cannot easily hold in their hands. Because thinking-process instruction, technology, and problem-based learning demand conceptual development, visual tools are more necessary than ever. For more information on teaching for conceptual understandings, Lynn Erickson's book *Concept-Based Curriculum and Instruction* is a good up-to-date reference for this field (Erickson, 2002). Erickson makes the case that knowledge is structured hierarchically, with facts at the bottom, leading up through topics, concepts, principles, and finally theoretical claims. This view of knowledge reflects a traditional view of how information is transformed into knowledge (Figure 6.1) by way of ever more inclusive categories. It is important to also notice that this visual map is central to the power of conceptual mapping. Conceptual maps are tools based on visually representing conceptual growth and inductive and deductive development of concepts. These tools provide a more concrete way to work with complexity, matching the capacities of our brains to see both the big picture and the details in linear and holistic form.

Figure 6.1   Structure of Knowledge

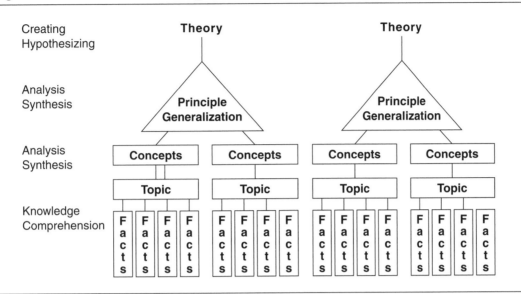

As we look at different examples of conceptual maps, which include nonhierarchical patterns such as systems thinking, we will see that most require both consistent graphics *and* flexible use. This relationship matches, at the deepest levels, the structure *and* dynamism of the brain. We can see that the brain thrives on a consistent structure that easily evolves dynamically, as do fractals, toward novel configurations. With the most richly developed conceptual maps, we see students' thinking at micro and macro levels of performance in a rigorous and reflective way.

NOVAK AND GOWIN'S CONCEPT MAPPING TECHNIQUES

Concept mapping is more than a tool: it is a symbolic language, as Joseph Novak describes. There are many references to concept mapping as basically "webbing" concepts, but this reference does not reflect the depth of this language. The text box describes the hierarchical and integrative processes of concept mapping as well as students' abilities to use it effectively.

> "Concept maps are a tool for representing some of the concept-propositional or meaning frameworks a person has for a given concept or set of concepts. If a person could draw all possible concept maps in which a given concept is related to other concepts, for all possible contexts, we would have a good representation of the meaning the concept has for that person. This is obviously impossible. . . . None of us knows the full potential meaning for concepts we have because a new context or a new, related proposition could yield meanings we had never thought about before" (Novak, 1998, p. 40).

Now look at one student's work (see Figure 6.2), which used concept mapping in a very sophisticated way to map out a summary of algebra that evolved through many iterations of the map over the course of a full year in the class (Novak, 1998; Novak & Gowin, 1984). Return to Figure 6.1 as a guide for thinking about the qualities of conceptual mapping: *defining, expanding, building, evaluating, reflecting* as you look at the algebra example.

This student was fully trained in this process, starting with **defining** concept mapping as based on a theoretical view of thinking as primarily hierarchical. The student thus started at the top, with the umbrella concept of "algebra."

This student was also flexibly **expanding** the concept map from the top down, with more inclusive concepts at the top and details below.

The interconnecting links within the maps give a visual tool for **building** simple mental models of algebra to a more complex, interdependent, holistic view of knowledge. This took not only an extensive amount of training but also a whole year or more of algebra to facilitate this final configuration of concepts and details.

This student was also **evaluating** the development of the map throughout the year by way of a scoring rubric provided by the teacher. As shown at the bottom, this concept map was given points by the teacher for the quality of "relationships," "hierarchy," and "cross links."

One of the key aspects of the use of concept mapping—not explicitly shown by this one example—is that students are constantly **reflecting** on the configuration of their maps, and thus seeing how their frames of reference and mental models influence their perceptions.

Though every student is ultimately responsible for his or her own concept maps, students are constantly comparing and sharing mapping information and their unique configurations. There is no ultimately "correct" map, as knowledge may be "correct" even when configured differently. Because of the flexibility of patterns of these multiple "correct" versions, Novak and Gowin called them "rubber maps," because they stretch in different ways to hold similar concepts or to find new understandings. Figure 6.3 offers an overview and starting points for concept mapping.

With just a glance, the algebra illustration may look like well-developed Mind Mapping, but it should become obvious on close scrutiny that this is a tool of a different kind. This is obviously *not* simply a rich brainstorming of what a student knows about algebra, but a highly evolved conceptual description. This explanation was possible only after a teacher and then this student were fully trained to make hierarchically interrelated links of concepts and details, starting from a blank page. The concept map starkly shows that there are fundamental differences between conceptual maps and other forms of visual tools. This also shows the power of an elegant mental tool in the hands and mind of a student who has practiced this technique over multiple years. This visual tool for mapping concepts is a promising tool and technology for investigation and concept development, and for lifelong learning in fields such as scientific discovery.

THE INDUCTIVE TOWER

Another example of concept mapping is the Inductive Tower developed by John Clarke (Clarke, 1991). There are many examples of conceptual maps based on hierarchical reasoning that help students see the main idea and support ideas and details

Figure 6.2   Algebra Concept Map Completed by a Tenth Grader

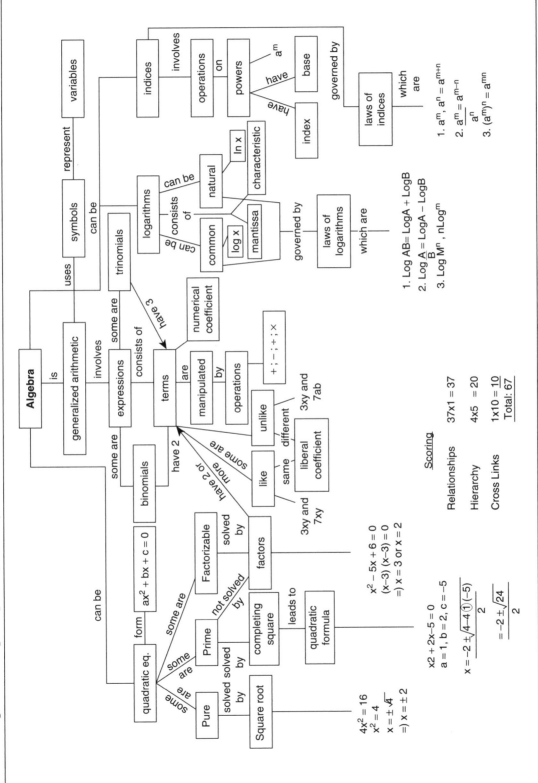

Source: J. D. Novak & D. B. Gowin. (1984). *Learning how to learn* (p. 179). Cambridge, England, and New York: Cambridge University Press. Copyright © 1984 by Cambridge University Press. Reprinted with permission.

Figure 6.3   Concept Mapping Overview

> **Background** Concept mapping was developed by Joseph Novak and Robert Gowin, both of Comell University. The term "concept mapping" is often used incorrectiy as a generic term for any kind of semantic map, but as shown below the processes for using this tool have been systematically developed and researched. Novak and Gowin believe that concepts are linked together in the mind in a hierarchical system of relationships and interrelationships. New information is assimilated under an umbrella of more generalized concepts. The same array of concepts may be mapped differently and still be conceptually correct.

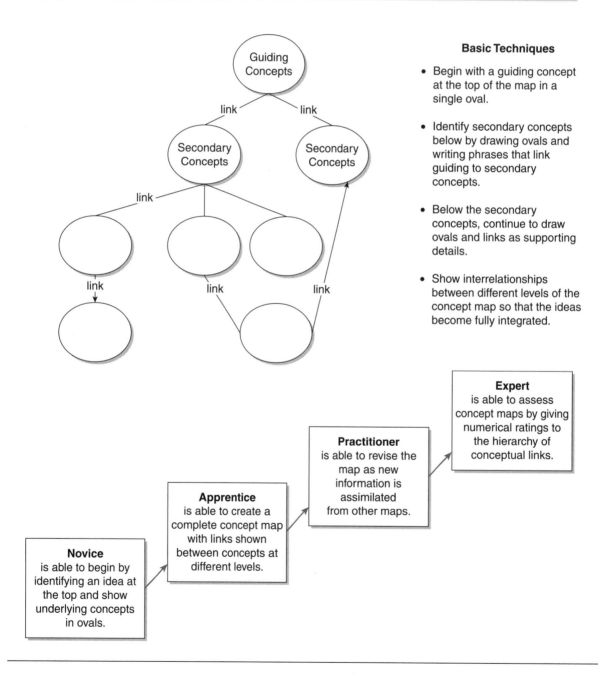

Basic Techniques

- Begin with a guiding concept at the top of the map in a single oval.

- Identify secondary concepts below by drawing ovals and writing phrases that link guiding to secondary concepts.

- Below the secondary concepts, continue to draw ovals and links as supporting details.

- Show interrelationships between different levels of the concept map so that the ideas become fully integrated.

Expert
is able to assess concept maps by giving numerical ratings to the hierarchy of conceptual links.

Practitioner
is able to revise the map as new information is assimilated from other maps.

Apprentice
is able to create a complete concept map with links shown between concepts at different levels.

Novice
is able to begin by identifying an idea at the top and show underlying concepts in ovals.

Figure 6.4   Inductive Tower Overview

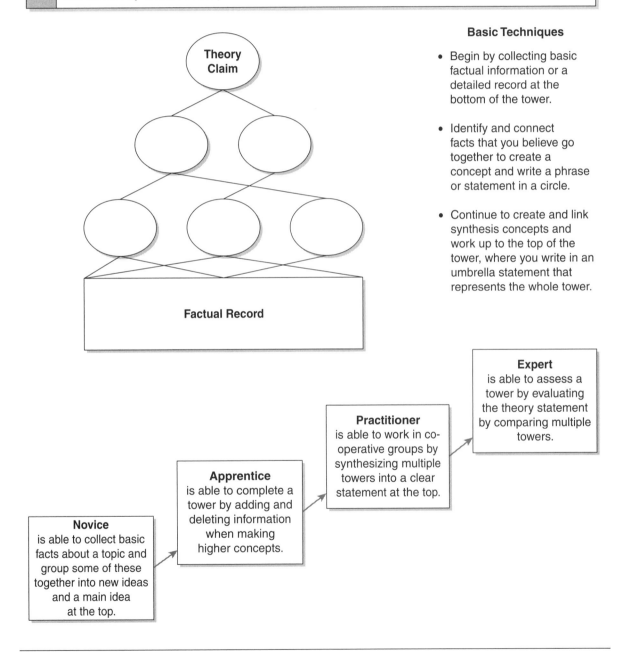

Background The inductive tower was developed by John Clarke, Professor of Education at the University of Vermont. The tower is based on inductive, hierarchical reasoning. Students are often asked to develop details about a topic starting with a main idea at the top of a map. This thinking-process map provides a tool for building categories or groups of ideas from an array of information at the bottom of the maps. Students then build the tower upward to the top. With each grouping at different levels of the map, students are constructing more inclusive and abstract concepts. At the top of the map is a generalization or category heading that represents the multiple levels of facts and inductively created concepts.

Theory Claim

Factual Record

Basic Techniques

- Begin by collecting basic factual information or a detailed record at the bottom of the tower.

- Identify and connect facts that you believe go together to create a concept and write a phrase or statement in a circle.

- Continue to create and link synthesis concepts and work up to the top of the tower, where you write in an umbrella statement that represents the whole tower.

Novice
is able to collect basic facts about a topic and group some of these together into new ideas and a main idea at the top.

Apprentice
is able to complete a tower by adding and deleting information when making higher concepts.

Practitioner
is able to work in co-operative groups by synthesizing multiple towers into a clear statement at the top.

Expert
is able to assess a tower by evaluating the theory statement by comparing multiple towers.

on, respectively, the top, middle, and bottom of the map. Yet the top-down design also replicates the kind of deductive reasoning that we often ask of students and does not engage students in more generative, inductive reasoning. The Inductive Tower supports students in starting at the bottom of the page and developing conceptual categories as they proceed up the tower. Figure 6.4 explains how the Inductive Tower process works, as well as descriptions of students' abilities to use the process effectively.

Because concept mapping requires training and support over time, it is not surprising that students are challenged to go beyond brainstorming ideas to more rigorous conceptual development of ideas. In Chapter 4, we reviewed software programs, such as Inspiration Software, that offer open-palette graphics. There are approaches that ensure a common graphic language beyond the idiosyncratic graphics found in open-palette programs, thus supporting unified translation of forms and ideas. A new software program, Rationale®, is used at the secondary and college levels, and was developed out of the need for students and thinkers in business and the law to both develop and critique arguments through dynamic, structured conceptual mapping. The capacity to develop concise and effective arguments in our society often leads to hierarchical reasoning, and as Tim Van Gelder discusses in the following section, this process requires a level of complexity and patterned thought that promotes critical thinking.

Argument Maps and Rationale, by Tim Van Gelder

An argument is a set of claims with a structured relationship devised to support or reject a contention. An argument map is a visual representation of an argument, such that one is able to view the reasons and objections being asserted and visualize how they are structured with respect to the main contention.

The argument mapping software Rationale guides and scaffolds effective argumentation and helps with the development of reasoning skills. It provides the means for thinkers to locate, systematically structure, evaluate, and clearly communicate arguments.

The argument map is no mere teaching appendage aimed to incorporate multiple intelligence forms for visual-spatial learners. Indeed, the essence of the mapping format takes advantage of our cognitive capacities for visual apprehension while assimilating complex arguments in a format that imposes less of a cognitive burden on the thinker. For example, the argument map counters the difficulties inherent in prose communication by

- instantaneous communication of the structure of an argument;
- illustrating logical relationships between claims while providing systematic lines or branches of reasoning to ensure reasoning remains directed and "on track";
- color coding and icon use for detailing the evaluation of individual claims, thus providing immediate understanding of the grounds for accepting a claim as true (or rejecting as having no grounds or false) and the degree of support a claim provides;
- requiring less memory retention by the thinker than that required by lengthy and/or complex prose argumentation; and
- providing a visual and structured guide to ensure communication in prose is equally structured, systematic, and considered.

Outcomes and Success

Computer-based argument mapping greatly enhances student critical thinking, more than tripling absolute gains made by other methods.

—Charles R. Twardy

The quantifiable success of this program is demonstrated by the outstanding student results provided by the California Critical Thinking Skills Test (CCTST), which is an international assessment standard designed to demonstrate reasoning and critical thinking skills. The statistical gains of critical thinking skills for the first year of university is typically 0.2 to 0.3 standard deviations, whereas the Rationale method at the University of Melbourne has achieved 0.7 to 0.85 standard deviations. (As Twardy explains, the gain or improvement relates to pre- and posttests students take. The raw gain is standardized so that it can be compared with other test scores. The standard deviation is the measure of variability and is achieved by the division of the average gain by the variance.)

Such statistics are useful guides to confirming anecdotal experience, which demonstrates that by using argument maps and related teaching resources, students become more rigorous critical thinkers by an increased ability to

- locate arguments in texts;
- refine claims;
- logically structure arguments using appropriate conceptual frameworks;
- identify copremises and hidden premises;
- consider and integrate independent claims;
- ascertain the grounds for accepting premises as true or false;
- evaluate the strength or support a reason or objection provides to another claim;
- analyze one's own cognitive bias (metacognition) and how to address this within the selection of information and the construction and evaluation of an argument;
- evaluate the main contention of an argument; and
- communicate the argument in prose, such that the claims and the argument structure and evaluation are clear, systematic, and rigorous.

Applications and Scope

Argument maps are not limited to a particular group of learners. Maps reflect the level of thinking skills attained, the sophistication of the reasoning, and the required purpose or educational outcome. As a consequence, Rationale maps are used at all levels of education and for professional decision making and report writing. At primary level, children are introduced to constructing hierarchical grouping diagrams, key reasoning concepts, and construction of basic argument maps. These skills are advanced into secondary years where more sophisticated argumentation, consideration of alternative viewpoints, and reflection are instigated.

At higher secondary and tertiary levels, higher-order thinking skills are developed by refining claims, analyzing arguments and their hidden assumptions, organizing a hierarchical structure to claims, and creating argument maps to advocate or inquire into a given issue or contention and communicate this argument in a systematic and clear essay form. For example, the continuing arguments about the authoring of Shakespeare's plays can be more fully analyzed with Rationale Software, as shown in Figure 6.5. It is important to recognize that this kind of hierarchical structuring of reasoning is foundational to every content area. When students write persuasive essays about literature, write pro-con essays in social studies on current controversial issues, or present findings in science based on experiments, the capacity to develop and show their ideas, and counter other arguments, is absolutely essential.

(Continued)

(Continued)

Figure 6.5 Shakespeare Map

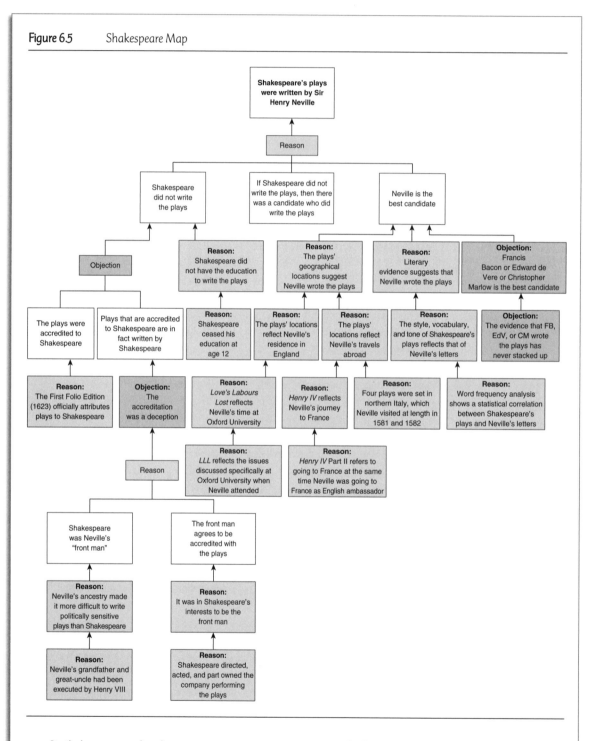

Similarly, a group of students may create an argument map, transfer this to prose, and have another group reconstruct a map from the given prose. This is an excellent activity for peer learning and demonstrating the problematic nature of interpreting prose and the requisite tools for ensuring effective communication.

Business and management professionals find argument maps useful in establishing systematic and exhaustive processes for individual and group decision-making models. Moreover, the communication of business information to other professionals or customers is oftentimes a critical factor in the success of a business, and so communicating an idea or argument from a refined, systematic, visual structure facilitates this process.

Argument maps, whatever the desired outcome, enforce a critical perspective on the quality and exhaustiveness of reasons while decreasing the cognitive strain of retaining copious quantities of information. In a world of information, arguments are often complicated, poorly structured or reasoned, and leave crucial premises unthought of or unstated.

FEEDBACKS AND FLOWS IN THE SYSTEM

Another form of conceptual mapping is based on "interdependent flows" and a theory of *systems dynamics* and not *conceptual hierarchies* found in the previous examples such as Concept Mapping, Rationale Software, and Inductive Towers. This approach starts with simple feedback loops and can be richly developed using a process developed by Connection Circles (Quaden & Ticotsky, with Lyneis, 2004/2007) on the way to more complex applications using STELLA software (Richmond, Peterson, & Vescuso, 1998).

It is odd that we all work in school "systems," but few of us ever fully learn how to *investigate* systems. We can talk about and blame "the system," tweak or shake up "the system" by changing specific parts, and totally transform larger sections of "the system" through symbolic acts or concrete decisions. We have also become quite fluent with talking about "systems," "feedback loops," and change over time. This is a starting point for real change, but like the parable of the elephant the blind men— each of whom believes he knows the whole animal by touching just one part—we are even further from the truth and lack the concrete tools to see the whole pattern as it exists *over time, as decisions have ripple effects and feedbacks over time in a system.*

The key to understanding knowledge from a systems approach is recognizing feedbacks in a system. For example, during any given day we become hungry, and we feed ourselves. We choose from foods that are available, prepare and eat the food, and then the food begins to travel through our system. Both physical and psychological responses (or feedbacks) tell us that we are satisfied or not, and the instinctual fear of starving dissolves. We become comfortable as our body sends feedback signals, but if we eat too much food, the feedback comes too slowly, so we feel bloated. Many parts of the body system work in this process, performed primarily within the digestive tract but centrally driven by the brain. Of course, the nutrients, in the short and long term, directly influence the whole body and mind. Though some of the processes seem linear, this is not a linear process; rather, the body as a system is responding dynamically to internal and external systems.

Furthermore, our whole body system is being driven by a mental model for eating. We have habitual practices that are framed by cultural influences, socioeconomic class, regional differences, and personal tastes. That most Americans eat meat, have three meals a day, have their heaviest meal in the evening, and now eat many more processed foods and "fast food" all influence not only when we get hungry but what we desire to eat and where, such as in our cars. An example of the power of these mental models can be seen in Atlanta, where a city councilman attempted to have fast-food "drive-thru" windows outlawed to reduce the high smog levels in the city. He believed that the mindset of fast-food patrons, who didn't want to get out of their idling cars to get their food, was both a symbolic and a real influence on the overall smog problem. This example shows that systems are indeed connected in ever more complex ways: what and how we eat is directly influencing other systems, such as the air quality.

Importantly, the preceding example was presented in a purely linear form, through a logical progression of sentences. In the linear attempt to describe the situation, I linked interconnected ideas and concepts grammatically, not spatially. The use of feedback loops and systems approaches results in a diagram of interconnections that is a graphic grammar for revealing interdependent relationships. In the next section, we look at a process developed by Rob Quaden and Alan Ticotsky that uses Connection Circles to support teachers and students in building their capacity and shifting their thinking from hierarchies and linear thinking to a systems dynamics approach. You can download the complete unit design and many others from their book *The Shape of Change* (2007) for educational purposes from www.clexchange.org and introduce this approach with students at any grade level. Here is their work in an abbreviated form.

Connection Circles, by Rob Quaden and Alan Ticotsky

Ecosystems are built on complex interrelationships among organisms and their habitats. Often, a change in the population of one species causes unexpected changes in other species. Understanding and representing a web of changes is challenging for the scientists who study them, let alone for readers who try to comprehend these complex situations. In this lesson, students read a chapter from a skillfully written science book and use connection circles to unravel a mystery of nature. In her informative and entertaining book *The Case of the Mummified Pigs and Other Mysteries in Nature*, Susan E. Quinlan (1995) has written 14 true stories that describe the research of ecologists who puzzle out how and why ecosystems behave as they do.

Readers discover the interesting and often surprising connections among organisms through the work of "detectives," who find clues to nature's riddles. "The Case of the Twin Islands" examines why the ecosystems in the waters off two islands in the same chain are so different. As students use Connection Circles to trace causal relationships in the story, they discover the role of a keystone species, a species vital to the balance of the whole ecosystem.

Procedure 1. Read "The Case of the Twin Islands." Students may read independently, share reading, or listen to it read aloud.

Procedure 2. Create Connection Circles summarizing the situation described in the story. Let students present their own ideas. Also encourage them to weigh the ideas of others. Students are always free to change their drawings as they continue to refine their mental models together. Here are the **Connection Circle Rules**:

1. Choose elements of the story that satisfy *all* these criteria: They are important to the changes in the story; they are nouns or noun phrases, and they increase or decrease in the story.

2. Write your elements around the circle. Include no more than 5 to 10.

3. Find elements that cause another element to increase or decrease. Draw an arrow from the cause to the effect. The causal connection must be direct.

4. Look for feedback loops.

Procedure 3. When students have drawn their Connection Circles with causal arrows, share them as the focus of a class conversation. Draw a large circle on the board or overhead projector. Have each team suggest an element to put on the circle. As a class, refine the list to include no more than 5 to 10 elements. Ask each team to describe a causal arrow and explain their reasoning for direct causality. Encourage other teams to ask clarifying questions. Students should refer to the text when explaining their reasoning. Figure 6.6 shows one example of a Connection Circle for "The Case of the Twin Islands." Drawings vary widely.

Figure 6.6   Connection Circles

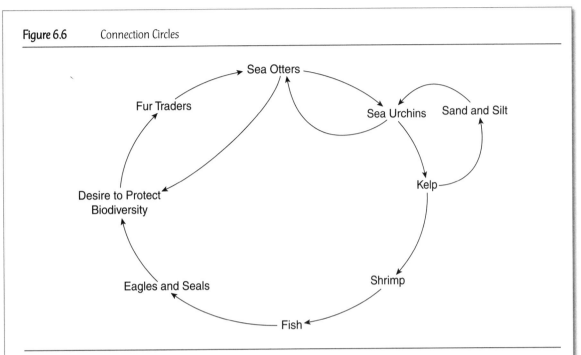

Source: Reprinted from *The shape of change* (2007) by Rob Quaden and Alan Ticotsky, with Debra Lyneis, published by Creative Learning Exchange (www.clexchange.org).

Ask students to explain their arrows: How did a change in one element directly cause a change in another? An increase in the number of fur traders caused a decrease in the number of sea otters because traders hunted and killed sea otters. Also, a decrease in traders caused an increase in sea otters because sea otters could multiply unharmed.

An increase in the shrimp population caused an increase in the number of fish because fish eat shrimp. A decrease in the number of shrimp caused a decrease in the number of fish. An increase in kelp plants caused an increase in sand and silt because the kelp calmed the waters, allowing sediment to be deposited. Notice that increased sediment then buried the sea urchins, causing them to decrease. Students might draw an arrow suggesting that an increase in kelp caused a decrease in sea urchins, but this is not a direct cause. Remind students to be very careful in their thinking about what caused what.

Procedure 4. Ask teams of students to trace a closed "loop." Can they start at one element, follow the arrows around the circle, and return to where they started? Each of these pathways is a feedback loop that tells part of the story. Trace each loop in a different color. After students trace a loop, ask them to make a simplified drawing that includes only the elements from the traced loop, as shown in the following examples. Again, student drawings will vary. The circle below shows one large feedback loop. Tracing it reveals a story.

Starting at the top, an increase in sea otters caused a decrease in sea urchins because sea otters eat sea urchins. Fewer sea urchins allowed the kelp plants to increase. An increase in kelp caused an increase in shrimp, which then caused an increase in fish, which then caused an increase in eagles and seals. With abundant wildlife, people were less worried about biodiversity. A decrease in the desire to protect biodiversity allowed the number of traders to increase, so the number of sea otters began to decrease.

This is a balancing loop. We started with an increase in sea otters, but going around the loop, the chain of events caused sea otters to decrease. If we traced the loop again, the decrease in sea otters would then become an increase, balancing back and forth each time around the loop.

(Continued)

(Continued)

Sea Otters and Fur Traders: Here is another possible loop about the links between sea otters and fur traders. Again, tracing the loop, we see that an increase in fur traders in the 19th century caused a decrease in sea otters to dangerously low levels. An awareness of the decline caused an increase in the desire to protect biodiversity. This led to a decrease in hunting. This is also a balancing loop: Any change works to restore itself around the loop again. The story gets complicated, but don't worry. It is easier when students construct and talk about their own circles. This is the reason for doing Connection Circles in the first place: Students can understand and communicate ideas that are difficult to express using more conventional tools.

Procedure 5. While sharing feedback loops with the whole class, look for elements that appear in more than one loop. Most stories contain overlapping loops. This diagram connects all the previous loops. Tracing the intertwined loops, notice how kelp plants provide food for shrimp, triggering increased biodiversity while also causing sand and silt to build up. The sand and silt loop drives the sea urchin population down, further enabling the kelp to grow. In this diagram, sea urchins and sea otters both have two arrows leading from them, signifying multiple outcomes caused by changes in their populations. An ecosystem is a delicate balance of many feedback loops. As students uncover these interdependencies, they begin to appreciate the complexity of natural systems.

Procedure 6. Have each team choose an element from the circle and draw a behavior-over-time graph of how things changed from the time when hunters arrived in the late 1800s to the time when "The Case of the Twin Islands" was written. Emphasize that the general shape of the graph is important—it cannot be precise because we have no specific data. Share the graphs and ask students to explain how they relate to their Connection Circles.

SYSTEMS THINKING

This highly defined language of interdependent feedback loops helps students show and analyze mental models of dynamic systems—eco-, body, economic, political, social, and solar *systems*—without having to rely solely on linear writing to convey interdependent systems. The "limitations of the linear" are revealed when we begin to create a visual representation of these intertwined systems. Let's look at how students took on the issue of hunger in a school that uses systems thinking and diagramming as a central tool for learning. For an overview, here is a simple diagram of feedback flows (Figure 6.7).

Every school has implicit and explicit ways of nurturing learning and measuring progress. Often the differences from school to school are impossible to see. But at the Murdoch Middle School, Peter Senge's Five Disciplines (Personal Mastery, Mental Models, Shared Vision, Team Learning, Systems Thinking) are posted in every classroom, and systems feedback—and the language of systems thinking—is used as a common thread for instruction and learning. Approximately 175 middle school students are housed in this innovative school located in the lower floor of a nondescript office building in Chelmsford, a suburb of Boston. The school's "charter" states that students leaving the school will be proficient problem solvers who

- think systemically,
- investigate options,
- test mental models,

Figure 6.7 Systems Feedback Loops Overview

Background Systems feedback loops have been used in many fields to show cycles: a simple feedback loop that every elementary child learns about is the precipitation cycle. When students learn about predator-prey relationships and food chains, feedback loops may be used to show the dynamic interrelationships among the variables in a system. Systems thinking as a way of understanding the world has evolved from business and industry applications in the 1950s and has gained visibility in the field of education through the work of Peter Senge of MIT. While systems thinking does not absolutely require mapping using feedback loops, it is hard to imagine representing a system and all its complex interdependencies other than through visual means.

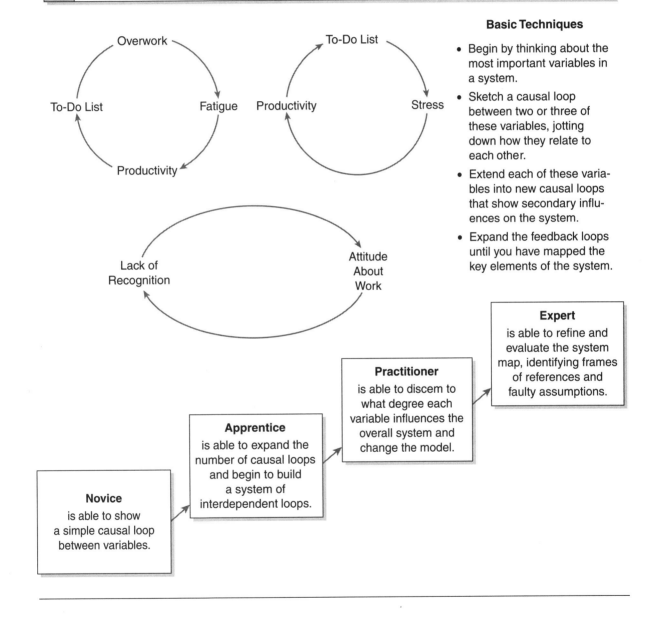

Basic Techniques

- Begin by thinking about the most important variables in a system.
- Sketch a causal loop between two or three of these variables, jotting down how they relate to each other.
- Extend each of these variables into new causal loops that show secondary influences on the system.
- Expand the feedback loops until you have mapped the key elements of the system.

- develop and ask relevant questions,
- make informed decisions,
- evaluate their process, and
- apply their knowledge to real-world situations.

These aims are accomplished through many means, including full training for staff in systems thinking and feedback flow diagramming and Peter Senge's Five Disciplines, a focus on interdisciplinary topics, and with accountability to the standards set by the State of Massachusetts Department of Education. On entering the school some years ago, when I met with the principal and began a tour led by two students, few things seemed different from any other school. At the first turn, two teachers entered a classroom, asking for one of the students. "Whooooaaa!" roared a room full of typical seventh graders in unison, expecting the girl to be reprimanded. One of the teachers laughingly said: "You're going to have to check your mental models—we want to talk to her about an award she will be receiving." The classroom went silent.

Mental models have been described in many ways by linguists, cognitive scientists, and business management theorists and consultants. Basically, a mental model is the theory or framework that a person—or a group—has for *how a system or part of a system works*. It consists of a mindset and overlapping frames of reference for how things or people act. In this example, the students knew the basic definition of a mental model, so when the teachable moment arrived, they were dealt a wake-up call: They had been going along blindly interpreting the situation without reflection.

This first step in systems thinking is an awareness that our prior experiences, knowledge, culture, and belief "systems" deeply influence what and how we learn new things. A system is not simple, and our mental models of it can wreak havoc on our ability to see the whole picture and shift our insights out of poorly formed assumptions.

Systems thinking—represented by modeling tools—requires us to build, challenge, and evaluate our mental models through feedback loops. At the time of this visit, Murdoch students were immersed in a unit on hunger. Several students were investigating India and the dynamics of hunger in this vast country. While most students also use brainstorming webs for generating ideas, systems loops and diagramming are, as one student said, "harder." For example, one eighth grader created a basic feedback loop to show one set of dynamic relationships as a starting point (see Figure 6.8). The two central loops are mutually reinforcing: As construction of farms increases, so too does food and, most likely, the number of healthy people. At the same time, new farms also create increased employment and expansion of land use. A "balancing" loop, in this case the available land, may have negative or positive influences on new construction.

The student, Matt Lowe, then created an extension of the problem of hunger in India. Rather than looking at supporting programs, such as the development of agriculture, Matt examined the problem of money being invested in nuclear testing (Figure 6.9). Again, this is a starting point from which we can see a wide number of feedback loops linking into each of these variables. Matt defines a problem, then analyzes it using a linked array of loops. Ultimately, he offers a solution with its implications. Importantly, this student is analyzing interdependencies in the system, and the loops could be integrated as his analysis grew. Matt was not just attempting to name parts of the problems but was showing them in relation to the whole system. In feedback form, these relationships appear much more complex, yet on another level the complexity is much easier to understand than if the problems were

Figure 6.8   A Feedback Loop: India's Employment/Nutrition Success by an Eighth
Grader at Murdoch Middle School

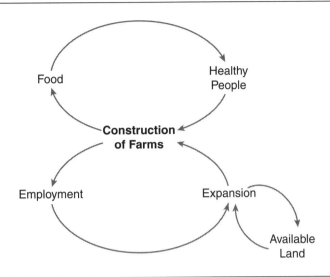

Created by Matt Lowe, student at Chelmsford Public Charter School, Murdoch Middle School.

presented in a linear fashion. Of course, our most interesting and important problems are complex and exist in systems.

LEAVING TRACKS

It would seem odd if students, teachers, and administrators at the Murdoch School didn't also walk the talk of thinking systemically about their own environment and interactions, and, in fact, plenty of evidence indicates that this form of thinking takes shape in the day-to-day lives of learners. House meetings are held regularly, where the whole school population gets together to discuss their needs.

Because each person is part of the "system," if the school doesn't pay attention to each person, the whole system—not just the person—may suffer over time. For example, when one student in the school was diagnosed with severe allergic reactions to perfumes and scented oils, everyone in the school came to a consensus (the school runs on a consensus model for decision making) that no one in the building would wear perfumes, scented lotions, or cologne. While this systems approach seems to be an analytical way of understanding empathy, it may be a much deeper, more fully integrated way of understanding empathy than trying to reinforce "caring" in a school through character development programs.

At Murdoch Middle School, issues such as attendance, conflicts, and behaviors among adolescents and adults in the building are often talked about with the language and the analytical understanding of the dynamics of complex systems and of the implications for behaviors, not just in the moment, but over time. Problem-based learning and real-world issues are thus extensions of the microcosm of this school in its attempt to understand systems.

One of the phrases that seems to embody this understanding—and that is heard in classrooms, meeting rooms, and hallways—is "actions leave tracks." This is much

Figure 6.9 Feedback Loop: India's Nuclear Testing Effects by an Eighth Grader at Murdoch Middle School

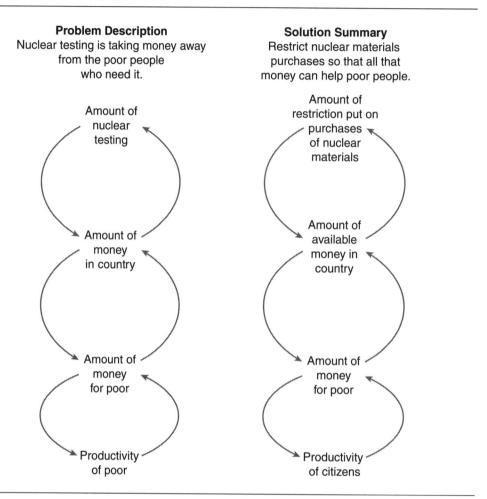

Problem Description
Nuclear testing is taking money away from the poor people who need it.

Solution Summary
Restrict nuclear materials purchases so that all that money can help poor people.

Amount of nuclear testing

Amount of money in country

Amount of money for poor

Productivity of poor

Amount of restriction put on purchases of nuclear materials

Amount of available money in country

Amount of money for poor

Productivity of citizens

Created by Matt Lowe, student at Chelmsford Public Charter School, Murdoch Middle School.

like the metaphor of the ripple effect from a stone thrown into a pond. But in the case of leaving tracks, consider systems thinking: Actions often do not ripple for a short time, in a uniform way, and then disappear. The idea of leaving tracks is consonant with a new paradigm of science and with common sense; what we do may have profound effects in the short term and forever influence future actions and behaviors across systems.

The "leaving of tracks" may be positive or negative. For example, that a whole school agreed to refrain from wearing perfumes left tracks in the short term by making one student feel welcome and healthy. The process of this decision set a precedent about the importance of process, of relationships in the school, and taking concrete actions in response to different needs within the school. This action will leave tracks for future students in the school and in the future lives of many of these students.

Leaving tracks also creates a metaphor for thinking systemically: that mental models can be traced and changed; that change happens over time; that change is complex with innumerable pathways, feedbacks, and flows; and that attempting to see the whole of an idea, concept, feeling, or action makes each part that much more important. It simply helps us realize that the whole is greater than the sum of its parts because of all the interdependent relationships between and among the parts. These patterns as processes are what is worth thinking about.

AN INTEGRATION OF VISUAL REPRESENTATIONS: TEACHING WITH *UNIT VISUAL FRAMEWORKS*

From across these last three chapters, we have surfaced examples of brainstorming webs, graphic organizers, and now conceptual mapping tools that become essential scaffolds for learning for students as teachers facilitate patterns of thinking through lessons or units of study. None of these tools, as presented, are used in isolation, and all require that students become independent in their application and transfer of these tools across disciplines. In a sense, the visual tools presented focus directly on facilitating conceptual understandings of either the micro or macro elements of a unit of study. Let's now consider what would happen if the use of visual tools became the overarching medium through which, in collaboration, students and teachers created an evolving visual representation of whole units of study as well as the micro level of the parts of the unit.

This level of use and sophistication is what Christine Allen Ewy offers through a process she calls teaching with Unit Visual Frameworks (UVF). Through a cogeneration process, students and teachers create a working draft on a classroom wall that visually displays the important elements of the unit of study. Students work as individuals, in small groups, and as a whole class to develop and update the display, so that the meaning and representation of concepts, and the relationships among them, are negotiated and commonly understood by all participants as they integrate their learning experiences and deepen their understandings.

Below are the definitions of the terms *unit, visual*, and *framework* that ground UVFs, also represented in visual form in Figure 6.10. These definitions are taken directly from Ewy's well-documented book for teachers who want to learn how to practice this approach, *Teaching With Visual Frameworks* (2002):

> **Unit.** A UVF organizes a whole unit of study from its beginning to end. A unit is defined as a progression of learning experiences that work together to ensure deep learning of clear targets.
>
> **Visual.** Students and teacher codevelop an ongoing class wall display (or other format where wall space is scarce) including a core visual with illustrations and text. They also make portable versions of the core visual for individual use.
>
> **Framework.** The UVF provides and maintains a clear focus on instructional targets, so that students and teachers have ongoing awareness of what they are learning, relative to what they will be held accountable for, as they pursue multiple teaching and learning experiences.

As Ewy describes and well illustrates in her text, UVFs are "organic"—evolving from the unit's concrete learning experiences—while also focusing to a high degree on the content and concepts that are the center of the unit. The teacher is the

Figure 6.10   Teaching and Learning With Visual Frameworks: My Mental Picture

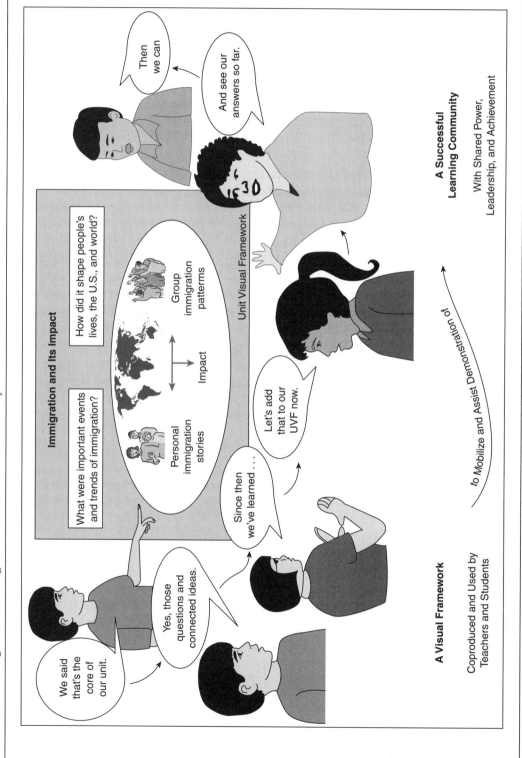

facilitator and mediator of the students' individual and group work, as well as of the students' development of drafts of the evolving group graphic on the wall. Students adapt the class UVF by developing their individual "portable" UVFs to ensure personal meaning, and through them they can expand their ideas on their own. This "demonstration" through the visual processing of and integration of content knowledge and conceptual understandings becomes a center of assessment for the unit of study.

An example of this cogeneration of work by students and teachers is offered by Ginger Benning, a sixth-grade teacher, who notes its importance to her: "Making the concepts visual helped me see the big picture. I also saw student learning of the facts and big ideas, and their enthusiasm at being part of the process and empowered to make decisions" (Ewy, 2002, p. 143). A complete chapter in Ewy's book follows the evolution of an earth science unit, "earth as a system," led by Ginger. It reveals the effectiveness of a process that follows this general sequence: Elicit the students' image of the unit of study; display the students' image organized to show the unit focus; expand the students' image; and update the displayed image (the UVF). Incomplete class and sample student portable UVFs from Ginger's earth science unit are shown in Figure 6.11. The unit focus questions are not depicted on these versions.

It is important to recognize that in the sequence of development of the class and student UVFs, student and teachers are accessing information from many of the same sources that any good teacher would bring forward, and what the UVFs do is unite the unit in a range of visual ways so that all the learning can be synthesized meaningfully. Within any UVF, the students and the teacher may use brainstorming webs, graphic organizers, and conceptual mapping along with illustrations and, of course, text to conceptually integrate content learning. Notice in the example in Figure 6.11 that both student UVFs are combined in hierarchical displays of information (types of earthquakes and types of volcanoes) shown side by side with a systems dynamics view of the interdependency of knowledge. These student documents are then integrated, in part, into the evolving class UVF, through discussion and negotiation based on the unit focus questions. The richness of this focused negotiation of ideas and concepts cannot be underestimated, because students have before them a range of meaningful representations of how the content fits together conceptually within a broad unit of study. This means, ultimately, that a unified understanding of the concepts in a classroom can be held together, improved, and recalled by students' conceptual display of knowledge.

The cogeneration of knowledge among students and teachers when creating UVFs shows a qualitative shift toward learning at the higher end of Bloom's taxonomy and to a level of systematic reflection on patterns of thinking (metacognition) rarely evident in classrooms. The UVF processes and product enable teachers and students to step back from and look more closely at not just what knowledge they have acquired but how they have synthesized their understandings. While students may move toward another product of learning, such as an essay, report, or oral presentation, the UVF acts as a resource for any further application or assessment. Key to this whole process, as it is with all the other conceptual mapping approaches surfaced in this chapter, is the significant role of focus questions in both planning and guiding work with students (Ewy, personal communication, 2006). Using questions that lead to the heart of the unit's learning is central to developing and effectively using UVFs and to furthering the capacities of students' asking themselves these questions in the future.

Figure 6.11 Earth Science Class and Portable UVFs

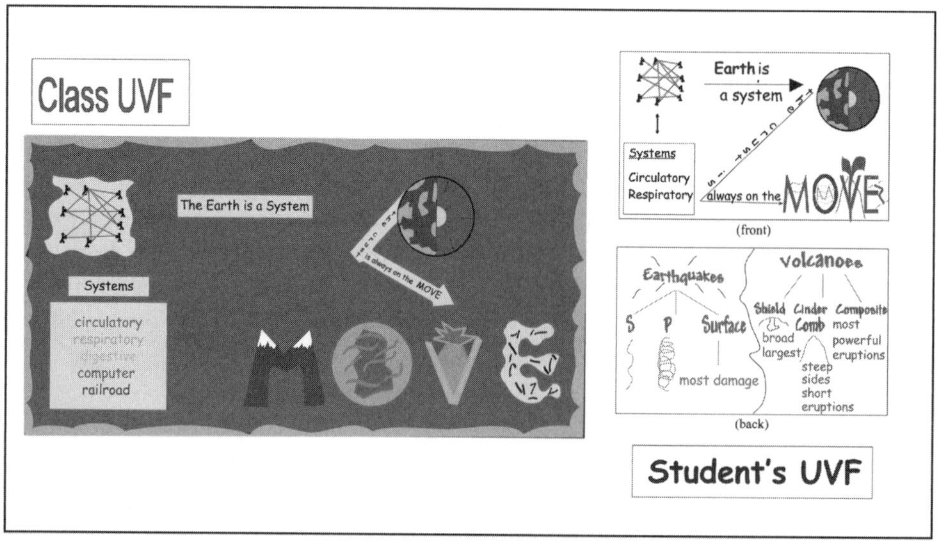

Source: Copyright © 2003 by Christine Allen Ewy. All rights reserved. Reprinted from *Teaching with visual frameworks: Focused learning and achievement through instructional graphics co-created by students and teachers*, by Christine Allen Ewy.

This exemplar brings this chapter to a close, integrating and reflecting its key points on visual tools for conceptual mapping: student ownership of the tools, practical and collaborative use, conceptual depth, and ultimately the facilitation of students' metacognitive abilities. It also reveals, by positive example, the inadequacy of or concerns we may have with using just one type of visual tool, or one type of conceptual mapping. By introducing and modeling the use of multiple visual tools as a grounding for learning, students will not see and act on the world of concepts through one lens. They will see the world across a range of conceptual structures and thus be adaptive to content learning requiring a differentiated range of thinking patterns. We now turn to another integrative example of visual tools, a language of differentiated forms, through which students, teachers, and leadership teams negotiate and transform information into meaningful knowing.

7

Thinking Maps

A Synthesis Language of Visual Tools

The full range of visual tools has been presented in the last three chapters as patterns for thinking creatively, organizationally, and conceptually. We can see how students are making sense of their own stored knowledge in displayed "visual schemata" and how they accommodate and assimilate new information and concepts through these richly developed visual tools: Brainstorming webs foster creativity, graphic organizers explicitly model more analytical content processes, and mapping tools explicitly focus on deeper conceptual understandings. So it is reasonable—practical really—to consider and question how this wide range of tools could be synthesized, coordinated, and offered to students in a practical and meaningful way so that they could ultimately take control of their own patterns of thinking.

- How could student-centered visual tools be coordinated in ways that they are generative like webs, analytical like organizers, and focused on conceptual learning?
- What would theoretically ground this organization of visual tools? How would we organize and link the visual tools?
- How would this work in practical ways for students, teachers, and school leaders?

These are the questions I asked myself long ago, and this chapter offers an answer drawn from 20 years of theoretical research, demonstrated quantitative and qualitative results, and practical experiences of implementing a common visual language of visual tools called Thinking Maps across whole schools, from preschool to college.

The evidence found in research across educational domains identifies nonlinguistic representations as key to student learning. *Classroom Instruction That Works* (Marzano, Pickering, & Pollack, 2001), *Building the Reading Brain* (Wolfe & Nevills,

2004), and the *Put Reading First* (Armbruster et al., 2001) research all conclude that *nonlinguistic representations* are essential vehicles for improving students' learning. These researchers and others from over 75 years of cognitive studies and the neurosciences also identify *fundamental cognitive patterns* as the foundation to student learning. This nexus of patterns of thinking and nonlinguistic representations is the foundation of Thinking Maps as a language of eight nonlinguistic representations defined by fundamental cognitive skills. This chapter introduces a common visual language for thinking, learning, teaching, and leadership practices that brings together nonlinguistic representations and fundamental cognitive skills in a theoretically sound and classroom-tested language for learning to integrate creative, analytical, and conceptual thinking for all students.

First conceived of in 1986, Thinking Maps* are a language of visual-verbal-spatial cognitive patterning tools that has now been implemented through required professional development training and systematic follow-up coaching in over 5,000 schools across the United States and internationally since 1990 (Hyerle, 1988–1993, 1990, 1993, 1995, 1996; 2000b; Hyerle, Curtis, & Alper, 2004). Teachers, students, and administrators in elementary, middle, and high schools are introduced to this language in the first year of implementation through a professional development process that includes training days, follow-up coaching, and the development of deep applications in reading, writing, mathematics, and technology. The primary outcome of the interactive professional development is that teachers work together over multiple years to *explicitly* teach all their students how to become fluent independent and collaborative users of this language for in-depth content learning and to transfer the same language of thinking across all content areas and grades levels, thus enabling continuous cognitive development for all students.

The effectiveness of Thinking Maps has been established through the scientifically based research cited in this book on nonlinguistic representations and graphic organizers, and extensively documented through test scores and qualitative evidence in academic publications since 1990. Most recently, over a dozen authors from the United States, New Zealand, and Singapore—from high- to low-achieving schools and from inner-city to rural schools—presented the documented results of Thinking Maps implementation in the book *Student Successes With Thinking Maps: School-Based Research, Results and Models for Achievement Using Visual Tools* (Hyerle, Curtis, & Alper, 2004).

In this chapter, we first look at the historical background of Thinking Maps and definition of this language. Then we will look at the implementation rubric for Thinking Maps that shows the development of student, teacher, administrator, and whole-school targets at five levels, as this language becomes a common foundation for learning, teaching, and leadership over multiple years. This will provide the framework for looking at three roles (students, teachers, leaders): student

---

*The term "Thinking Maps" and the term "Thinking Maps" with the graphic forms of the eight Maps have registered trademarks. No use of the term "Thinking Maps" with or without the graphic forms of the eight Maps may be used in any way without the permission of Thinking Maps, Inc. Specific training is required before Thinking Maps are implemented in the classroom. Inquiries regarding Thinking Maps and training can be made to Thinking Maps, Inc., 1-800-243-9169, www.thinkingmaps.com.

performance in schools with large populations of English-language learning in high-poverty areas; teachers using Thinking Maps for content deep applications through *Mapping the Standards*; and the evolution of a learning community using Thinking Maps for leadership practices. The last chapter of this book reveals the bigger picture of what happens to student and teacher performance when Thinking Maps are implemented for multiple years in a school that is exclusively for students with language and learning disabilities.

A SHORT HISTORY OF THINKING MAPS

The Thinking Maps were created as a language during the generative stages of my writing a student workbook for facilitating thinking skills at the middle school level called *Expand Your Thinking* (Hyerle, 1988–1993). There were four significant experiences that grounded my theoretical and practical development of Thinking Maps as a language for learning, teaching, and leadership.

First, in the early 1980s, I learned from my teaching credential processes and student teaching with the Bay Area Writing Project (University of California, Berkeley) that my students could visually represent their thinking in *every* discipline using brainstorming webs. As shown in Chapter 4, when students surface their conceptions and misconceptions of the content they are learning and writing, we can assess what and how we are connecting content ideas. I taught my students Tony Buzan's Mind Mapping techniques and their writing and thinking improved. Then my students and I hit a wall. Every web started in the center and branched out. The repetitive visual pattern being developed did not reflect a rich range of thinking patterns in the content areas; too much irrelevant information was scattered across a page, with not enough coherence of ideas. I asked myself of brainstorming: What happens after the storm?

In 1983, after attending seminars led by Dr. Arthur Costa, I learned that the direct facilitation of fundamental cognitive skills and habits of mind (then called *intelligent behaviors*) supports student learning at every level of Bloom's taxonomy. I learned from this second experience that it was central to education for teachers to coach these cognitive skills *explicitly*, mediate students' thinking, and ask reflective questions of students so they would become metacognitive, self-assessing, independent learners. If this did not happen, students would be overwhelmed, as they are today, with information and conceptual challenges without conscious tools for thinking on their own. Sometime after these seminars, I was invited to be a part of the newly formed Cognitive Coaching® group led by Drs. Art Costa and Robert Garmston, focused on supervision and coaching in schools. Here I could see that the very same kinds of reflective questions we may ask of each other through supervision, mentoring, and coaching of colleagues reflect the kinds of questions we ask students to facilitate their thinking processes. I also realized that responses to these complex questions could be held in visual maps facilitating metacognition.

A third influential experience occurred during my two years in the early 1980s with the federally funded Teacher Corps, which focused on bringing new teachers into urban education. I was given the opportunity to pilot two comprehensive programs intended to systematically integrate content learning with thinking skills development. One of the programs was called *THINK!* with a scope and sequence that moved from phonemic awareness to full reading comprehension at the eighth-grade level. The second was called *Intuitive Math,* and its scope and sequence moved from basic number identification through eighth-grade math and prealgebra. Both of these programs focused on three outcomes: content learning, basic skills in each area of content, and the explicit teaching of a model of fundamental cognitive skills developed by a relatively unknown semanticist and professor, Dr. Albert Upton. Here I learned that we could *explicitly* teach children cognitive skills *simultaneously* with content knowledge and basic skills and that this *combination* is the key to learning.

Upton's theoretical work *Design for Thinking* (1960) describes six fundamental cognitive skills: defining "things" in context, describing, classifying, part-whole spatial reasoning, sequencing, and analogous thinking. Although these *foundational* thinking processes were well known to all cognitive psychologists and educators, Upton's definitions of these cognitive processes and his capacity to reveal how these skills work independently and interdependently—*along with a few key graphic representations*—showed me that these ways of thinking were at the center of every level of complex thinking from early childhood through adult learning. These cognitive skills work at every level of complexity, and they never go away.

I taught this approach in inner-city Oakland, California, at a Grades 4 to 8 school with a student population that was predominantly African American, most of whom were scoring in the lower two quartiles in reading and mathematics. Within weeks, the students thrived and I could *see* their rich thinking, which was not reflected on their previous test scores. As time went on, these students significantly shifted their test scores upward and began matching the high quality of their thinking with testable performances. This experience in the early 1980s gave me, at a very early stage of my career, an up-close view of the great disparity called the *achievement gap* and the structural inequities of school segregation and inequities of funding, which are still well documented in education today (Kozol, 2005). I also saw the fallacy of the "bell curve" mindset and became an advocate for improving thinking performance for all children. This reframing of the bell curve also led me to reject the culturally narrow framework for the intelligence "deficit model" that presupposed, with blinders on, that African Americans and other racial and ethnic groups were intellectually inferior to the dominant white culture in America. These structural and institutional frames still influence education today, but through my teaching experiences back then, I could see the glimmer of a way through the dire state of many urban classrooms. Students needed explicit tools for thinking through and transforming isolated information into mapped knowledge.

The last experience that captured me occurred while completing doctoral studies at the University of California at Berkeley, through my courses and guidance from Dr. George Lakoff. His research helped me to understand the influence of metaphor, mental models, and "framing" on human cognition. Specifically, frames of reference, whether belief systems, primary discourses in language, or the wealth of culture, directly and deeply influence how each of us as human beings *see* and *think* about the world. Lakoff's cross-cultural research and writings show that fundamental cognitive skills such as categorization, comparison, sequencing, and causality are all framed by our experiential base. This experiential base is found in language, culture, and cognitive structures (Lakoff & Johnson, 1980). The theory of *frame semantics* became a guiding concept for me in learning how cognitive processes and dynamic schemas work together in an often awkward dance to make sense of incoming experiences to the brain and mind.

As described in the following sections, and drawing from Art Costa's insights on metacognition, each cognitive pattern within the model of Thinking Maps is grounded explicitly by the visual rectangular "frame" of reference. After students map content, they may draw the frame around the map and write within the frame any information or experiences that may be influencing their point of view. This establishes a metacognitive stance in relationship to the *thinking* held in each *map*.

The four experiences described above—visual brainstorming, cognitive skills, the link of content learning and literacy to cognitive skills, and metacognition frame theory—all drew together around my interest in improving thinking abilities and learning for *all* students and for providing myself and other teachers with tools to help mediate student thinking.

DEFINING THINKING MAPS AS A LANGUAGE

The language of Thinking Maps is first and foremost based on eight fundamental cognitive skills. These eight cognitive skills, as shown in Figure 7.1, are based on a synthesis of cognitive science research, models of thinking developed for psychological testing and educational programs, and a transformation of Dr. Upton's early work. This model is neither linear nor hierarchical. The eight cognitive skills are defining in context, describing attributes, comparing and contrasting, classification, part-whole spatial reasoning, sequencing, cause-and-effect reasoning, and reasoning by analogy. This language is not a comprehensive view of thinking; it identifies the coherence and interdependency of the eight *fundamental* cognitive skills that ground thinking and learning.

This model is somewhat analogous to the eight parts of speech of the English language, which are used in a unifying way to produce sentences and sonnets and have no hierarchy or linearity in their use. Although it is dangerous to proclaim universals—which may be disrespectful to different cultures, language, and cognitive styles represented around the world—the eight cognitive primitives that ground Thinking Maps have found resonance and relevance as we introduced the tools in places like Singapore, Japan, Mexico, and, of course, in U.S. cities and districts of New York City that work with students speaking at least 150 languages and dialects.

The claim offered here is that around the world, like universal human emotional patterns such as love, joy, and pain, there are also basic universal cognitive processes: Every child born into this world, for example, comes to learn how to *sequence* the day, *categorize* ideas and objects around them, break down objects *whole to parts* and assemble them parts to whole, survive by causal reasoning, and reason by *analogy*. For example, there is no doubt that every human being has a visceral if not always conscious understanding of the causes and effects of actions; we would not survive physically, socially, or emotionally in the world if we did not reflexively and reflectively use cause-and-effect reasoning.

Key to understanding each of the eight cognitive processes is the essential interdependence among them. For example, as we saw in Chapter 2, Robert Marzano and his team have identified *comparing and contrasting* as one of nine strategies that work consistently well in classrooms. When students and teachers become aware of the eight Thinking Maps, including comparing and contrasting, it is clear that to do a high-quality level of comparison, one *must* be able to describe the qualities of the two items being compared. As an extension of this rule, to classify at a higher order rather

Figure 7.1   Thinking Maps Overview

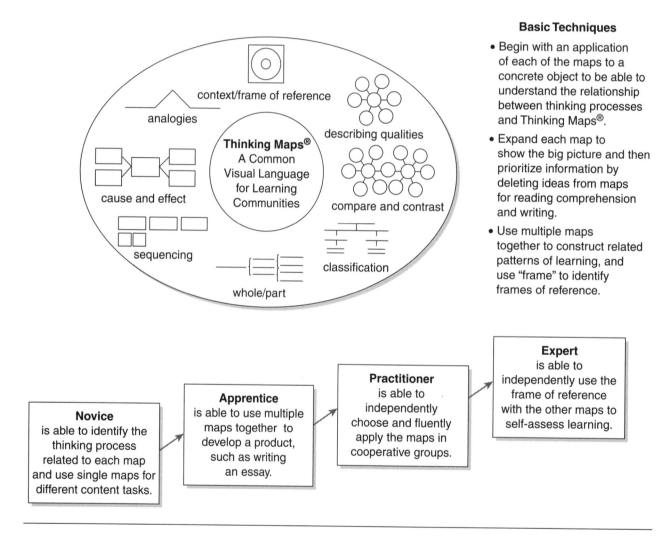

Background Thinking Maps® is a language, or toolkit, of eight thinking-process maps, developed by David Hyerle. Each map is graphically consistent and flexible so that students may easily expand the map to reflect the content pattern being learned. Thinking Maps® are introduced to students as tools for reading and writing, content-specific learning, and for interdisciplinary investigations. Over time, students learn to use multiple maps together and become fluent in choosing which maps fit the immediate context of learning. Thinking Maps® and Thinking Maps® Software are used in whole schools through faculty training and follow-up.

context/frame of reference

analogies

Thinking Maps®
A Common
Visual Language
for Learning
Communities

describing qualities

cause and effect

compare and contrast

sequencing

classification

whole/part

Basic Techniques

- Begin with an application of each of the maps to a concrete object to be able to understand the relationship between thinking processes and Thinking Maps®.

- Expand each map to show the big picture and then prioritize information by deleting ideas from maps for reading comprehension and writing.

- Use multiple maps together to construct related patterns of learning, and use "frame" to identify frames of reference.

Novice
is able to identify the thinking process related to each map and use single maps for different content tasks.

Apprentice
is able to use multiple maps together to develop a product, such as writing an essay.

Practitioner
is able to independently choose and fluently apply the maps in cooperative groups.

Expert
is able to independently use the frame of reference with the other maps to self-assess learning.

than through one-shot thinking, a student may need to compare items or ideas to determine in which category they belong and for what purpose. This awareness by students of the *interdependency* of thinking skills is, I believe, a missing link in classrooms today. Educators at every level, and psychologists and researchers, simplify these processes by teaching and testing thinking skills in isolation and imply the use of thinking skills rather than explicitly teaching them to students. Thinking is reduced to isolated skill development rather than a complex of cognitive processes that must work together to enable students to think at every level of Bloom's taxonomy. My critique of graphic organizers in Chapter 5—as being often static and isolated, teacher rather than student centered, and task specific rather than transferable—is resolved when teachers teach students how to use and transfer Thinking Maps independently as a language of multiple dynamic cognitive maps across content areas and their educational experience, K–12.

This introduction reveals why the name of this language uses the terms *thinking* and *maps*, in that order and not the reverse: The visual form of each map follows from the cognitive function of each map. *Form follows function.* The eight visual maps are a language of nonlinguistic representations for fundamental cognitive patterns that unite with and explicitly support spoken, written, and numeric representation systems. Each of the graphic primitives that visually define and animate each cognitive process is closely attuned to and reflects the cognitive pattern. Without going into lots of detail on the development of each graphic for each of the eight maps, it is obvious that the Flow Map was derived from flow charting, the Tree Map for classifying came from a traditional diagram for hierarchical reasoning, and the Brace Map for physical analysis of part-whole spatial relationships came from the classic text *Gray's Anatomy*. Each of the other map configurations, as expanded from visual starting points, were derived during my process over many years of developing a graphic primitive that any learner could use from simple to complex applications in every discipline. The main criterion in generating the visual form was that it as closely as possible followed the functioning of the cognitive processes defined by our evolving history of cognition.

As noted earlier, what is important is that each of the cognitive processes is influenced, animated, and transformed by the cultural frames that surround these behaviors. This means that everyone may understand and utilize the cognitive process of categorization, but the categories carry a different language, content, processes for development, and forms within and across cultures. After playing with and rigorously testing the eight maps as individual tools and as a language of interdependent tools, I realized what was missing: a way for learners to name and visually represent what was influencing, or framing, the thinking patterns they had developed using each Thinking Map. Inherent in the metaphor of "frame" was the visual needed for facilitating reflection: Learners could draw a rectangular frame, like a window frame, around any of the maps and thus ask many reflective questions such as:

- What is influencing how I am seeing this information?
- What prior knowledge is helping or getting in the way of my understanding this new content knowledge?
- Why did I choose this Thinking Map?
- Is there another or several other Thinking Maps I should use to understand this idea?

In retrospect, and from what we now know about the effectiveness of Thinking Maps from close to 20 years of implementation in whole schools, the eight cognitive processes grounding the visual representations are most powerful when the learner adds this metacognitive frame of reference around the map being created. This is because we not only want students to be self-assessing and metacognitive, but we want them to understand that other learners in the classroom or school will create different maps of the knowledge. Respecting and having empathy for another person's view of knowledge and frames of reference enhance knowledge creation in classrooms and communication across languages and cultures.

While there are only eight maps—and the "metacognitive" frame that surfaces the culture, belief systems, and perspective of the maps' maker—each map has an infinite number of configurations, much as the English language has only eight parts of speech but a vast number of combinations that create an infinite number of simple to complex variations. Five essential qualities of Thinking Maps are key to their being infinitely expandable and capable of being used simultaneously, as a carpenter uses multiple tools in constructing buildings (Figure 7.2). For example, using the Flow Map as an example, the map is

- *graphically consistent,* as the flow is created with boxes and arrows only and can show substages;
- *flexible,* as the graphic primitive expands so the flow can be linear and cyclical, or have multiple parallel flows connected;
- *developmental,* as it can be used at any age level and is responsive to simple to complex applications;
- *integrative,* as it is used across disciplines and for interdisciplinary problem solving; and
- *reflective,* as learners uses it to assess how they are thinking and share and compare the visual representations with one another and teachers.

These qualities of the tools, used individually and together as a language, lead immediately and directly to more complex orders of thinking, such as problem solving involving evaluating, thinking systemically, and thinking analogically. When students are given common graphic starting points, *every* learner is able to detect, construct, and communicate different patterns of thinking about content concepts, as shown in the figure within the frame of reference surrounding the Bubble Map. This is especially true when Thinking Maps are used as a language, keyed to thinking skills vocabulary for learning and assessing, and when they are used with Thinking Maps Software and other technologies, and, most important, when they are reinforced over multiple years across disciplines.

In summary, as a *language* of visual tools, each of the eight Thinking Maps embodies the creative quality of *brainstorming webs,* the organizing and consistent visual structure of *graphic organizers,* and the deep processing capacity and dynamic configurations found in *conceptual maps.* At any time, learners can access this thinking language—on paper or through software—to construct and communicate networks of mental models of linear and nonlinear concepts. As explored in the following sections, using the language of eight graphic primitives, learners and teachers identify the questions and cognitive skills needed to solve a problem, complete a task, answer a question, or write an essay and identify which Thinking Map or most likely *multiple maps* will be useful for the problem before them.

Thinking Maps, as a language of visual tools based on fundamental thinking skills, have been proven as one route for *unifying* content and process instruction and

Figure 7.2   Bubble Map of Five Qualities of Thinking Maps

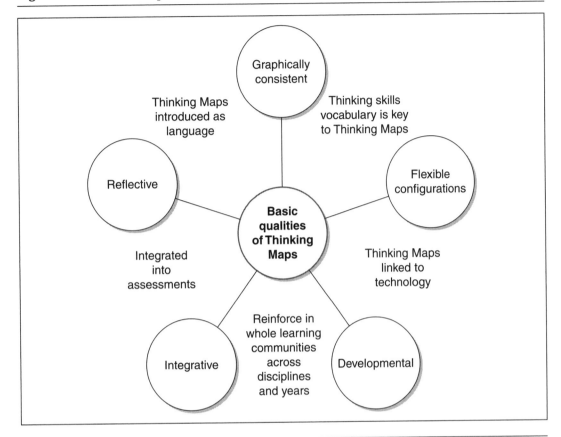

assessment of products. As students across whole schools become fluent with Thinking Maps, this array of eight visual tools becomes a common visual language in the classroom for communication, cooperative learning, and facilitating a deep empathy for how others think as well as for the *continuous cognitive development* of every child over a lifespan of learning.

FIVE LEVELS OF THINKING MAPS IMPLEMENTATION

After participating in a Thinking Maps "Day 1 Training" and coaching conducted over a year, teachers and students become independent and cooperative tool users, fluidly linking content knowledge and working together to build maps on the way to final products. Many of these schools integrate Thinking Maps Software® (Hyerle, 2007) into the routines of classroom and computer lab experiences, creating a seamless web connecting the mind of the learner, the content being taught interactively by teachers, and technology.

Thinking Maps are used for reading comprehension and writing across disciplines. The training manual *Thinking Maps: A Language for Learning* (Hyerle, 1995; Hyerle & Yeager, 2007) contains content correlations and examples of Thinking Maps applications to literacy development and mathematics, science, social studies, reading, and writing and the full range of activities in schools from the arts to physical education. As described below, teachers move from novice to expert users of these tools by directly linking the content they are teaching and the questions they are asking to their own local, state, and/or national standards. This occurs through collaboration with outside consultants and their own in-house trainers who have been certified to conduct Thinking Maps follow-up. Though each map is based on a defined thinking process, teachers and students use this correlation to fully integrate the reading, writing, and thinking connection necessary for full comprehension and expression of ideas.

Over the past 15 years, the processes of implementing Thinking Maps over multiple years have surfaced a common evolution across schools and states in which we have worked. Because the implementation model is based on whole-school use over time and the direct involvement of all students, teachers, and administrators, a clearly defined rubric for implementation has been developed as a guideline for long-term implementation (Figure 7.3). As you can see, there is an evolution for students, teachers, administrators, and whole-school development across five levels:

1. Introducing the big-picture concept of Thinking Maps to all participants in the school so that there is a readiness to fully implement the tools

2. Teaching and reinforcing the basic use of Thinking Maps to all participants

3. Horizontal transfer of Thinking Maps as a language across disciplines and communication by teachers and administrators in the school

4. Vertical integration of Thinking Maps and software into students collaborative work and homework as well as within instructional strategies and programs

5. Executive control of Thinking Maps so that all participants are experts in this language and able to independently and collaboratively use the tools for novel applications in any setting

Because Thinking Maps are a visual *language* and is not an add-on program of activities, materials, or worksheets, this rubric is based on the evolution of all participants in a school toward fluency with the tools as applied to what they are already doing in classrooms and in professional meetings. The Concerns Based Adoption Model (CBAM) may be used as a filter for decoding or understanding this innovation across whole schools: participants in the school learn the language, begin to see the implications for the maps for their own work, learn the language from outside experts, develop expertise within their own community of learners, and thus are empowered to more complex and novel applications as they take "executive control" over the content, processes, products, and assessment of the work.

Figure 7.3 Five Levels of Thinking Maps Implementation

	1 Introducing the Knowledge Base	2 Teaching the Skills and Maps	3 Horizontal Transfer Across Disciplines	4 Vertical Integration	5 Executive Control and Assessment
STUDENT	• Is aware of the impending implementation	• Correctly applies and constructs all 8 maps with support • Recognizes maps as teacher applies them in new situations • Identifies appropriate TM in response to prompt or question	• Uses thinking-process vocabulary • Accurate and independent selection of TM for communicating thoughts and ideas in all subject areas • Applies multiple maps to analyze and comprehend information for learning	• Uses TM collaborative group work to expand, revise, and synthesize ideas • Collaborative problem solving • Applies TM to homework, projects, etc., for a variety of purposes and through a variety of technologies, including TM software	• Fluid, independent use of language of TM across disciplines • Uses TM for metacognition, self-reduction, and assessment • Self-selected artifacts for student portfolio of Thinking Maps • Novel applications beyond academic areas
TEACHER	• Has attended Day 1 TM training • Established a plan for systematically introducing TM • Has met with colleagues (grade level, content area) to review plans for implementation • Discussed with students the plan for implementation	• Explicitly introduces and reinforces all 8 maps • Models and applies multiple maps to demonstrate and introduce content and concepts	• Uses TM to guide questioning and responses • Encourages and models thinking-process vocabulary for the transfer across disciplines • Explicitly scaffolds map(s) for improvement of students' thinking abilities	• Uses TM in collaborative work for instruction and assessment • Collaborative problem solving and curriculum planning • Uses TM in and for curriculum planning, cooperative learning, and assessment through a variety of technologies, including TM software • Embeds Thinking Maps in other instructional strategies, structures, and initiatives	• Fluid use of map(s) instruction and assessment • Uses TM for metacognition, self-reflection, and assessment • Self-selected collection and documentation of Thinking Maps integration • Novel application to instructional opportunities beyond academic areas

(Continued)

Figure 7.3 (Continued)

	1 Introducing the Knowledge Base	2 Teaching the Skills and Maps	3 Horizontal Transfer Across Disciplines	4 Vertical Integration	5 Executive Control and Assessment
ADMINISTRATOR	• Has a clearly developed plan to support TM implementation • Uses TM for basic agendas or to display data such as agendas, roles (if leadership training has preceded TM implementation)	• Uses TM to plan and facilitate small- and whole-group meetings • Models multiple maps to introduce and generate information about topics or issues	• Uses TM for coaching and supervision • Uses TM for long-term planning and school improvement • Encourages and models thinking-process vocabulary for transfer across the learning organization	• Uses TM In collaborative work for instruction and assessment • Collaborative problem solving and curriculum planning • Uses TM in and for curriculum planning, cooperative learning, and assessment through a variety of technologies, including TM software • Embeds Thinking Maps in other instructional strategies, structures, and initiatives	• Fluid use of maps in collaborative problem solving, coaching, and supervision, etc. • Uses TM for metacognition, self-reflection, and assessment • Schoolwide documentation of applications across grade levels and disciplines • Novel application to administrative duties
SCHOOL	• Leadership Team, including Trained Trainers, established to guide implementation • All resources and TM software, if acquired, are distributed to faculty • Central area established to share/display TM work	• Displays evidence of student, teacher, and administrator applications • Parents are made aware of the implementation of the maps and opportunities are provided for them to become oriented to their use	• Sharing, discussing, and collecting map applications and media across all grade levels and positions to promote the schoolwide common language • Uses TM for schoolwide data analysis and action planning	• Uses TM in grade-level, department, parent, and volunteer meetings for collaboration problem solving • Integrates TM as a tool within other communication frameworks through a variety of technologies, including TM software	• Fluid use of maps for communication between all members of learning community, parents • TM technology used to facilitate higher-order thinking across school • Schoolwide assessment of implementation indicating patterns of use, growth and next steps • Novel applications outside of school building (in the wider community

Source: Copyright © 2006 by Thinking Maps, Inc. All rights reserved. From *Thinking Maps®: A language for leadership,* by Larry Alper and David Hyerle. Reprinted with permission.

The last cell of the rubric, at the bottom right, is the ultimate goal of implementing Thinking Maps: an evolved capacity for a community of learners to use Thinking Maps as a true language for communication, higher-order thinking, and problem solving, and for assessment at every level of the learning community and thinking organization. Ultimately, as we shall see, this means a leveling or flattening of the typical school hierarchy of empowerment, with the principal at the top, the students at the bottom, and teachers caught in the middle. This is because Thinking Maps offer a common visual language that brings people together around questions, concerns, and problems that reveal patterns from simple to complex and create a visible public space that is cogenerative and not positional (Alper & Hyerle, 2006).

The maps, as shown in the following examples, energize thinking and emotional states by explicitly centering on surfacing and thus honoring the frames of reference of every participant—students, teachers, and administrators—in the processes of learning and leading in schools.

In the first example, principal Stefanie Holzman of Roosevelt Elementary School in Long Beach, California, describes how Thinking Maps have become a "first language" for thinking across the whole school and as a bridge for students between their primary language, Spanish, and their second language, English. This writing is excerpted from Holzman's complete chapter in the book *Student Successes with Thinking Maps* (Chapter 10 in Hyerle, Curtis, & Alper, 2004). In the beginning of the implementation, all teachers and administrators attended Thinking Maps training, and with each year a new cluster of teachers attend a regional, in-depth training of trainers so that expertise is continuously being developed within the school. Roosevelt is now at the highest level of the CBAM model: step into any classroom and you will see, as I did, that teachers are creating novel applications with the tools and are focused on the adaptive and systematic use of Thinking Maps as fully integrated with their complete instructional program, specifically for language development and content learning.

Also, interview almost any student in the school and you will find them fluent with the Thinking Maps for their own learning across disciplines. I interviewed students from one fifth-grade classroom during the 2004 school year, and many stated that they regularly use the maps independently from teacher prompting, that the maps have directly helped their performance—especially in writing—and some even confessed to using the maps at home for working out problems. One student successfully taught the Thinking Maps to his older, high school sister who was having difficulty with writing.

The classroom experiences, transformation of teacher instruction and leadership, and performance results of students at Roosevelt and schools in Los Angeles have led to the in-depth training of over 300 Thinking Maps Trained Trainers in the Language Acquisition Division of the Los Angeles City Schools. Stefanie Holzman's insights offer a window into the idea of differentiated thinking patterns for all students, independent of level of language use, cultural background, and socioeconomic status. The improvement in test scores that she details in the next section—a gain of 182 points over the past three years when the state expectation was 30 points—is highly significant as each year student performance well exceeds state expectations.

Differentiated Thinking Patterns for English-Language Learners, by Stefanie Holzman

Learning content while learning a second language is a complex process. It is frustrating for a child to have ideas, vocabulary, and rich patterns of thinking in one language that are not immediately translated and understood by teachers in the context of the classroom. This is because the acquisition of a second language obviously gets in the way of our thinking and learning. The Thinking Maps become a translator of language and thinking from one language-mind (Spanish) to another (English). Thinking Maps became our first language for thinking, thus supporting the languages, content learning, and cognitive development of our multilingual population. Importantly, Thinking Maps were used to promote critical thinking skills even for students who were still acquiring English.

All students in our school, Roosevelt Elementary, in Grades 1 to 5 were tested on a standardized test in reading and math, and Grades 2 to 5 were also tested on the California standards test. Much of the math section includes reading. The teachers taught students to analyze the type of math question it was (for example, comparison, whole to part/part to whole, relationships, patterns) and the map associated with each. Once the students understood the five kinds of "story problems," they were able to tease out their critical attributes and apply them to the test. For example, in response to a word problem, one first-grade student selected the key information from the problem using a Circle Map and then used the Flow Map to show the steps and the strategies involved in solving the problem based on the information from the initial Circle Map. The change in students' ability to do these problems made a significant difference between last year's and this year's school scores.

Over 85% of the students who enter kindergarten in our school speak Spanish as their primary language. By law, we are required to differentiate the instructional practices based on the level of English-language proficiency of students. Theoretically, differentiation is simple: Teach differently to different students based on their individual needs. Easier said than done. However, one of the differences that Thinking Maps has made at my school is that teachers teach the same content to various groups in their classroom, but they have begun to provide alternative means for students to access content and to show what they know. For example, some teachers expect students to use the Thinking Maps as processes to a final product, whereas others expect students to use the tools as a final product to demonstrate their thinking and comprehension of the content.

In one of the third-grade classes, the students were expected to understand the similarities and differences between two planets. All students were required to complete a Double-Bubble Map comparing and contrasting the two planets, which was the stated outcome of the lesson. However, to differentiate the lesson, students who were fluent in English were also expected to write a report containing this information. Students less fluent in English needed only to create the Double-Bubble Map. The teacher was able to evaluate every student's factual and conceptual learning using either strategy (the map alone or the map and writing). With fluent English speakers, she was also able to evaluate their ability to communicate their learning in writing, something she already knew the less fluent English speakers would not yet be able to do. Of course, it is also essential to have the students who are not fluent in English begin to write from the Thinking Maps, as this provides the bridge from their primary language to the mainstream spoken and written form. As a first language for thinking, the maps became vocabulary builders, visible organizers, and starting points for writing in a second language.

The numbers are in from the standardized tests given in California. The state has a very complicated formula to determine expected growth. Roosevelt School was expected to gain 11 points overall in year 2003. We exceeded that goal with a 60-point gain. Not only did the school as a single unit make improvement, but so did our significant subgroups: Hispanic students, English-language learners, and students of low socioeconomic status as determined by free lunches. In 2003–2004, we gained 18 points on the California assessments and last year we gained another 28 points. We have also been identified as a CA Title 1 Academic Achievement Award winner for 2006. And we are still not satisfied. We've made a total of 182 points on the California assessment system; the expectation was about 30.

The important point here is that the teachers are able to assess content learning and use student maps as data points to see whether or not it is language that is getting in the way of understanding or if there are content misconceptions that need to be retaught. It is often difficult to determine how much limited English-proficient students understand of what is taught. If a teacher wants to know what a second-language learner has learned, does the teacher ask the student to use the second language if the student does not have verbal or written fluency? If assignments require writing what they know, these students often drown in the English language. They have to figure out the vocabulary, the syntax, the spelling, and the punctuation of English and at the same time remember the content they have learned. The results are that teachers often evaluate the students' English skills and sentence construction and not their content knowledge or their reasoning. However, when teachers ask students to use Thinking Maps to demonstrate what they know, then the students do not have to focus on English and can use their mental energies to communicate what they know about the content. They do not even have to use words to convey this information. In most cases, Thinking Maps lend themselves to visuals (e.g., drawings or pictures from magazines) to communicate the content.

Source: Copyright © 2004 by Corwin Press. All rights reserved. Reprinted from *Student successes with Thinking Maps: School-based research, results, and models for achievement using visual tools,* edited by David Hyerle, Sarah Curtis, and Larry Alper.

ESSENTIAL COGNITIVE QUESTIONS BASED IN STANDARDS

The kind of performance gains documented in Roosevelt School and many more are attained through focusing on essential questions that teachers ask of students on a day-to-day basis in classrooms. These types of questions also show up at the end of chapters in textbooks and in guides for teachers in published programs. These questions, based on fundamental patterns of thinking, are also the basis for questions found in local, state, and national standards.

These questions are also the foundation for Thinking Maps as shown in the following. Like the preceding questions, each Thinking Map—along with the "frame" of reference around them—represents a reflective question:

1. Circle Map: How are you defining this (concept) and in what context?

2. Bubble Map: What are the attributes?

3. Double-Bubble Map: How are these alike and different?

4. Tree Map: How are these grouped together?

5. Brace Map: What are the parts of a physical whole object?

6. Flow Map: What was the sequence of events?

7. Multi-Flow Map: What were the causes and effects?

8. Bridge Map: Is there an analogy between these ideas?

By grounding the Thinking Maps in fundamental cognitive skills, this language becomes the cognitive bridge to literacy between these questions and the reciprocal processes of reading comprehension across disciplines and writing prompts. As shown in Figure 7.4, the Thinking Maps key students and teachers to this bridge.

Figure 7.4   The Cognitive Bridge to Literacy

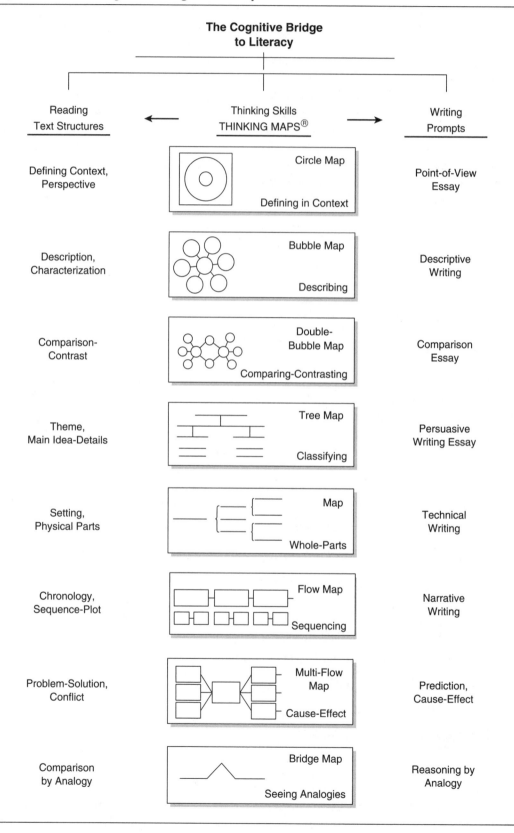

By linking concrete maps with essential questions and abstract thought processes, students can deal with more complex thinking because they know *what it looks like*. Importantly, they come to know how to link multiple Thinking Maps together in response to the *multiple* essential questions that teachers ask almost every day.

In the following section, Sarah Curtis, former teacher and lead author of the Mapping the Standards project, details how these exemplar lessons guide teachers and students to see how Thinking Maps bridge their own knowledge and skills base with standards-based questions and performances. Of course, it is the student who must perform independently on the gatekeeping tests in our educational system, and Sarah shows how Thinking Maps become the tools not only to meet the cognitive demand for each standard but also to exceed the standards and develop a deeper understanding of content knowledge. This section also reveals how Thinking Maps Software for students, teachers, and administrators offers a seamless connection between classroom practice, higher-order thinking, and this cognitive tool–based technology.

Again, return to the rubric to consider which of the five levels of implementation of Thinking Maps are being attained by integrating these tools into the core learning and teaching practices of a school, when these tools are focused on *meeting the standards by mapping the standards*.

Using Thinking Maps Software to Map the Standards, by Sarah Curtis

Most educators can remember their first attempts to decipher the standards for their grade level or content area. Furrowed brows and signs of exasperation greeted those unappetizing documents that outlined with confounding verbiage what students of a particular age needed to know and be able to do. Perhaps you can recall your own reaction to your state or district standards: anger, rejection, defeat, denial, or overwhelming frustration. Rarely did these documents, intended to provide and promote consistent benchmarks of achievement, leap from the page and into practice across the nation.

Thinking Maps and Thinking Maps Software are useful as tools for instruction and assessment for prioritizing standards across subject areas, and for developing conceptually and cognitively based lessons that address the standards. This provides both teachers and students with a means to translate the complex language of the standards into a tangible form of instruction and assessment for an array of different outcomes, as schools tried to adapt to the standards movement. Thinking Maps offer a vehicle for understanding the standards, constructing meaningful lessons targeting the learning outcomes, and a form of representation of what that learning might actually look like as students progress through their academic careers (Figure 7.5). The Thinking Maps Software provides the technology to archive and distribute these lessons across sites and to document student thinking over time.

When approaching the standards from a thinking-process lens inherent in the design of Thinking Maps, the cognitive processes of the standards emerge to the forefront while the content or topic moves in parallel to the side. Examining the standards in this manner helps shift the focus from an overload of content to be memorized toward a consistent pattern of how to think about content. Continuing to sift through subject matter, this cognitive filter illuminates a new way to see the content. The question changes from "What content needs to be covered?" to "How are the students asked to think about the content, to what degree, and from what angle?"

During the initial professional development day described earlier, when the Thinking Maps are introduced to teachers, teachers spend part of the day analyzing their local and/or state standards by looking at the types of thinking processes that students would use to meet the standard(s). If teachers have acquired Thinking Maps Software, they may begin to map out lesson plans by using this technology. See the example provided of a fifth-grade history lesson in Figure 7.6a–c.

(Continued)

(Continued)

Figure 7.5   Mapping the Standards Outcomes

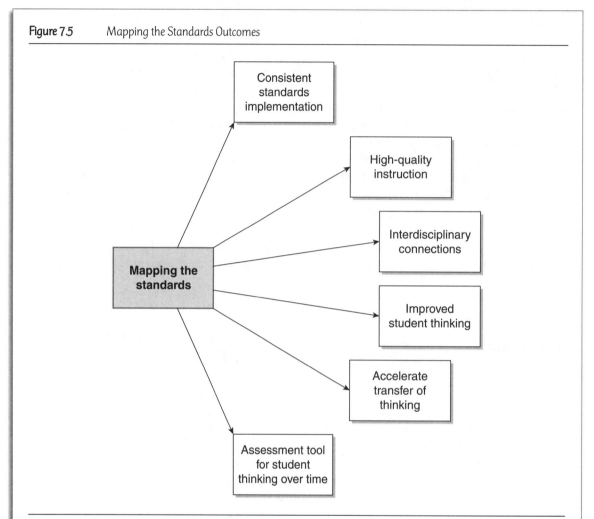

Thinking Maps® is a registered trademark of Thinking Maps, Inc.

Thinking Maps Software shows how the thinking processes embedded in the standards lead to the creation of essential questions and the application of a series of multiple Thinking Maps to develop that understanding. Partially completed Thinking Maps in the Map Window feature possible maps that correspond to the questions during the lesson. These maps may be used for pre- and postassessment and as scaffolds for a final project.

If the final demonstration of understanding is a written assignment, then the Writing Window of the software can be opened next to the Map Windows, and the information can be composed in the Writing Window as a word-processing document. Each lesson may include maps to activate prior knowledge, support student processing, assess content understanding, and extend knowledge. Educators can access the database of standards-based lessons by grade level, content area, or standard and select the lesson that meets their requirements.

In structuring lessons from concept to content—focused on essential questions and the cognitive pattern embedded in the questions—this professional development process aims to provide a model of high-quality instruction for teachers and the explicit pathways for students to exceed the standards. In the history lesson, students are asked to think about the concept of exploration, not just regurgitate names, places, and dates from a random period of time. Presenting this concept invites students to bring their prior knowledge to bear on learning the new information. Most students have some degree of familiarity with exploration, whether they have explored a sibling's room, their neighborhood, or a new landscape in a video game.

Figure 7.6a   Mapping the Standards Example

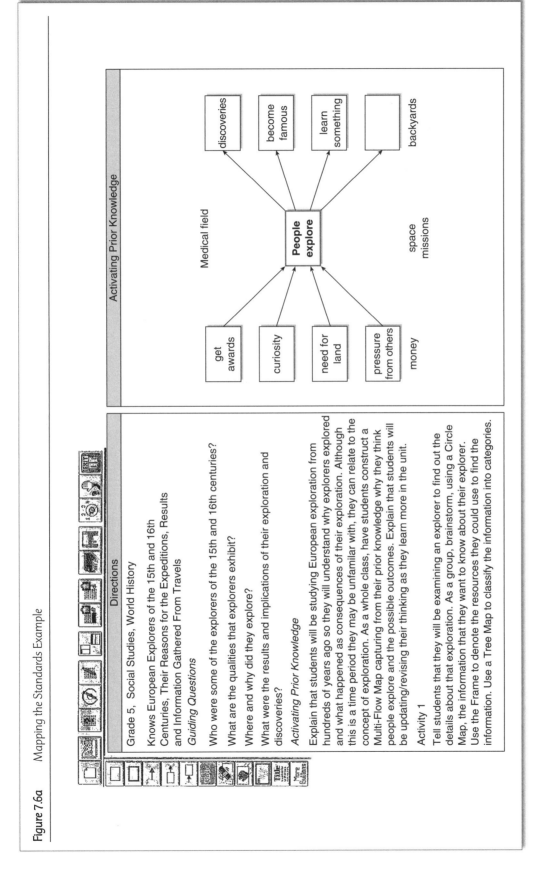

(Continued)

133

(Continued)

Figure 7.6b

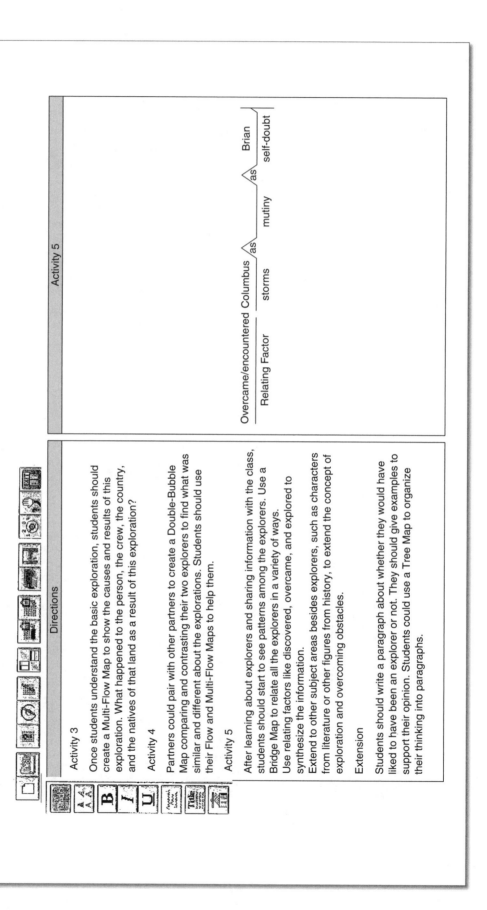

Directions

Activity 3

Once students understand the basic exploration, students should create a Multi-Flow Map to show the causes and results of this exploration. What happened to the person, the crew, the country, and the natives of that land as a result of this exploration?

Activity 4

Partners could pair with other partners to create a Double-Bubble Map comparing and contrasting their two explorers to find what was similar and different about the explorations. Students should use their Flow and Multi-Flow Maps to help them.

Activity 5

After learning about explorers and sharing information with the class, students should start to see patterns among the explorers. Use a Bridge Map to relate all the explorers in a variety of ways.
Use relating factors like discovered, overcame, and explored to synthesize the information.
Extend to other subject areas besides explorers, such as characters from literature or other figures from history, to extend the concept of exploration and overcoming obstacles.

Extension

Students should write a paragraph about whether they would have liked to have been an explorer or not. They should give examples to support their opinion. Students could use a Tree Map to organize their thinking into paragraphs.

Figure 7.6c

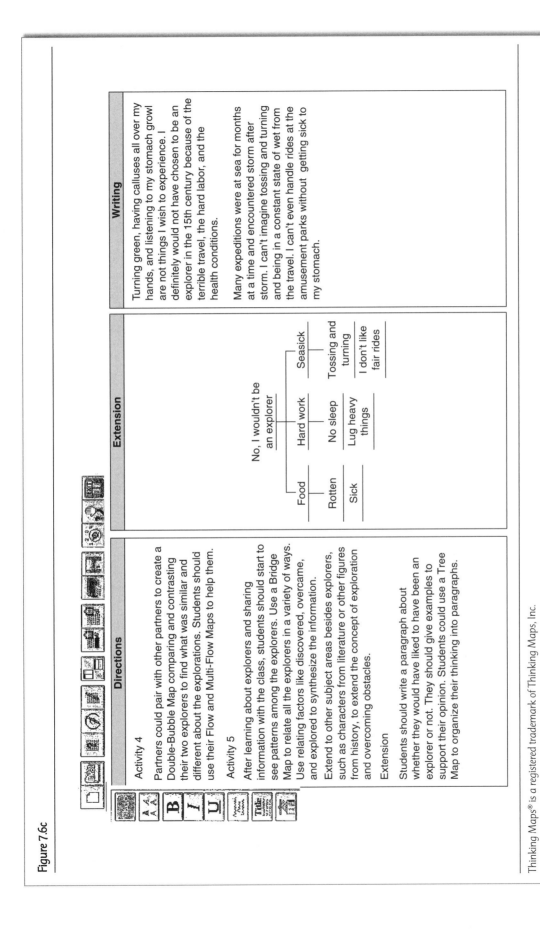

Directions

Activity 4

Partners could pair with other partners to create a Double-Bubble Map comparing and contrasting their two explorers to find what was similar and different about the explorations. Students should use their Flow and Multi-Flow Maps to help them.

Activity 5

After learning about explorers and sharing information with the class, students should start to see patterns among the explorers. Use a Bridge Map to relate all the explorers in a variety of ways. Use relating factors like discovered, overcame, and explored to synthesize the information.

Extend to other subject areas besides explorers, such as characters from literature or other figures from history, to extend the concept of exploration and overcoming obstacles.

Extension

Students should write a paragraph about whether they would have liked to have been an explorer or not. They should give examples to support their opinion. Students could use a Tree Map to organize their thinking into paragraphs.

Extension

No, I wouldn't be an explorer

Food — Rotten / Sick

Hard work — No sleep / Lug heavy things

Seasick — Tossing and turning / I don't like fair rides

Writing

Turning green, having calluses all over my hands, and listening to my stomach growl are not things I wish to experience. I definitely would not have chosen to be an explorer in the 15th century because of the terrible travel, the hard labor, and the health conditions.

Many expeditions were at sea for months at a time and encountered storm after storm. I can't imagine tossing and turning and being in a constant state of wet from the travel. I can't even handle rides at the amusement parks without getting sick to my stomach.

(Continued)

(Continued)

The Multi-Flow Map stimulating cause-and-effect reasoning about why people explore and the possible consequences can bridge these thoughts from self (what is known) to historical content (what is unknown). The Bridge Map, used for analogous relationships, deepens the concept from that historical time period to other aspects of history, literature, and science, as demonstrated in Activity 5. The Bridge Map is the concrete visual tool that breathes life into Stephanie Harvey's comprehension strategy of making connections among self, other texts, and the world (Harvey & Goudvis, 2007). In these lessons, explicit interdisciplinary links are offered for students as comprehenders of any subject matter. By focusing on both the cognition and the concept, this process of using Thinking Maps Software not only meets but exceeds the standards.

The Multi-Flow Map highlights some of the key outcomes related to instruction and assessment. From the teaching perspective, this process happens over multiple years in a school or school system as teachers begin to develop, pilot, and distribute the lessons to colleagues at their grade level and within their content area, providing teachers with multiple examples of Thinking Maps embedded into curriculum in meaningful ways, supporting the implementation of both Thinking Maps and standards at a site for teachers at different points in their careers (as new hires, transfers, and veterans). The more comfortable practitioners are with the tool, the more fluent they will be with the language of thinking. The cognitive and conceptual focus provides a model for teaching any content and offers a method for thinking about lesson design. These key questions for uniting standards-based instruction with the language of thinking may serve as guides to streamline the teaching-learning cycle:

1. How are the students asked to think about the content now and over time?

2. What questions, content and cognitive patterns, or links emerge?

3. What concepts or themes are present?

4. How might these patterns, concepts, or themes connect across different disciplines and cultures?

The last question is particularly important as we strive to have students transfer their learning across content and contexts. Teaching for both thinking skills and concept transfer has been the subject of many educational books and articles. The potential for this process described here focuses explicitly on transfer of concepts across content areas and grade levels, but cognitive development over time for each student as well. As students move through school, the topics may change, but the ways in which students are asked to engage in the subject are remarkably similar. The Thinking Maps, as a highly flexible and rigorous language of interdependent visual tools, are easily applied in different content areas and contexts. The recurring use of fundamental cognitive skills as patterns also enables higher-order skill development. For example, the Multi-Flow Map for cause-effect in the Exploration unit, is the same type of thinking necessary for logic problem solving in math, problem solution in literature, and physical change in science. Therefore, this ongoing process of using Thinking Maps and software offers a way to view the standards not only by content or concept but by cognition as well. It is this marriage that makes the potential for teaching for transfer possible.

Thinking Maps® is a registered trademark of Thinking Maps, Inc.

FROM STUDENTS AND TEACHERS TO LEADERSHIP DEVELOPMENT AND WHOLE-SCHOOL TRANSFORMATIONS

In the preceding two pieces by Stefanie Holzman and Sarah Curtis, the focus is primarily on shifting student performance and teachers' instructional approach. The focus, in both cases, is also on content learning, language development, and the transfer of Thinking Maps across disciplines and conceptual work required in each content area.

In the final section of this chapter, Larry Alper, a former principal and lead author of *Thinking Maps: A Language for Leadership*, shows how these tools are used across a whole school to create and sustain a learning community. Larry and many other principals who have ushered Thinking Maps into their schools and guided their use have done so with hope, belief, and anticipation that the maps would directly improve students' thinking and performance as well as elevate teacher performance to a higher order. What they don't often expect is what Stefanie Holzman describes:

> Ironically, my intent as the instructional leader of Roosevelt School was initially isolated on these tools for a direct and immediate impact on student performance. What I didn't realize and could not foresee were the deeper effects upon the development of teachers across our year-round, multitrack school as a result of the use of Thinking Maps in their classrooms. I discovered that from an administrator's point of view, Thinking Maps did much more than what I had understood from both practical and theoretical points of view.
>
> First, there are changes in how teachers learn and teach and evaluate student work, especially with differentiated processes for our second-language learners.
>
> Second, there have been shifts in the culture and climate of our school, most obvious in the quality of professional conversations that now rise to the surface.
>
> Third, there is a new level of access and discourse in the areas of teacher evaluation and accountability, which has led to a higher quality of teacher decision making. All of these changes—often referenced as keys to school change—will continue to have a long-term positive outcome on the academic achievement of the students at my school beyond the direct application of these tools by students to academic tasks and tests. (Holzman in Hyerle, Curtis, & Alper, 2004)

Let's turn to yet another level of the implementation rubric: administrator leadership and instructional leadership across whole schools. Larry Alper, lead author of *Thinking Maps: Language for Leadership* (Alper & Hyerle, 2006), guides us through an example of multiple maps used to engage in improving parental involvement.

The Role of Thinking Maps in the Process of Becoming a Professional Learning Community, by Larry Alper

The community aspect of learning is a critical dimension of the conceptualization of schools as learning communities. It recognizes that knowledge is as much a social construct as it is an individual one, mediated through the interaction of ideas and experiences shared by people within the community. A unifying feature of communities is the language it speaks. As a common, visual language for thinking, Thinking Maps offers all members of a school community a shared way to elicit, discuss, and examine the individual and collective wisdom within the organization. It provides the community with a common tool for lessening the impulse to arrive too quickly and superficially at a solution before fully surfacing the range of possibilities beyond those immediately evident.

(Continued)

(Continued)

The phrase *professional learning community* has become common in describing our aspirations as educators for working most effectively on behalf of students. It feels quite natural to apply the act of learning to the work adults within a school environment engage in to address the complex challenges of educating children. However natural the association of this term is to the practices of teaching and leading, too much of what transpires in the professional realm of the school community fails to reflect the qualities of learning. Whether it is because of the pressures of time, or the weight of expectations, or the habits developed from many years of working in hierarchical organizational settings, identifying schools as professional learning communities does not necessarily make them so.

Learning is propelled by curiosity, by the confidence to embrace and enter the unknown and accept ambiguity, and by the willingness to or even the delight in loosening the conventions of one's knowledge and experience to entertain the possibility that there is something new to discover. Frequently, understanding is more about compartmentalizing—associating something new with the familiar and pulling it back toward the established constructs of our thinking or schema, rather than relaxing the boundaries of our ideas to enlarge our field of vision and allow new possibilities to emerge. In professional learning communities, Thinking Maps can provide visual pathways to enter a lush landscape of ideas previously unimagined.

Consider the following selected examples in which a leadership team used multiple Thinking Maps to create an engaging and productive process of inquiry and decision making for improving the involvement of parents in the education of their children and with the larger school community. These examples are excerpted from a new seminar guide for school leadership, *Thinking Maps: A Language for Leadership* (Alper & Hyerle, 2006). Notice how questions were used to guide the process and direct the selection of the particular Thinking Map in response to the thought process reflected in the question. Notice, too, how multiple frames of reference were surfaced to ensure that the fullest possible representation of the topic is presented for consideration.

In the first example (Figure 7.7a), the leadership team began by responding with a partial Multi-Flow Map to the question, What would the outcomes (effects) be if parents were fully involved in their children's education? This question and the ensuing responses allowed the team to surface and clarify its purpose before moving to the next stage in the process (Figure 7.7b).

At a later point, recognizing that not all families are the same, the team used a Double-Bubble Map (Figure 7.7c) to examine how some of these family types might be similar and different to identify the prevailing needs of the various families represented in their school community. The question, "In what ways are the needs of grandparents raising grandchildren the same as and different from a single parent?" helped to inform the team's thinking as they prepared to identify meaningful topics and structures for meeting the different needs within the school community.

Recognizing the need to retrieve information directly from the people they wanted to reach, the team chose to use a Circle Map (Figure 7.7d) to generate the questions to be used in a survey and interviews. The Frame of Reference was used by the team to identify the "parents" in the school community and to stimulate more questions with the needs of those people in mind.

Having gathered information from the parents within the school community, the leadership team used a Tree Map (Figure 7.7e) to organize the data and looked for patterns and connections from which to begin to formulate effective action steps. The use of the Tree Map allowed the team to also identify what was missing and to consider the reasons for the absence of these topics.

As shown, Thinking Maps allow for a fundamental shift in the nature of discourse within a community of learners. Rather than expecting people to establish positions and defend or justify them, Thinking Maps invite the members of the organization to identify the multiple ways a topic can be approached to fully understand it, to sift through its complexity, or to simply allow it to reveal itself to us through the nature of its patterns. Thinking Maps inherently place trust in the ability of members of the professional learning community to think deeply about a topic and to arrive at a collective knowing and decision through a process of inquiry. This shift affirms learning as a core value of the school community. It demonstrates and places confidence in the members of the organization to arrive at meaningful and effective solutions through a genuine process of learning. And it does so by establishing a schoolwide language for thinking, uniting all members, children and adults, in this common pursuit.

Figure 7.7a   The Effects of Full Parent Involvement

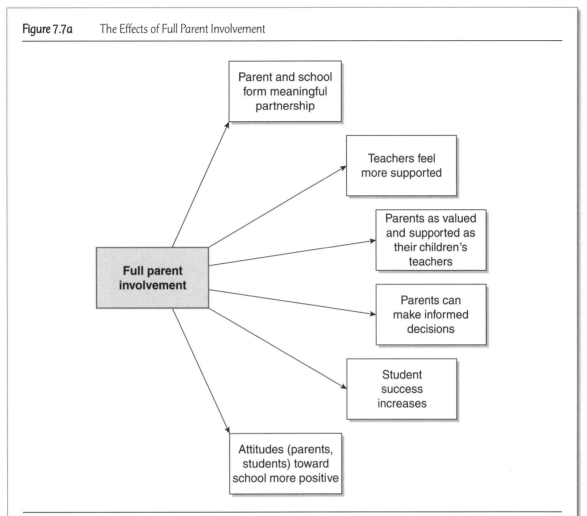

Successful schools not only have the ability to adapt to circumstances, they are able to generate new directions and design novel solutions to complex and changing situations. They not only respond effectively to current realities, they help shape and influence the very circumstances within which they exist in line with their values and beliefs. Thinking Maps help capture and communicate the texture of experiences as they unfold. How we think about a topic, problem, or event shifts as we become fully engaged with constructing meaning and guiding others in a similar process. As tools for learning, Thinking Maps used in combination with each other enable us to enter the varied and shifting landscape of any situation with confidence and the anticipation of discovery. And with adults and children sharing a common language for thinking across an entire school, we create a powerful and compelling culture for learning.

(Continued)

(Continued)

Figure 7.7b How to Create Parent Involvement and the Effects

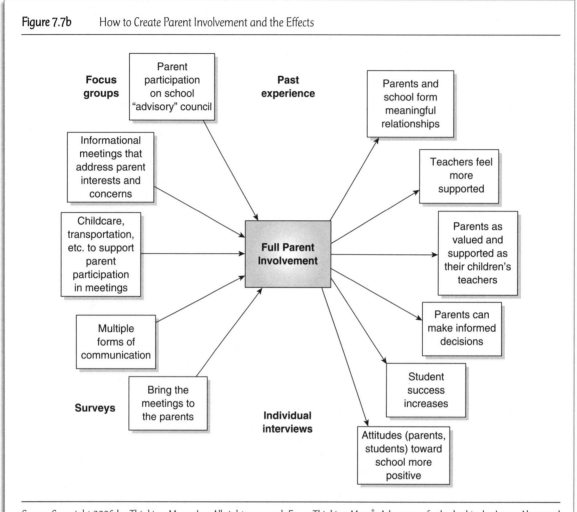

Figure 7.7c   Comparing Single Parents and Grandparents Raising Children

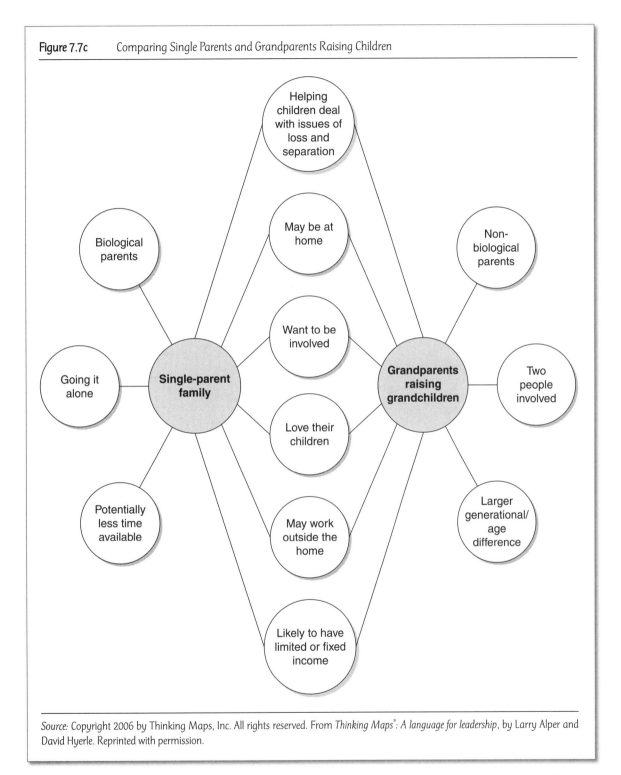

(Continued)

(Continued)

Figure 7.7d   Generating Information Needed From Parents

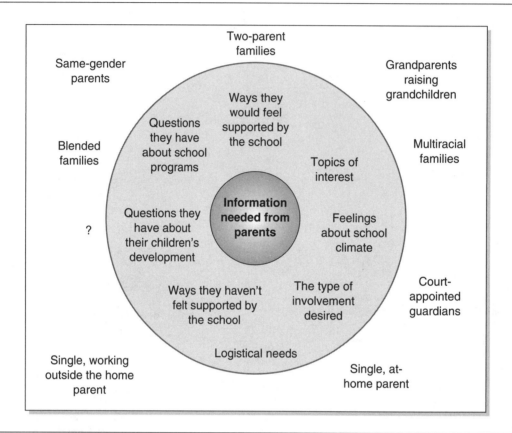

Figure 7.7e   Categorizing Parent Involvement Topics and Details

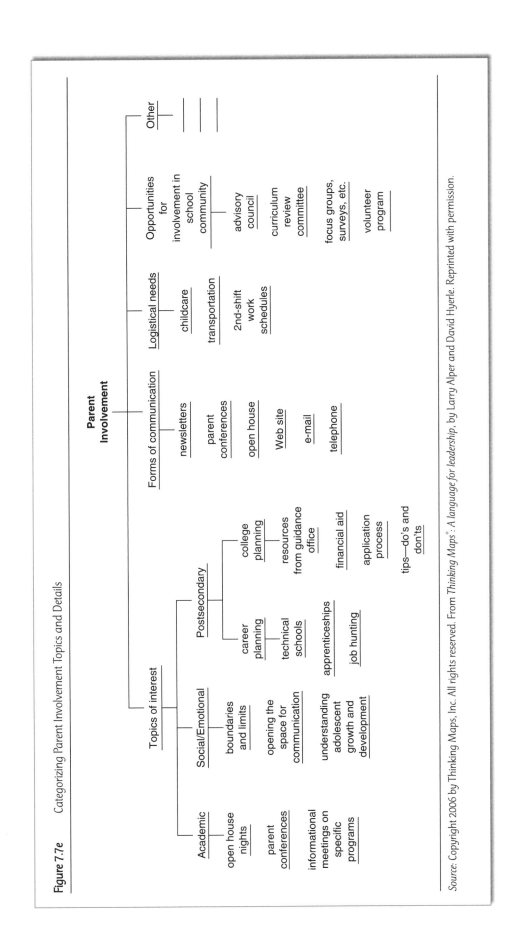

WHOLE SYSTEM CHANGE

The visual tools and language of Thinking Maps presented in this chapter provide a new avenue for student, teachers, administrators, and the whole community of learners in a school, including parents. In the examples described, we see that students can develop their capacities to be creative and flexible, to persevere and be systematic, and to be reflective and self-aware of cognitive patterns to the degree that they can readily apply these patterns to challenging performance. Yet we also now know that, like the inner working of our brain, our students must continue to grow and adapt over their lifespans. In this chapter, we presented evidence of significant changes in performance for students, in the one case by students, most of whom come from a low socioeconomic area. On entering the school, they also had low levels of English-language usage. But they did not have low cognitive abilities. When we return to the research, we find that the explicit and dynamic blending of nonlinguistic representations and cognition is a vital intersection for students of poverty, in first- and second-language discourses, and their capacities to decode text structures, write in meaningful response to prompts, and problem solve in math and science.

When we look forward to the decades of the 21st century, we realize that explicitly supporting students in their capacities to think and problem solve independently and collaboratively across content areas, languages, and cultures may be the linchpin to an evolution in how they transform information into meaningful knowledge.

Thinking Maps for Special Needs

Cynthia Manning

To close this book, we now turn to one of the most profound concerns we have as educators: How do we scaffold learning, language development, and cognitive abilities for those students who, on comprehensive evaluation, are found to have severe language and learning disabilities? This complete chapter, written by Cynthia Manning, vice principal and supervisor of Thinking Maps at Learning Prep School in Massachusetts, resonates across all the pages of this book as it demonstrates what happens when a common visual language of cognitive tools becomes a foundation for learning. The director of Learning Prep School, Nancy Rostow, and the faculty, students, and parents offer us an open door for transforming teaching, thinking, and learning for children placed in "special education." This writing demonstrates what can happen when visual tools, based on cognitive skills, become a language for learning in a whole school for children who are rarely perceived as having a good chance of "making it" in our educational system and in our society.

THINKING MAPS GIVE ME A CHANCE TO LEARN: LEARNING PREP STUDENT

Ralph Waldo Emerson wrote that "The task ahead of us is never as great as the power behind us." For many students with severe learning disabilities and for all those students who never make it out of the lower tracks of our educational processes, the task ahead is often daunting and perceived by many as insurmountable. They never see the power behind them; their self-concept is low because they rarely if ever *see* and fully apply the power of their own abilities to think through content information, conceptual challenges, and even social problems. The task of explicitly improving students' cognitive abilities and language performance toward a higher order—and empowering students who often are perceived as incapable of improved thinking and learning—is being accomplished at our school because of the power of Thinking Maps behind our students, faculty, and parent community.

Thinking Maps are one of the most powerful tools that Learning Prep School uses to facilitate learning for students who have been unable to succeed in other educational environments. Four years ago, we felt we served our students well, but they were not where we knew they could be in their daily performance and their abilities to perform on the Massachusetts exam, the MCAS. We now *see* the significant results of our students' performance through the use of these visual tools integrated into our overall program, and students can *see* themselves differently, as independent learners capable of "getting it," as one student declared:

> *Thinking Maps give me a chance to learn.* I couldn't get it when one of my old teachers talked to me all day and then wanted me to write a lot of words. At this new school, I can understand the teachers when they use the maps. And I can finally do the work because I get it!

This qualitative and quantitative view of our experiences shows how Learning Prep began by implementing Thinking Maps in our elementary through high school curricula and then fully integrated these tools consistently and flexibly across grade levels and content areas to give students with learning disabilities clear pathways to think on their own and process information independently.

BACKGROUND ON LEARNING PREP SCHOOL

All Learning Prep School (LPS) students have language-based learning disabilities as their primary challenge. Many also have tangential issues or diagnoses that interfere with their ability to learn, such as a lack of social communication skills; attention deficit disorder; and visual, perceptual, auditory processing, or motor deficits. Because of these challenges, most students who enter typically demonstrate a two-year delay compared to peers who possess age-appropriate academic skills, and they are unable to utilize reading as a functional learning tool. Direct teaching methods, language strategies, and coordinated adaptive and social services are employed consistently to help students become independent learners; so that they may lead productive lives, students also master the skills necessary for independent living. On the average, 90% of Learning Prep's graduating seniors progress to college, vocational training, or post–high school transition programs. Learning Prep provides services to 360 students in its elementary, middle, and high school programs. Since 1970, it has been the only school specifically designed for language-impaired students within the region. Students, many of whom live in inner cities, come from more than 140 communities throughout Massachusetts, New Hampshire, and Rhode Island. A quarter of the LPS population consists of students of African American, Hispanic, and Asian descent.

Because of the students' unique and diverse learning challenges, Learning Prep must carefully examine potential curriculum programs. Each approach must be flexible, focused on skill development, able to accommodate a variety of modifications mandated by Individual Education Plans (IEPs), and, most important, be effective instructional tools. Thinking Maps initially appealed to the school's director, Nancy Rosoff, because they complemented the curriculum and could be used at any academic level. Nancy was impressed by the Thinking Maps as a model and the objectives of implementing the tools: for students to be able to use the tools—based on thinking processes—to extract salient information from different forms of text and present it clearly and concisely in a visual context. She also came to believe that the success of implementing Thinking Maps into any educational setting depends on having one certified Thinking Maps Trainer to be responsible for program coordination for teachers, students, and parents. My role as supervisor of Thinking Maps in Learning Prep has enabled me to support the implementation and comprehensive use of these tools throughout the entire curriculum. This position has also given me a unique opportunity to observe and then document how the maps may be used with flexibility and depth across this whole learning community.

As we have progressed over the years and evaluated the effectiveness of Thinking Maps, it has become mandatory for all staff to use the maps as a foundation for teaching and learning. This fits into the implementation design first established in 1990 by the professional development group, Thinking Maps, Inc. Thinking Maps are normally introduced as a common language for whole schools and require all faculty to undergo an initial training and follow-up coaching to ensure that the implementation focus is on the sustained use of the tools by all students over multiple years as they move among teachers across disciplines and grades. Of course, this focus on schoolwide use makes eminent sense for Learning Prep, because the tools are based on *the direct facilitation of specific cognitive skills,* which is an essential part of the primary mission of the school. Beyond the core curriculum, the maps are now infused into all aspects of the student's school life, including occupational and speech therapies, electives (such as computers or art), prevocational classes, counseling, and social skills groups. Without this consistency, students will identify the maps only with a certain subject area or therapy and not be able to make the generalizations or transfer of cognitive skills that ensure learning.

This comprehensive vision of the power of Thinking Maps as a language for the school has led to teachers, students, and parents receiving ongoing coaching and support over the past three years as summarized in the following text.

Teachers receive ongoing instructional training, and all new teaching staff receive an orientation workshop. Refresher training sessions and curriculum development meetings are scheduled for all returning staff during the year. Supervision of staff is given as needed to integrate Thinking Maps within all aspects of the curriculum, which includes observation of all staff to ensure that maps are being taught and integrated correctly and to the maximum capabilities. This supervision is supported by model lessons using Thinking Maps within classrooms to demonstrate consistent and deeper uses related to students' different needs.

Students receive an initial introduction to the maps and Thinking Maps Software by their teachers. Tutoring sessions for new students identified as having specific learning needs and refresher training and reinforcement exercises for all students are performed at the beginning of each school year, focusing on each of the eight cognitive processes and maps, and how to use the maps and frame of reference in each discipline.

Parents are offered two training sessions during the year to help reinforce the maps and Thinking Maps Software within the home environment and community. These sessions support further meetings with parents as needed to develop maps for targeted use within the home (e.g., chores, homework, task completion, vacation planning, budgeting income from afterschool jobs, etc.). Regular communication with parents and students via the Web and a monthly published newsletter ensures that parents are aware of and actively supporting Thinking Maps use at home.

Many prospective parents have expressed a strong interest in Learning Prep because they have read about Thinking Maps on our Web site, and they hope that the maps will benefit their children by teaching them to organize and process information more efficiently. Ms. Rosoff, as director of the school, believes that Thinking Maps oftentimes have been instrumental in gaining the interest of potential students and their families. In fact, Ms. Rosoff believes that "Thinking Maps have been responsible for putting Learning Prep on the map."

DEVELOPING THE FUNDAMENTAL PSYCHOLOGICAL PROCESSES THROUGH THINKING MAPS

According to the American Psychological Association's *Journal of Experimental Psychology: Learning, Memory, and Cognition*, there are 10 basic psychological processes: *cognition, knowledge acquisition, memory, imagery, concept formation, problem solving, decision making, critical thinking, reading,* and *language processing.* Without continuing development of these characteristics, learning cannot take place. Thinking Maps have been essential in helping Learning Prep develop our students across these characteristics and metacognitive abilities, thereby demystifying learning, increasing intellectual capacities as measured by increased MCAS scores, and enabling our students to engage in higher-order thinking. A close look at these processes related to Thinking Maps shows the versatility of these tools.

Cognition includes our "fund of information about the world and our mastery of problem-solving skills," in addition to executive functioning skills, which are "our capacity to initiate, sustain, inhibit, and shift in our problem-solving efforts" (Bolick, 2004, p. 15). Children with low cognition scores have difficulty with input controls ("sustained attention to preferred tasks") and output controls ("sustained effort regarding topics of interest") (Levine, 2003). This salience determination—what is important to maintain attention, develop executive functions, and complete tasks—is especially challenging to individuals with low cognition because they may not be able to self-regulate to eliminate what is irrelevant or identify what is salient. Consequently, input control can be difficult; they do not know what to look for or listen to without their attention being framed accordingly, but as one of our students noted, "It's easy for me to pick out the important parts of something and put them into a map. Sometimes I use Thinking Maps for work without even knowing it—I just draw them automatically."

With output control, it is easy to assume that because a child may not able to demonstrate cognition, knowledge is not present. This inhibition of output merely indicates that the child cannot encode and "show what he knows" (Bolick, 2005; Levine, 2003). Another student reveals, "I have trouble coming up with information without them, when all I have in front of me is a blank sheet of paper and a whole lot of questions to answer. When I draw a map to answer a question, it's easier for me to remember information. It's almost like having a teacher there to cue you. They help me work independently." This comment leads us to another misconception, which parallels that of cognitive output control, and this is *memory*. Many people, including parents, mistakenly equate rote memory with knowledge. However, if children cannot integrate and apply their knowledge, then learning connections are not being made, and the disparate details cannot be encompassed into a gestalt that is meaningful, relevant, and informative (Bolick, 2005). These two comments by students reflect a common view among our learners using the maps: "They keep all your good ideas in one easy place so you don't lose them," and "They turn a whole bunch of information that gets me confused into a few simple steps."

For LPS students who show "low cognition," as identified by specific test items that isolate certain cognitive skills and levels, Thinking Maps have been an essential tool for success. This shows that these students, who may be perceived in other settings as having a static intellectual capacity, can shift to higher-order thinking through the use of Thinking Maps as tools for cognitive mediation *over time*. In addition to being taught in all academic subject areas, maps also are used by elective vocational classes, which can present a challenge to these students because of the lack of structure normally present in an academic classroom. The maps assist with salience determination and self-regulation; they provide the necessary structure and a visual component that is easily transferable (allowing generalizations to be made and learning connections to be established). Thus, this student could say, "The maps help me identify what is important and what isn't. If it doesn't fit in the map, then it's not important. They also help me stay focused so I can get my assignments done; they're easy and fun to draw, and they're kind of like a puzzle. I don't need to worry and stress about if what I did is correct. I can read over my map and know if I did it correctly or not. They're easy to proofread." When students are able to demonstrate increased input controls—sustained attention and task completion—because they understand the process (such as *how* to complete a map), the cognitive load is lowered and thus their minds are freed to focus on *knowledge acquisition* (*what* to use to complete the map) and further develop and demonstrate their cognitive skills.

Other aspects of cognition—visuospatial processing, visuomotor output, and sequential processing—also affect children's awareness of their bodies in relation to other objects, making them clumsy and unable to complete certain motor tasks. These functions furthermore impact their ability to attend to multistep tasks, recall sequences, and understand parts-to-whole (or whole-to-parts) relationships (Bolick, 2005). The use of the Flow and Brace Maps, in conjunction with scheduled Occupational Therapy sessions on campus, have assisted our students greatly by increasing their ability to complete these motor tasks. Thinking Maps are integrated into treatment plans, allowing students to immediately understand what they will be working on and why. By incorporating the facilitation of a metacognitive stance in an occupational therapy (OT) setting, students are better able to plan and execute a task as well as evaluate their progress. These kinds of processes require students to analyze a problem or a topic, as one student conveys explicitly in this comment: "Thinking Maps help break down topics. I can express my ideas using them, even though I can't do that with essays. They make things easy to understand, and I use them to help me study." Another student surfaces the importance of organizing information, a key dimension of executing complex tasks such as writing: "The maps make me a stronger writer. I never was able to write before I learned the maps. But now I get main ideas and supporting facts; the way the maps are drawn and organized helps me to see these things now." Thinking Maps Software has also been distributed to students, allowing them to customize the maps to their lesson requirements and for writing assignments. The software has proven to be a particularly effective accommodation for dysgraphic students who have difficulty constructing the maps independently.

An additional component of cognition that impacts students with learning disabilities is higher-order thinking, which includes *problem solving, critical thinking,* and *concept formation.* It has been a joy to hear students in our school respond as this one did recently: "Thinking Maps get me to think." Difficulties with higher-level cognition arise as these children increase in age. They often surpass their peers at rote academic tasks common in early elementary grades, and their self-esteem is based on their clever reputation. As they begin to encounter academic failure in the fourth or fifth grade, coinciding with an increase in tasks that require higher-order thinking processes, children with learning disabilities can feel depressed or anxious. Written expressive skills are deficient, inferential knowledge is challenging, and predicting or estimating can be impossible tasks for these individuals. Learning inevitably is impeded by the child's inadequate cognition (Bolick, 2005).

One of Learning Prep's main goals is to increase cognitive development. As our students become fluent in Thinking Maps, they are able to develop their cognitive skills and metacognition, to "think about thinking," and apply these cognitive skills to problem-solve and develop higher-level, abstract thought. The value of these tools is that when students begin to choose which map they are going to use, it is not a random decision; it is because of the thinking *they* see is required of the task. As a student observed: "I love Thinking Maps because I can choose which one I want to use sometimes. That makes me feel like I'm responsible for my learning. And some kinds of learning are easier for me than others. This way I get to learn how I learn best." By doing so, some students have been able to progress independently to a more complex level of map usage—using multiple maps in unison to solve multistep assignments. In March 2004, after demonstrating competency with all eight maps, teachers and students were trained in multimapping, or using two or more kinds of maps together to organize information. This strategy is particularly effective at facilitating higher-order thought. Because the maps draw on the integration and application of multiple thinking processes, the concepts presented are elevated from the concrete level to abstract and inferential patterns of thinking, thus developing higher-level cognition.

Another direction staff have taken is developing and reinforcing skills using cooperative learning strategies to teach Thinking Map lessons. Interactive activities, or group work, augment cognitive skill acquisition using a method that facilitates social skills development. As shown in the training manual for Thinking Maps, these tools can help teachers mediate student behaviors through conflict resolution. One student recalled that "I got into a fight with my best friend, and our counselors used maps to help us work things out. I realized why I shouldn't tell lies about her when I'm mad at her." Learning how to work with others is a life skill that is as important as mastering curriculum, and cooperative learning is an effective way for students to learn turn-taking, role-playing, self-control, cooperation, responsibility, and problem-solving skills.

Imagery can be difficult for learning disabled students, but using Thinking Maps to break down stories and make them more concrete also has enabled students to form mental images of people when using Bubble Maps for characterization. One student commented that "I *see* my Thinking Maps, and what they contain, in my mind, when I need to remember the information for tests or quizzes. If I just have a large page of notes, I can't remember the information as easy. Because I drew the map and used it as a study guide, I can remember the information and see it in my head when I need it." A clear example of this capacity to visualize information and connect the visual to the verbal is shown in a high school student's multiple Thinking Maps used for comprehending a story by P. R. Giff, *Pictures of Hollis Woods*. While rarely do students use all the maps at one time for comprehending text, this is a high-quality example of how students may become fluent in using all the maps at any time, independently, to surface patterns of thinking from linear text (see Figure 8.1).

Because decoding and encoding language is challenging for all our students, they often balked at one of the most critical basic processes, ***reading***, in addition to writing open responses to short-answer or essay questions. Anxiety can set in and sabotage their ability to complete the task at hand. Students might know the structure of a paragraph, but when they have to integrate that knowledge along with decoding what the question is asking, they become easily and quickly overwhelmed. If, however, they recognize the thinking process within the context of the question, and the reading text structures, they can relax and focus their efforts on understanding the question. The student example shown in Figure 8.1 reveals how basic text structures such as comparison, narrative sequencing, and causes and effects of main events in a story become both visible and accessible for students. The dual coding and processing of the vocabulary and visual structures of cognitive patterns reveal the practice and effectiveness of nonlinguistic representations for learning (Marzano & Pickering, 2005).

This kind of depth of processing and fluency with linking content-specific questions with cognitive processes and Thinking Maps has a direct impact on students responding to isolated questions on a test. For example, if the prompt reads, "Explain the main causes of the Civil War as well as its effects on slaves," a student who is fluent with Thinking Maps will immediately associate the cues "causes" and "effects" with a Multi-Flow Map and begin working. Before students had learned the maps, they would struggle, refuse to work, or even experience an emotional meltdown. Now students will attempt to complete the assignment independently. Their familiarity with the maps provides them with the structural knowledge necessary for task completion, and with that familiarity comes increased self-esteem. "I know how to answer questions now," one elementary school student proudly reported this year. Maps are also an integral part of teaching *Wilson Reading Program* lessons in reading and language arts classes, as students rely on the completed maps to reinforce concepts and phonetic rules, and they file them in their binders as reference tools.

Language processing has been perhaps the most important fundamental process for our student population. Because they all possess language-based learning disabilities, this is the area in which they are most challenged, and this deficit has repercussions on all other aspects of learning. Students might be highly effective decoders, but if they cannot comprehend what they are reading, then they cannot process or organize the information they are reading, and learning does not take place. Another difficulty our students experience is that they know the information but they are unable to communicate effectively what they are thinking. One student stated what could be true of most students using these tools: "They help get the ideas out of my head and onto an empty sheet of paper." Thinking Maps have facilitated learning for our students in both oral expressive and written expressive language; they are able to process speech or written text more easily when interpreting it through the context of the common visual language they share with their teachers and develop interactively with their peers.

Figure 8.1 Student Example of Applying All Eight Thinking Maps

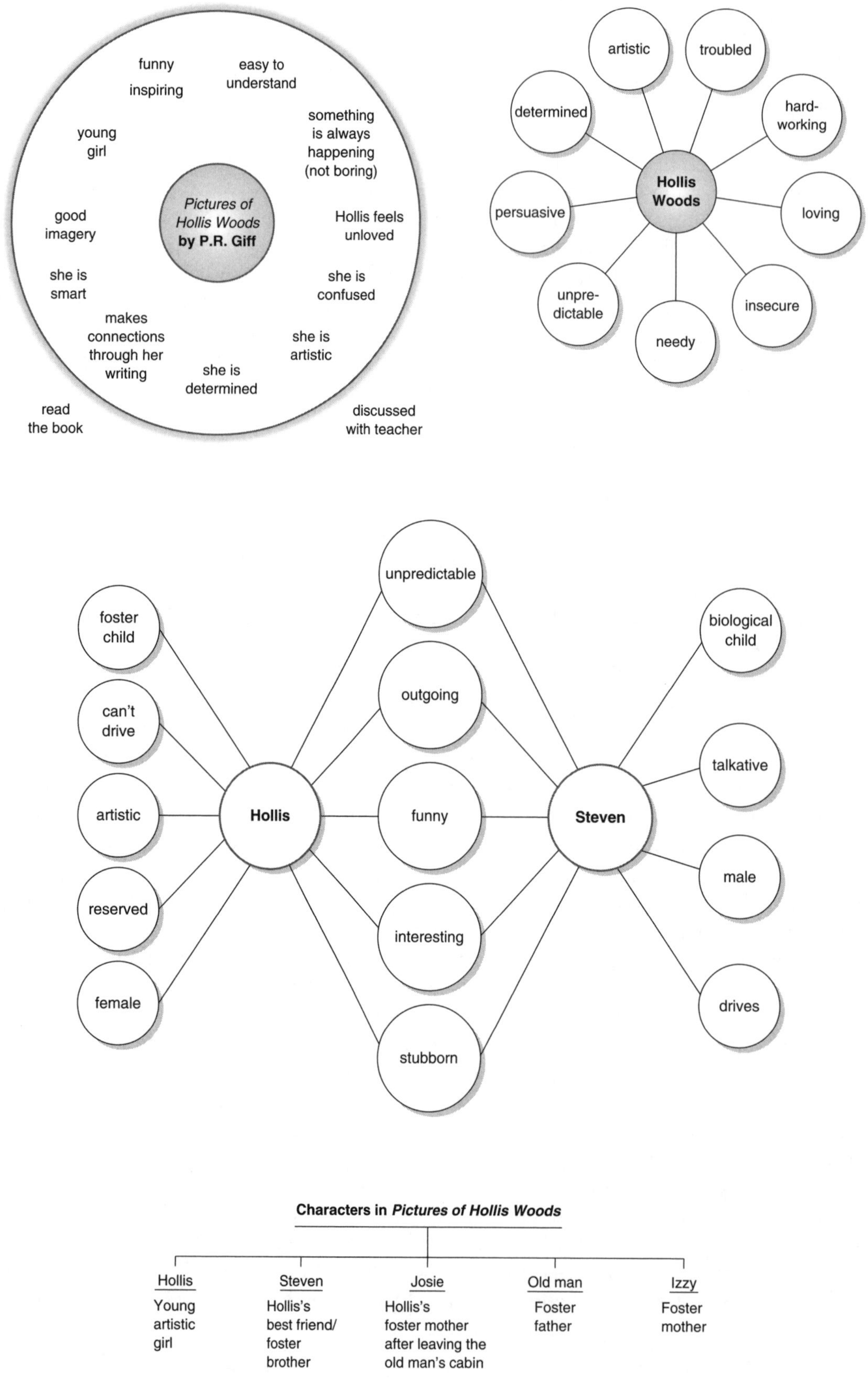

Circle Map (top left):

Pictures of Hollis Woods by P.R. Giff

- funny
- inspiring
- easy to understand
- young girl
- something is always happening (not boring)
- good imagery
- Hollis feels unloved
- she is smart
- she is confused
- makes connections through her writing
- she is artistic
- she is determined

Frame of reference: read the book / discussed with teacher

Bubble Map (top right):

Hollis Woods
- artistic
- troubled
- determined
- hard-working
- persuasive
- loving
- unpredictable
- insecure
- needy

Double Bubble Map (middle):

Hollis:
- foster child
- can't drive
- artistic
- reserved
- female

Shared (Hollis and Steven):
- unpredictable
- outgoing
- funny
- interesting
- stubborn

Steven:
- biological child
- talkative
- male
- drives

Tree Map / Brace Map (bottom):

Characters in *Pictures of Hollis Woods*

Hollis	Steven	Josie	Old man	Izzy
Young artistic girl	Hollis's best friend/ foster brother	Hollis's foster mother after leaving the old man's cabin	Foster father	Foster mother

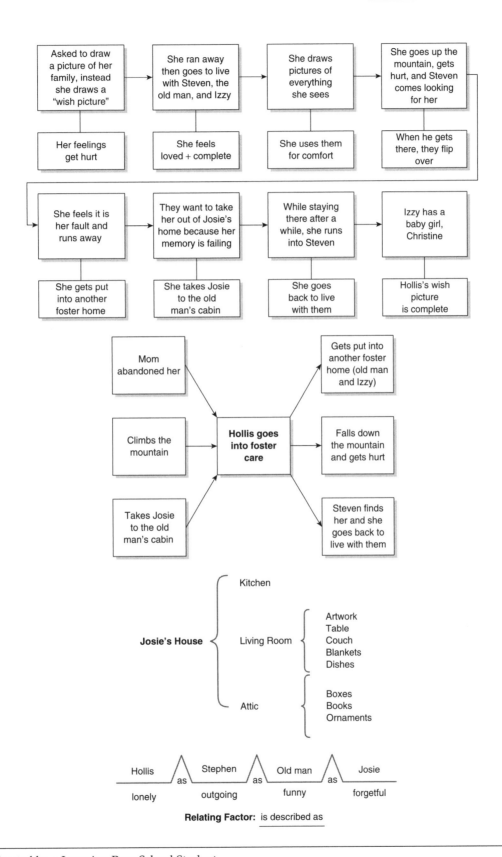

Created by a Learning Prep School Student.

THINKING MAPS AND HIGH-STAKES TESTING

Thinking Maps are best validated when the results can be quantified. Learning Prep has been tracking student progress using scores from a high-stakes test, the Massachusetts Comprehensive Assessment System (MCAS) exam, as an indicator of cognitive development. The majority of test scores since Thinking Maps were implemented indicate an increase in receptive and written expressive language skills, such as comprehending, processing, and organizing information.

Since December 2001, when the introduction of Thinking Maps had been completed, students have become fluent with all eight maps, using them to analyze information and develop writing assignments. When taking the MCAS exam, a majority of students use various maps to answer both open-response and multiple-choice questions. Before Thinking Maps were introduced, students would demonstrate low frustration tolerance levels and heightened anxiety, writing protest messages in their answer booklets instead of attempting to answer the questions. Now that students have a familiar strategy that helps them tackle the open-response questions, they are significantly more calm and confident during test administration. Angry statements have been replaced by paragraphs or essays responding to the English Language Arts writing prompt. In the last three years, not a single complaint was written on the test, nor did any student experience an MCAS-related emotional meltdown. It is important that students perceive that the Thinking Maps directly affect their performance in classrooms, as one student stated: "Thinking Maps make good study guides. I used to get C's and B's on tests, but now I get A's and B's." And they also influence their performance on high-stakes testing, as another student noted: "Thinking Maps make work easier and less stressful for me—especially tests and the MCAS exam."

Before Thinking Maps were introduced, most Learning Prep students were unable to pass the MCAS exam. For the spring 2001 Mathematics test, 4 students passed, and 28 failed; on the English Language Arts test, 3 passed, and 29 failed. For the fall 2001 Mathematics test, 5 students passed, and 41 failed; on the English Language Arts test, 10 passed, and 33 failed. As shown in Figure 8.2, after the students had learned all eight maps, the numbers dramatically reversed.

For the spring 2002 Mathematics test, 24 students passed, and 19 failed; on the English Language Arts test, 34 passed, and 9 failed. Since the introduction of the maps, eight MCAS exams have been administered; students overall have fared better on the English portion of the exam than the math. On 50% of the mathematics tests administered, the number of students who passed exceeded the number who failed, whereas the number of students who passed exceeded the number who failed on 87% of the English Language Arts tests administered. We are proud to report that, for the first time since Learning Prep began administering the MCAS exam, 100% of the students who took the English Language Arts portion of the fall 2005 test achieved passing scores.

Learning Prep administrators have observed that the most notable change in the results was the increase of students who not only passed but achieved *advanced* scores (ranging from 260 to 280) or *proficient* scores (ranging from 240 to 258) on the spring exams (fall exams are retests that are condensed versions of the MCAS). Prior to using Thinking Maps, only a few students were barely able to pass, scoring in the *needs improvement* performance level (ranging from 220 to 238); the vast majority of our students failed the exam, with scores of 218 or below. According to the

Figure 8.2 MCAS Test Results

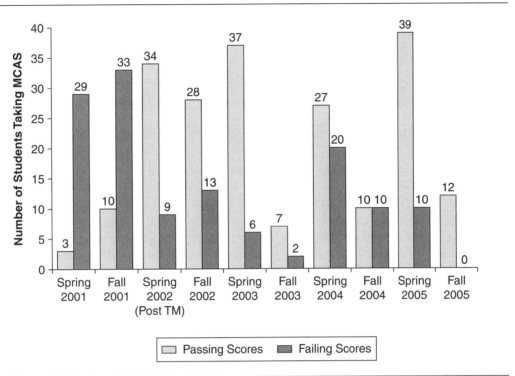

Created by Cynthia Manning.

Massachusetts Department of Education's *Guide to Interpreting This Report* (which accompanies all MCAS score reports), students who are able to score *proficient* "demonstrate a solid understanding of challenging subject matter, and solve a wide variety of problems," and those who score *advanced* "demonstrate a comprehensive and in-depth understanding of rigorous subject matter, and provide sophisticated solutions to complex problems." There was also substantial improvement in the levels of reading comprehension, higher-level cognitive thought, and written expressive skills, as evidenced by the continued rise in open-response scores, increasing from *0, 1,* and *2,* to *2, 3* and *4* (with *0* equaling *low* and *4* equaling *high* ratings).

Use of Thinking Maps is one major difference that accounts for the increase in test scores. When Thinking Maps are integrated schoolwide throughout the curricula, as they have been at our school, test scores demonstrate considerable gains. Additional benefits, other than improved scores on high-stakes testing, have become apparent throughout Learning Prep and have been documented through student work, the interviews referred to earlier, and faculty observations over time:

- Students and teachers share a common language that improves communication and facilitates the learning process.
- Students are developing a higher level of thinking (application and evaluation) while working on recall and comprehension skills.
- Many students' attitudes have become more positive toward learning.
- Most students have demonstrated improvement in their ability to organize thoughts.

- The quality of learning has been taken to a higher level, as activities have become more meaningful and relevant.
- Many students demonstrate a greater retention of knowledge.
- Teachers have observed improved quality and increased quantity of writing.
- Teachers using Thinking Maps have noted improved organization and focus in their lesson plans and curriculum development.

TEACHERS AND STUDENTS SEE THE SUCCESS

An integral part of the program's success is teachers embracing the maps and realizing how instrumental they can be in their teaching. Nancy d'Hemecourt, an LPS high school teacher of Language Arts and Literature, is one of their most staunch advocates: "After much modeling (direct, explicit instruction or spiraling review) and practice (generated during classes and for homework assignments), students are empowered to expand their thoughts from low-level thinking to higher-level thinking. Not only are the maps great for assignments at home and during class, they also aid tremendously when writing a five-paragraph MCAS essay."

Gia Batty, department chair for literature in the high school, believes that "the maps provide a language that we all speak together—teachers, students, counselors, administrators. This language allows us to converse about our thinking and writing in a visual and organized way. When we use the maps, we are essentially thinking in the same way. This is pretty amazing when you think about it—to be standing in front of a bunch of kids who all think and learn in vastly different ways, and then to use the same map on the board that they are all visualizing in their minds. The maps are wonderful and versatile teaching tools."

When asked why they thought Thinking Maps were so beneficial, teachers in the elementary, middle, and high schools agree that they are highly effective for teaching students with varied learning styles. Differentiated instruction is one methodology LPS uses; the average class size is six students in a homogenous group. If a teacher is introducing fractions, but one group is composed of visual learners and another has strong auditory processing skills, the instructional methods used to impart the content can vary substantially. *Thinking Maps are flexible enough to be used with all kinds of learners who possess a variety of profiles*, because the maps are not just visual, they are visual-verbal-spatial frames that support all learning modalities.

When I polled 186 Learning Prep students to find out how the maps helped them learn, the most popular answer given by 124 students, or 67% of the student body, was that "Thinking Maps help me organize my writing." Some students replied that "answering the question is too hard; can I draw a map instead?" Almost a third of the students—58 children—first drew a map and used it to formulate their response. Many students stated directly that Thinking Maps were very effective for them during the MCAS test.

THINKING MAPS AND "THE REAL WORLD"

One aspect of our school that is different from most others is that we offer a 5-year high school program. Students attend their standard freshman and sophomore years, and then spend much of their middle year preparing for working and attending school on alternate weeks during their junior and senior years. This work/study program better prepares students for "the real world" by imparting job skills, identifying realistic educational and career goals, and teaching strategies for self-advocacy and disclosure and providing additional structured time for the student to develop compensatory strategies in school as well as in the workplace. This transfer of the tools outside formal academic work was noted by one student who said: "Thinking Maps help me to not only be a better student, but they make my whole life easier. I use them for everything at home, too." According to Lois Gould, the supervisor of transition planning, Thinking Maps have been highly beneficial with

- transition planning (now mandated by the government);
- formulation of advocacy statements;
- appropriate accommodation requests within the workplace;
- job counseling and coaching;
- processes of conducting job searches and succeeding in job interviews;
- task sequencing;
- senior portfolios (used for transition planning and college admissions);
- career education classes;
- identification of personal learning styles;
- assistance with matching skills and abilities with interests;
- development and application of social intelligence and acceptable behaviors that foster social interactions;
- mastering of transferable skills for specific jobs; and
- recognition of what is essential to success in the workplace.

Some students choose on their own initiative to use the maps outside of school—at home, in an afterschool program, with a tutor, in religious education classes, or in outside therapy. Parents of LPS students have been impressed by their children's willingness to use the maps in other environments, demonstrating fluency and total integration of the maps into their repertoire of problem-solving strategies; that the children can recognize on their own accord the effectiveness of these visual tools is a powerful testimony to their efficacy. Some children draw maps to help them choose a family pet or what activity to do over the weekend; others rely on a laminated map task card with instructions on how to make an afterschool snack or complete a household chore. A middle school student recently used a series of maps to help him during his Bar Mitzvah, and another student has been drawing maps in outside counseling to help her accurately express her feelings about a difficult family situation.

IN CONCLUSION

After LPS students become fluent in Thinking Maps as a common visual language for learning, they are able to apply multiple thinking skills to problem-solve and develop higher-level, abstract thinking. By implementing this language schoolwide across the curricula, students learn more effectively and efficiently, thus enabling learning objectives to be covered in less time and with greater retention. In addition to promoting integrated thinking and interdisciplinary learning, Thinking Maps are used by teachers to assess student progress, gauge student knowledge, track student performance, and even assess their own teaching lessons as they discover what students have learned from class by viewing the maps.

These powerful tools combine to comprise a comprehensive, cognitive-based visual language that works in every grade, in every subject, and at any level of academic activity. This is because the focus is on the fundamental cognitive processes defined and activated by each map. Students are able to organize and see their own thinking; teachers can then use the completed maps to observe the students' thinking processes and assess student language and content learning at the same time. This dual lens—thinking processes and knowledge content—enables the kind of feedback and in-the-moment assessment rarely found in schools, and it has become a foundation for success in our school. As our students continue to internalize the thinking processes taught within the context of the maps, we believe that additional benefits will become increasingly evident as we evaluate our approach. We greatly anticipate watching our students grow as they become more fluent with this language for learning.

Harkening back to Emerson's quote, many if not all of our students can say with self-assurance and with a determination rarely shown by students with special needs that . . . *the task ahead of us is never as great as the power behind us.* With Thinking Maps as a common language of visual tools in hand and behind us as tools for mindful teaching, learning, and assessing, we have empowered our children to think for themselves, and maybe most important, *to think about themselves as especially adaptable thinkers and high-achieving learners for the rest of their lives.*

References and Further Reading

Alcock, M. W. (1997). Are your students' brains comfortable in your classroom? *Ohio ASCD Journal 5*(2), 11–14.

Alper, L., & Hyerle, D. (2006). *Thinking Maps: A language for leadership*. Cary, NC: Thinking Maps, Inc.

Ambrose, S. E. (1996). *Undaunted courage: Meriwether Lewis, Thomas Jefferson, and the opening of the American West*. New York: Simon & Schuster.

Anderson, L., Krathwolh, D., et al. (Eds.). (2001). *A taxonomy for learning, teaching, and assessing (a revision of Bloom's taxonomy of educational objectives)*. New York: Addison Wesley Longman, Inc.

Armbruster, B., et al. (Eds.). (2001). *Put reading first*. Washington DC: U.S. Department of Education.

Ausubel, D. P. (1968). *Educational psychology: A cognitive view*. New York: Holt, Rinehart & Winston.

Ball, M. K. (1999). *The effects of thinking maps on reading scores of traditional and nontraditional college students*. Unpublished doctoral dissertation, University of Southern Mississippi, Hattiesburg.

Bartunek, J. M., & Moch, M. K. (1987). First-order, second-order, and third-order change and organizational development interventions: A cognitive approach. *Journal of Applied Behavioral Science 2.3*(4), 483–500.

Belkin, L. (1998, August 23). Splice Einstein and Sammy Glick. Add a little Magellan. *New York Times Magazine*, sec. 6, p. 26.

Bellanca, J. (1990). *The cooperative think tank: Graphic organizers to teach thinking in the cooperative classroom*. Arlington Heights, IL: SkyLight Publishing.

Bellanca, J. (1991). *Cooperative think tank, I and II*. Arlington Heights, IL: SkyLight Publishing.

Bolick, T. (2004). *Asperger syndrome and young children: Building skills for the real world*. Gloucester, MA: Fair Winds Press.

Bolick, T. (2005, October). *Clinical and educational assessment*. Lecture presented at Antioch New England Graduate School, Keene, NH.

Bromley, K., Irwin-De Vitis, L., & Modlo, M. (1995). *Graphic organizers*. New York: Scholastic.

Buckner, J. (1999). *Write from the beginning training manual*. Cary, NC: Innovative Sciences, Inc.

Buzan, T. (1979). *Use both sides of your brain*. New York: G. P. Dutton.

Buzan, T. (1996). *The mind map book*. New York: Plume/Penguin.

Caine, R. N., & Caine, G. (1994). *Making connections: Teaching and the human brain*. Menlo Park, CA: Addison-Wesley Pub. Co.

Capra, F. (1996). *The web of life: A new scientific understanding of living systems*. New York: Anchor Books.

Chase, M., & Madar, B. (2004). *Kidspiration in the classroom*. Portland, OR: Inspiration Software.

Clarke, J. H. (1991). *Patterns of thinking*. Needham Heights, MA: Allyn & Bacon.

Classroom ideas using inspiration. (1998). Portland, OR: Inspiration Software, Inc.

Costa, A. L. (Ed.) (1991a). *Developing minds: A resource book for teaching thinking* (Vols. 1 and 2, rev. ed.). Alexandria, VA: Association for Supervision and Curriculum Development.

Costa, A. L. (1991b). *The school as a home for the mind*. Palatine, IL: IRI/SkyLight Publishing.

Costa, A. L., & Garmston, R. (1998). Maturing outcomes. *Encounter: Education for Meaning and Social Justice 11*(1), 11.

Costa, A. L., & Kallick, B. (Eds.). (1995). *Assessment in the learning organization: Shifting the paradigm*. Alexandria, VA: Association for Supervision and Curriculum Development.

Costa, A. L., & Kallick, B. (2000). *Activating and engaging habits of mind*. Alexandria, VA: Association for Supervision and Curriculum Development.

Costa, A. L., & Kallick, B. (Eds.). (2008). *Thinking Maps®: Visual tools for activating habits of mind.* Alexandria, VA: Association for Supervision and Curriculum Development.

Costa, A. L., & Kallick, B. (In press). *Habits of mind.* Alexandria, VA: Association for Supervision and Curriculum Development.

Csikszentmihalyi, M. (1991). *Flow.* New York: Harper Perennial.

DePinto Piercy, T., & Hyerle, D. (2004). Maps for the road to reading comprehension: Bridging reading text structures to writing prompts. In D. Hyerle, S. Curtis, & L. Alper (Eds.), *Student successes with Thinking Maps®* (pp. 63–73). Thousand Oaks, CA: Corwin Press.

Erickson, L. H. (2002). *Concept-based curriculum and instruction.* Thousand Oaks, CA: Corwin Press.

Ewy, C. (2002). *Teaching with visual frameworks.* Thousands Oaks, CA: Corwin Press.

Fanelli, S. (1995). *My map book.* New York: HarperCollins.

Fauconnier, G. (1985). *Mental spaces.* Cambridge, MA: MIT Press.

Fincher, S. (1991). *Creating mandalas.* Boston: Shambhala.

Freire, P. (1970). *Pedagogy of the oppressed.* New York: Basic Books, Inc.

Friedman, T. (2005). *The world is flat.* New York: Farrar, Straus and Giroux.

From Now On: The Educational Technology Journal. www.fno.org.

Gage, N. L. (1974). *Teacher effectiveness and teacher education: The search for a scientific basis.* Palo Alto, CA: Pacific Books.

Gardner, H. (1983). *Frames of mind: The theory of multiple intelligences.* New York: Basic Books.

Gardner, H. (1985). *The mind's new science: A history of the cognitive revolution.* New York: Basic Books.

Gawith, G. (1987). *Information alive!* Auckland, NZ: Longman Paul Limited.

Gawith, G. (1996). *Learning alive!* Auckland, NZ: Longman Paul Limited.

Giamatti, A. B. (1980, July). The American teacher. *Harper's,* pp. 28–29.

Goleman, D. (1985). *Vital lies, simple truths: The psychology of self-deception.* New York: Touchstone.

Goleman, D. (1995). *Emotional intelligence.* New York: Bantam Books.

Grandin, T. (1996). *Thinking in pictures: And other reports from my life with autism.* New York: Vintage Books.

Harvey, S., & Goudvis, A. (2007). *Strategies that work* (2nd ed.). Portland, ME: Stenhouse Publishers.

Horton, M., with Kohl, J., & Kohl, H. (1990). *The long haul: An autobiography.* New York: Doubleday.

Hughes, S. (1994). *The webbing way.* Winnipeg, MB: Peguis Publishers Limited.

Hyerle, D. (1988–1993). *Expand your thinking* (Series: Pre-K–Grade 8). Cary, NC: Innovative Sciences, Inc.

Hyerle, D. (1990). *Designs for thinking connectively.* Lyme, NH: Designs for Thinking.

Hyerle, D. (1991). Expand your thinking. In A. L. Costa (Ed.), *Developing minds* (2nd ed., pp. 16–26). Alexandria, VA: Association for Supervision and Curriculum Development.

Hyerle, D. (1993). *Thinking Maps as tools for multiple modes of understanding.* Unpublished doctoral dissertation, University of California, Berkeley.

Hyerle, D. (1995). *Thinking Maps: Tools for learning training manual.* Cary, NC: Innovative Sciences, Inc.

Hyerle, D. (1995/1996). Thinking Maps: Seeing is understanding. *Educational Leadership, 53*(4), 85–89.

Hyerle, D. (1996). *Visual tools for constructing knowledge.* Alexandria, VA: Association for Supervision and Curriculum Development.

Hyerle, D. (1999a). *Visual tools and technologies* [Video]. Lyme, NH: Designs for Thinking.

Hyerle, D. (1999b). *Visual tools video and guide.* Lyme, NH: Designs for Thinking.

Hyerle, D. (2000a). *A field guide to using visual tools.* Alexandria, VA: Association for Supervision and Curriculum Development.

Hyerle, D. (2000b). *Thinking Maps training of trainers resource manual.* Raleigh, NC: Innovative Sciences, Inc.

Hyerle, D. (2000c). Thinking Maps: Visual tools for activating habits of mind. In A. L. Costa & B. Kallick (Eds.), *Activating and engaging habits of mind* (pp. 46–58). Alexandria, VA: Association for Supervision and Curriculum Development.

Hyerle, D. (Presenter). (2000d). *Visual tools: From graphic organizers to Thinking Maps* [Video] (elementary and secondary eds.). Sandy, UT: Video Journal of Education.

Hyerle, D. (2007). *Thinking Maps software* (Rev. ed.). Cary, NC: Thinking Maps, Inc. (Originally published 1999.)

Hyerle, D. (In press). Thinking Maps®: A language of cognition for facilitating habits of mind. In A. Costa & B. Kallick (Eds.), *Habits of mind.* Alexandria, VA: Association for Supervision and Curriculum Development.

Hyerle, D., Curtis, S., & Alper, L. (Eds.). (2004). *Student successes with Thinking Maps: School-based research, results and models for achievement using visual tools.* Thousand Oaks, CA: Corwin Press.

Hyerle, D., & Yeager, C. (2007). *Thinking Maps: A language for learning training guide.* Raleigh, NC: Thinking Maps, Inc.

Israel, L. (1991). *Brain power for kids.* Miami: Brain Power for Kids, Inc.

Jacobs, H. H. (1997). *Mapping the big picture: Integrating curriculum and assessment K–12.* Alexandria, VA: Association for Supervision and Curriculum Development.

Jago, C. (1995, December 27). Like drivers, schoolchildren require a clearly marked road map. *Los Angeles Times.*

Jensen, E. (1998). *Teaching with the brain in mind.* Alexandria, VA: Association for Supervision and Curriculum Development.

Jones, B. F., Pierce, J., & Hunter, B. (1989). Teaching students to construct graphic representations. *Educational Leadership, 46*(4), 21–24.

Jung, C. G. (1973). *Mandala symbolism.* Princeton, NJ: Princeton University Press.

Kozol, J. (1991). *Savage inequalities.* New York: Crown Publishers.

Kozol, J. (2005). *The shame of the nation.* New York: Crown Publishers.

Lakoff, G. (1987). *Women, fire, and dangerous things.* Chicago: University of Chicago Press.

Lakoff, G., & Johnson, M. (1980). *Metaphors we live by.* Chicago: University of Chicago Press.

Lakoff, G., & Johnson, M. (1999). *Philosophy in the flesh.* New York: Basic Books.

Lao-tzu. (1986). *The Tao of power: A translation of the Tao to thing by Lao Tzu* (R. L. Wing, Trans.). Garden City, NY: Doubleday.

Levine, M. (2003). *The myth of laziness.* New York: Simon & Schuster.

Lowery, L. (1991). The biological basis for thinking. In A. L. Costa (Ed.), *Developing minds: A resource book for teaching thinking* (Rev. ed., Vol. 1, pp. 108–117). Alexandria, VA: Association or Supervision and Curriculum Development.

Mahiri, J. (Ed.). (2003). *What they don't learn in school: Literacy in the lives of urban youth.* New York: Peter Lang Publishing Group.

Margulies, N. (1991). *Mapping inner space.* Tucson, AZ: Zephyr Press.

Margulies, N., & Valenza, C. (2005). *Visual thinking.* Bethel, CT: Crown House Publishing.

Marzano, R. J., Norford, J. S., Paynter, D. E., Pickering, D. J., & Gaddy, B. B. (2001). *A handbook for classroom instruction that works.* Alexandria, VA: Association for Supervision and Curriculum Development.

Marzano, R. J., & Pickering, D. (2005). *Building academic vocabulary: Teacher's manual.* Alexandria, VA: Association for Supervision and Curriculum Development.

Marzano, R. J., Pickering, D. J., & Pollock, J. E. (2001). *Classroom instruction that works: Research-based strategies for increasing student achievement.* Alexandria, VA: Association for Supervision and Curriculum Development.

Marzano, R. J., et al. (1997). *Dimensions of learning teachers' manual* (2nd ed.). Alexandria, VA: Association for Supervision and Curriculum Development.

McTighe, J., & Lyman, F. T., Jr. (1988). Cueing thinking in the classroom: The promise of theory embedded tools. *Educational Leadership 45*(7), 18–24.

Meier, D. (1995). *The power of their ideas: Lessons for America from a small school in Harlem.* Boston: Beacon Press.

Miller, G. A. (1955). The magical number seven, plus or minus two: Some limits on our capacity for processing information. *Psychological Review, 63,* 81–97.

Novak, J. D. (1998). *Learning, creating, and using knowledge: Concept maps as facilitative tools in schools and corporations.* Mahwah, NJ: Lawrence Erlbaum Associates.

Novak, J. D., & Gowin, D. B. (1984). *Learning how to learn.* New York: Cambridge University Press.

Ogle, D. (1988–1989). Implementing strategic teaching. *Educational Leadership, 46,* 57–60.

Parks, S., & Black, H. (1992). *Organizing thinking, Book I.* Pacific Grove, CA: Critical Thinking Press and Software.

Quaden, R., & Ticotsky, A., with Lyneis, D. (2007). *The shape of change: Stocks and flows.* Acton, MA: Creative Learning Exchange. (Originally published May 2004.)

Quinlan, S. E. (1995). *The case of the mummified pigs and other mysteries in nature.* Honesdale, PA: Boyd's Mills, Press.

Richmond, B., Peterson, S., & Vescuso, P. (1998). *STELLA.* Hanover, NH: High Performance Systems.

Rico, G. L. (1983). *Writing the natural way.* Los Angeles: J. P. Tarcher, Inc.

Robinson, A. H. (1982). *Early thematic mapping in the history of cartography.* Chicago: University of Chicago Press.

Roth, W.-M. (1994). Student views of collaborative concept mapping: An emancipatory research project. *Science and Education, 78*(1), 1–34.

Rowe, M. B. (1974). Wait time and rewards as instructional variables: Their influence on language, logic and fate control. *Journal of Research in Science Teaching, 11,* 81–94.

Secretary's Commission on Achieving Necessary Skills. (1991). *What work requires of schools: A SCANS report for America 2000.* Washington DC: U.S. Department of Labor.

Senge, P. M. (1990). *The fifth discipline.* New York: Currency Doubleday.

Senge, P. M., Kleiner, A., Roberts, C., Ross, R., & Smith, B. (1994). *The fifth discipline fieldbook: Strategies and tools for building a learning organization.* New York: Doubleday.

Shah, I. (1972). *Reflections.* Baltimore: Penguin Books.

Shenk, D. (1997). *Data smog.* New York: HarperCollins.

Sinatra, R., & Pizzo, J. (1992, October). Mapping the road to reading comprehension. *Teaching K–8 Magazine.*

Snyder, G. (1990). *The practice of the wild: Essays.* San Francisco: North Point Press.

Standing, L. (1973). *Quarterly Journal of Experimental Psychology, 25,* 207–222.

Stewart, D., Prebble, T., & Duncan, P. (1997). *The reflective principal.* Katonah, NY: Richard C. Owen Publisher.

Sylwester, R. (1995). *A celebration of neurons: An educator's guide to the human brain.* Alexandria, VA: Association for Supervision and Curriculum Development.

Teachers' Curriculum Institute. (1994). *History alive? Interactive student notebook.* Mountain View, CA: Teachers' Curriculum Institute.

Upton, A. (1960). *Design for thinking.* Palo Alto, CA: Pacific Books.

Vygotsky, L. S. (1986). *Thought and language.* Cambridge, MA: MIT Press. (Originally published 1936.)

Wandersee, J. H. (1990). Concept mapping and the cartography of cognition. *Journal of Research in Science Teaching, 27*(10), 923–936.

Wiggins, G., & McTighe, J. (1998). *Understanding by design.* Alexandria, VA: Association for Supervision and Curriculum Development.

Wolfe, P. (2004). Foreword. In D. Hyerle, S. Curtis, & L. Alper (Eds.), *Student successes with Thinking Maps®.* Thousand Oaks, CA: Corwin Press.

Wolfe, P. (2006). *Video interview introducing Thinking Maps®.* Raleigh, NC: Thinking Maps, Inc.

Wolfe, P., & Nevills, P. (2004). *Building the reading brain, preK-3.* Thousand Oaks, CA: Corwin Press.

Wolfe, P., & Sorgen, M. (1990). *Mind, memory, and learning.* Napa, CA: Authors.

Wycoff, J., with Richardson, T. (1991). *Transformational thinking: Tools and techniques that open the door to powerful new thinking for every member of your organization.* New York: Berkley Books.

Zimmerman, D. P. (1998). *The role of reflexivity in the orders of change: The unraveling of the theories about second order change.* Unpublished doctoral dissertation. The Field Institute, Santa Barbara, California.

Index

CORWIN PRESS

The Corwin Press logo—a raven striding across an open book—represents the union of courage and learning. Corwin Press is committed to improving education for all learners by publishing books and other professional development resources for those serving the field of PreK–12 education. By providing practical, hands-on materials, Corwin Press continues to carry out the promise of its motto: **"Helping Educators Do Their Work Better."**